American Bureaucracy

American Bureaucracy
Public Choice and Public Law

Glen O. Robinson

Ann Arbor

THE UNIVERSITY OF MICHIGAN PRESS

Copyright © by the University of Michigan 1991
All rights reserved
Published in the United States of America by
The University of Michigan Press
Manufactured in the United States of America

1994 1993 1992 1991   4 3 2 1

Distributed in the United Kingdom and Europe by
Manchester University Press, Oxford Road,
Manchester M13, 9PL, UK

Library of Congress Cataloging-in-Publication Data

Robinson, Glen O.
    Americn bureaucracy : public choice and public law / Glen O.
Robinson.
      p.   cm.
    Includes bibliographical references and indexes.
    ISBN 0-472-10243-5 (cloth : alk. paper)
    1. Administrative law—United States.   2. Law and politics.
3. Bureaucracy—United States.   4. Public administration—United
States.   5. Social choice—United States.   I. Title.
KF5402.R63   1991
342.73'06—dc20
[347.3026]   91-15395
                                                        CIP

British Library Cataloguing in Publication Data
Robinson, Glen O.
  American bureaucracy : public choice and public law.
  1. United States. Public administration. Accountability
  I. Title
  353.01

  ISBN 0-472-10243-5

For Kay

Acknowledgments

I began this book too long ago. Some of my original conceptions of the subject have changed. Some of the credit, and the blame, for this change is attributable to friends and colleagues. Naming the responsible parties is not easy. When a project lasts as long as this one, one accumulates a lot of debts that never get recorded, no matter how important they have been. Some debts are easy to recall. I owe a debt to two deans, Dick Merrill and Tom Jackson, who supported my efforts with generous research grants (much supplied by the Law School Foundation) and never asked when the research effort would bear tangible fruit.

Of the many intellectual debts incurred, foremost is one owed to Ron Cass, a scholar and practitioner of the subject, who contributed both by way of review and ongoing discussion over the years. Parts of the book borrow from earlier work that I have done with others, notably Peter Aranson, Hal Bruff, and Ernest Gellhorn, and they bear some conspiratorial responsibility on that account. They should be forgiven if they don't recognize what I have done with our joint efforts. Also, on specific parts of the book, Hal Bruff and Bill Stuntz gave very helpful advice. Review comments from anonymous reviewers of the entire manuscript have had a major impact on the organization and character of the argument throughout, as has Colin Day who believes, with most editors, in Mies van de Rohes' architectural edict that "less is more." (Lawyers, more than most folks, have to be reminded of this wisdom; even if we are not exactly paid by the word (as, say, Dickens), we are trained to think words do matter, from which we naturally, if incorrectly, infer more words matter more.) Finally, I must acknowledge, with appreciation, the clerical contributions of Elsie Hall and Karen Harper who suffered through numerous revisions of this manuscript.

Contents

Introduction

Alongside the ubiquitous phrase "welfare state," the phrase "administrative state" has become an increasingly popular label for modern American government. The two labels are related, of course; in the federal government, the welfare programs and activities comprise the largest activity of bureaucracy outside the domain of national defense. But administrative bureaucracy is a more pervasive phenomenon of modern government than welfare programs, and administrative state evokes distinctive images and opinions. The images and opinions are for the most part negative, just as the term *bureaucracy* is a term of scorn the world over. We endure it. The old saying that two things are unavoidable, death and taxes, is incomplete; in a modern society you can't have taxes without a bureaucracy (and vice versa).

If bureaucracy is inevitable, it is not inevitably autonomous, or self-regulating, however. Herein lies the challenge of a modern government: how it directs and governs its bureaucracy marks the character of a society more distinctively than any other attribute. Virtually all modern societies profess to control bureaucracy with law, but how they do it, or how seriously they try to do it, is what sets some apart from others.

Legal control of the bureaucracy has been an important concern in America since the New Deal era. One can find growing awareness of the problem before that; academic legal writing on the subject goes back at least to the turn of the century. But it was the sudden rush of new agencies and administrative programs in the New Deal that sparked national concern and prompted the first congressional attempt to get a legal grip on the subject at the national level. The initial legislation was somewhat overwrought in its effort to subject all federal administrative action to intensive judicial surveillance and, on that account, was vetoed by President Roosevelt. But it set the stage for more moderate legislation, the Administrative Procedure Act (APA), which came at the end of World War II. The APA provided a basic framework for federal administration and a model for state laws. The act itself was a modest effort toward control; it was little more than an outline, a structure, for the rule of law. One does not expect much from an outline; everything is in the implementation.

To say that we have effectively implemented the rule of law over bureaucracy would be controversial. Not the least of the controversy would be over what it means to establish such supremacy. Which is another way of asking the question, what are the law's ambitions? What do we expect of bureaucratic government? What, indeed, do we expect of government? In varying degrees this book is about each of these questions. To say that it is "about" them does not imply that it is a comprehensive treatment of them; it is, rather, an attempt to describe and assess in fairly condensed fashion the ways and means of American bureaucracy seen through the eyes of a conventional (more or less) administrative lawyer. I use the term *American bureaucracy* loosely here. In fact I deal almost entirely with the federal bureaucracy. This necessarily omits much that is interesting and instructive about state and local bureaucracy. But to include that domain would entail moving to a higher level of generalization, about both the law and the politics of bureaucratic activity, than seemed to me fruitful.

As an essay on government bureaucracy this is essentially a synthetic work. It contains no new political theories. The present need for new theories—paradigm shifts, as post-Kuhnian theorists like to say—seems to me quite limited. We are, in fact, awash in theories of bureaucracy, as will be illustrated in chapter 3. Some of the theories are quite powerful, but most of them are more interesting than useful. It is time we took stock of the theories we have and to see how they fit (or don't fit) the legal and political environment in which we live. I say fit advisedly; I mean two different senses of that term, depending on the nature of the theory. A descriptive or "positive" theory fits the world if it is reasonably accurate in describing what most of us accept at any given time as reality. A normative theory, of course, has a different purpose; its evaluation is necessarily more contingent insofar as it appeals not to some presently fixed perception of reality but to values that are highly subjective and protean. Nevertheless, we can and do judge the fit of a normative theory according to whether it appeals to ethical values that are attractive and useful, in the pragmatist sense of William James.

With respect to descriptive theory, the book deals frequently with modern public choice theory with its emphasis on instrumental, self-interested, rational political behavior. I find this perspective always interesting, frequently provocative, and sometimes useful. I find very dubious many of the scientific pretensions made for it by its more ardent exponents, but in political science, as in social science generally, the "science" component must be taken *cum grano salis*. The fact that three Nobel laureates in economics (Kenneth Arrow, George Stigler, and James Buchanan) were honored primarily for work associated with public choice theory is reason to take seriously this methodological perspective on the ways and means of government and its agents. In taking seriously the perspective of public choice theory, however, one needs to be particularly mindful of the distinction between positive and normative theory. Modern positive descriptions of political behavior are deeply disquieting to anyone who believes that politics ought to be more than legalized warfare by and between marauding interest groups. Several generations of "realist" political scientists, now joined by realist legal and economic scholars, have insisted with increasing influence and effect on public expectations that there is no exogenous "public good"; the public good is simply the product of struggle among individuals and groups in the political arena. Any other conception, we are told, is impossible to grasp without unacceptable sacrifice to the autonomy of the individual, which liberal societies presuppose. I accept the premises of liberal theory with its preeminent emphasis on individual choice, as against the communitarian perspective that insists that individuals locate their moral and social identity within the constraints of a community ethic. At the same time, I find unpalatable the notion, embraced by what is now mainstream modern political theory, that public choice must inexorably ratify the aggregate preferences of those groups or individuals who happen to dominate political institutions or processes at any given time.

Time was when even intensely practical men imagined a reconciliation of individual freedom with the public good. The tradition of civic republicanism, at least as adopted by American colonialists, embraced both ideals. It is sometimes supposed that this ideal was abandoned in the constitutional era. Madison's famous essay on factions in The Federalist No. 10 has often been seen as the new "realism." But even Madison, regarded by some as the archetypal political realist, imagined the possibility of keeping the republican ideal alive. Supported by appropriate institutional restraints Madison still had the notion that pursuit of a public, public choice could be made consistent with the rights and autonomy of the individual.

How to vindicate that notion has been the central puzzle of American constitutionalism and challenge to the rule of law ever since. No one reasonably could say the puzzle has been solved, but some persons still think that the liberal-republican vision was the right one, however fuzzy its vision of private and public good. Civic republicanism has been enjoying a rejuvenescence among constitutional legal scholars of late. It is too early to say whether it will have a lasting impact on constitutional law; it does have at least the virtue of challenging the trend of modern political realists who believe that notions of public interest are simply the residue of old-fashioned Wilsonian idealism.

Theory aside, this is a book about what law schools typically catalog as administrative law (although as a teacher of administrative law for over a score years, I still have difficulty explaining to my students what administrative law is and is not, so vague is its domain). This is not a textbook; it contains some of the subjects that go into such a course to be sure, but I have tried to suppress the urge to examine the law or legal commentary in either a detailed or a comprehensive fashion. My aim is to bridge the gap between those who read political science and those who read law, with a view to telling each something about the other while at the same time trying to advance my own arguments about the proper relationship of law and politics.

Chapter 1 opens with a sketch of some statistics and institutional landmarks in the relentless growth of what is now unlovingly called big government as symbolized, if not fully represented, by the federal government. Following that introduction I sketch some of the dominant styles of liberal political theory about the public sector. The message here is not complex; it also is not new. Government grows as a function of growth in the population and increased economic activity. Bureaucracy increases correspondingly, as a means of managing government tasks. This much is conventional and unproblematic, more or less. But it is not the whole account. Anyone who reflects on what has happened over the past sixty years or so will recognize that the pattern of government and bureaucracy reflects more than simple population growth and increased economic activity. It reflects, as well, a different conception of the role of government. One hesitates to describe this as a change in the public philosophy, for that implies a reflective, principled, coherent design. The doleful reality is that the public philosophy behind the trends seems to be mostly a contingent amalgam of political interests, each making increasing demands on the public fisc. Some of these demands have genuine elements of public welfare that commend them to our collective concern; some do not. The problem is that we seem to have no effective political mechanism that can reliably distinguish one from the other. That is, of course, what the political realists have been telling us for much of the modern period (at least for thirty to forty years); part of the burden of chapter 1 is to challenge the notion that we must accept this as "political reality."

Conflicting theories of what politics ought to be frame the discussion of constitutional limitations that follows in chapter 2. This is not a systematic review of constitutional law. The discussion is selective and aimed at advancing an argument for active judicial supervision of legislation. Conservative political rhetoric notwithstanding, liberal democracy is not threatened by constitutional restraints on legislative action, not even when the constitutional restraints are the creation of an "unwritten" constitution. Indeed, the opposite is more nearly true: liberal democracy is threatened by the absence of constitutional constraint precisely in the sense that the legitimacy of public choice is threatened by the absence of principled restraint on raw political power. This is not, I should emphasize, an argument *from* democracy; constitutional restraints are not justified by their democratic attributes. Constitutions are fundamentally antidemocratic (a proposition I once thought too obvious for dispute until I began reading conservative constitutionalists). Their acceptance by democratic republics is simply a matter of recognizing that a democracy without constitutional restraint is worse than one with it.

It is also important to recognize that, contrary to the claims of some constitutional scholars, the most important feature of American constitutionalism is not that it has been reduced to written form, but that its norms are preeminently defined by courts, rather than by the government or legislature as in the English system. As a historical matter, the American Constitution may have been unique in being embodied in written form, but what has made American *constitutionalism* special is less the product of its tangible form than the fact that it is judicially enforceable as a form of common law, with all of the undemocratic inventiveness that implies.

No matter how fundamental constitutional review may be in articulating a principled rule of law by which public power should be measured, it can never play more than a marginal role either legally or socially. Even liberal advocates of activist judicial review—whose unfashionable biases on this point I generally share—must concede that the rule of law is primarily a rule of nonconstitutional character and is thus directed not to the legislature but to the agents it creates, the administrative agencies. The remainder of the book is devoted to these creatures—which, as I said earlier, everyone seems to regard as an inevitable, if lamentable, attribute of modern society. As Justice Holmes once said of taxes, bureaucrats are the price we pay for civilization.

In chapter 3, federal bureaucracy and its political-legal environs are examined. My chief purpose is to review some of the modern political wisdom about bureaucrats, and their utility functions (to borrow the economists' ugly but convenient expression), and to relate this to the political and legal environment in which bureaucratic institutions are set. In particular I examine the relationship between agencies and special interests (industry groups are my model but not, of course, the exclusive exemplar), and between agencies and Congress, the president and the courts. The central issue is political responsibility and legal control. Consistent with my earlier argument, political responsibility is viewed as something transcending pluralistic accommodation of interests. As a practical matter, the notion of a transcendent responsibility—a public interest if you will—inevitably implies a conception of the rule of law as an active constraint on agencies.

Chapters 4 and 5 discuss functional elements of the rule of law, considered first as internal due process and second as judicial review. These are the core of administrative law as taught in the law school classroom, and my treatment here more or less parallels conventional exposition, without the doctrinal detail that one would encounter in a textbook. The discussion of due process comes in two parts, a constitutional part that focuses principally on the evolution of property and liberty rights that are the prescribed foundation of due process, and a discussion of basic elements of process and the purposes they serve. Of the two aspects, most of the attention has been given, by courts and commentators, to the rights issue, perhaps because it raises some interesting and subtle constitutional problems that have invited, and often frustrated, repeated intellectual efforts to solve. The nature of the process required has received less attention, perhaps because it has been buried under a rubric of balancing the interests, which has obscured some philosophical questions of purpose that are interesting and vexing in their own right. My aim in discussing these is exploration, not problem solving, though the analytical framework can find useful application in developing structures for the administrative process.

American discussions of the rule of law are quickly reduced to questions of judicial review. American constitutional law is a law of judicial review, and common law at that. Courts do not simply enforce the Fourteenth Amendment for instance; they invent it. The same is even more true of nonconstitutional review, the subject of chapter 5. To be sure, the jurisdictional framework, and to varying degree the basic substantive policy directions, are conferred by statutes (either a specific statute that underlies the claim for judicial relief or a general statute such as the federal Administrative Procedure Act). But within the usually capacious boundaries set by statutes, courts asked to review administrative action must define for themselves both the degree of access to the courts by aggrieved citizens and the nature and degree of scrutiny the courts give agency decisions. Though an activist judicial review of agency action is not uncontroversial, I believe it bears none of the burdens associated with the (overly) celebrated "countermajoritarian difficulty" (Alexander Bickel's phrase) of constitutional review. In reviewing administrative choices courts do not, formally or in effect, set themselves against popular cum legislative sovereignty or political responsibility. Nonconstitutional review is, after all, subject to legislative creation, direction, and override in the same way that agencies are. If it would be naive to pretend that courts here function merely as agents of the legislature, it would be equally foolish to suppose agencies do either.

Recognizing an active role for judicial review is one thing, crystallizing that role into functionally useful standards of review is another. The general verbal formulas we now have are not very useful as functional guidelines. But attempts to articulate fixed rules or functional criteria for allocating fact-finding and law-determining functions between agency and court are hopeless; given the varied character of agency decisions, how could one formulate generic standards of legal justification? The absence of a clearer allocation of decision-making authority between court and agency is sometimes frustrating, for it leaves room for endless argument about whether the courts have stayed within their proper realm. But no set of general rules is likely to end such argument, and the effort to devise such rules, across the board, is a waste of time and energy. In individual contexts it may be quite legitimate to define the task of review with greater specificity, but attempts to tinker with this by generic decree are futile. Lawyers, who have no legitimate pretensions to be scientists, should know better than to try to invent a science of review. Alas, it is not so. The quest for some algorithm of review continues, undiscouraged by repeated failure. If there is any important weakness in the present system of review, it comes not from the absence of specific rules but from the absence of strong consensus about the importance of judicial review and of the rule of law itself in our political system. Here is where we apologists for an activist conception of legal control of the bureaucracy need to concentrate our energies and our hopeful expectations.

CHAPTER 1

Government and Bureaucracy

In the British Museum's Far Eastern gallery there is an exhibit containing three pairs of terra cotta figures found in a Tang Dynasty (eighth century) tomb. The first pair of figures, of ferocious demeanor, reportedly represent thunder gods or similar nature spirits. They are accompanied by a pair of fierce looking warriors, guardians of heaven, who stand next to a pair of more placid but dignified figures, identified as civil servants. We are told by the exhibit card that it was customary for sets of these figures to be placed in the tomb of Chinese notables. Their function there is not explained, but we can guess what it must have been: the nature spirits and warriors protected the deceased's spirit on its journey to the other side, while the civil servants were there to see that all the necessary forms were filled out when they arrived.

At least two lessons from this Tang custom come immediately to mind: one, bureaucracy is ancient; two, it follows us to the grave. A cynic might also see in this ancient practice yet a third lesson. Observing that the figures were placed only in the tombs of Tang notables he might infer (*a*) that the civil servants only protected the notables; or (*b*) that only the notables needed it. It appears that ancient China has many lessons for contemporary civilization.

The Rise of National Bureaucracy

It is difficult to trace the evolution of American federal bureaucracy without writing a history of the United States. Government institutions reflect public programs that are but part of a larger set of social, economic, and political events. In most histories, the creation of bureaucratic institutions is scarcely noticed except as a passing incidental feature of the social landscape. To single out this particular government program or that particular agency from the larger historic setting thus risks some distortion. It is not simply that the institutional history can only be fully understood when the surrounding political events are examined, though that is true enough. It is also that the singling out of particular programs, policies, and institutions causes them to loom rather larger in the historic landscape than is justified. At the very least, the fixing of particular institutions or programs in one historic period or event can be misleading insofar as it tends to obscure the gradual evolution that characterizes most of our public programs and institutions. But my purpose here is not to write a history; I want merely to identify some institutional landmarks and central political themes.

Though bureaucracy is an ancient and, apparently, inevitable feature of social organization, as a feature of American government it is a relatively recent development.[1] Those who, in Gary Will's phrase, "invented America" did not attempt to invent an administrative structure to go with it. The Constitution itself is nearly silent on the subject. It vests "the executive power" in the president but does not define what functions that power embraces or how it is to be organized and used. The president is instructed to see that the laws are "faithfully executed," and to this end he is empowered to nominate executive officials and to receive advice from them. He is also designated commander in chief of the armed forces, a designation to which appeal has sometimes been made in support of general civilian executive prerogatives. That is, essentially, the substance of the executive power defined by the Constitution. It is scarcely a reliable indicator of what today the executive power and its attendant responsibilities encompass.

One would not, of course, expect a great deal of specificity in a constitution. The details of administrative functions and organization obviously have to be left vague in order to accommodate future political and social circumstances. Time has removed some of the vagueness of constitutional design, but not all of it. For instance, early dispute over the respective powers of the president and Congress in regard to appointment, control, and removal of executive officers has continued into modern times.[2] Other related controversies over the allocation of power between branches include efforts by Congress to give itself certain prerogatives with regard to executive functions, such as the appointment of officers or reserving control of executive implementation of legislative mandates.[3] It is a measure of the vagueness of the Constitution that such basic questions can still be raised two hundred years after its signing. It is also a measure of the pragmatic accommodation of American politics that such issues, while still alive, have not prevented the constitutional structure from holding up quite well after two centuries of wear and tear.

Of course, those two centuries have not been uniformly burdensome in the demands they placed on the administrative structure of government. Until very recently, the demands on the system were modest; the American government was a small affair. Indeed, in its first half-century the federal government was almost a personal affair; all major issues were reviewed by the president personally, acting on the advice of department and other office heads. For instance, Jefferson attended to all messages and directives on matters large and small, even down to specifying directions for the construction of river crossings for post roads in wilderness areas.[4]

Jefferson, as we know from countless biographical accounts, was by nature a detail man. But, of course, in those days the distinction between detail and grand design was not so apparent as it is now. In 1800, total federal expenditures were less than $11 million and the federal civilian workforce was about 4,000. This can be measured against a national population of 5.3 million and a GNP that I estimate (based on later GNP data and estimated growth rates) to be in the neighborhood of $400 million.[5] Perhaps needless to say, Jefferson's belief in small government was a good deal easier to sustain then than it would be in today's large, complex society. One naturally expects government to grow in some proportion to population and level of economic activity, so it is hardly cause for dismay that, with a present (1990) GNP of approximately $5.5 trillion and a (1989) population of 249 million, we see a rather larger federal establishment than in Jefferson's time.[6]

However, any inference that there is some necessary constant relationship between the size of government and the population or level of GNP would be misleading. In fact, for a brief period from 1870 to 1900 total government spending as a percent of GNP declined from 4.1 percent to 2.8 percent. Since 1900, however, the ratio of spending to GNP has risen steadily. For instance, in 1930 it was 3.7 percent; in 1960, 18.3 percent; in 1990 about 21.8 percent.[7] These figures may be somewhat misleading for they include both defense spending and interest on the national debt, neither of which are good indicators of bureaucratic or programmatic growth of the kind people think about when they express Jeffersonian concerns over big government. For instance, measuring bureaucracy by federal civilian employment, one finds rather little change over the past twenty years (fluctuating between 2.9 and 3.0 million), despite a continued increase in federal spending relative to GNP.[8] At the same time, if expenditure figures exaggerate government growth in one respect, they understate it in another. Concern over what government is doing, cannot be expressed as a simple function of what government is spending to do it. Surely it would be silly to measure the social effects (good and bad) of the Department of Agriculture, the Federal Communications Commission (FCC), or the Environmental Protection Agency (EPA) by reference to their budgets, just as it would be to assess the impact of presidential activities by the size of the White House budget.

If we put aside expenditure data as an unreliable measure of government institutions and their effects, we are left with no easy way to depict the ways in which government has changed since the days when Jefferson presided over the construction of wilderness river crossings—no simple way short of a detailed history that would be beyond the purpose of this book. Nevertheless, it may still be helpful to get a sense of the evolutionary path by noting a few landmarks of this history.

For nearly a hundred years after the inauguration of Washington the federal government remained a very modest affair, as I noted. While there were continuous adjustments and additions to the core executive departments and agencies with which the nation began (State, Treasury, War, along with two major offices, the Post Office and the Office of the Attorney General), it was not until the late nineteenth century that expansion of national institutions took secure hold. For many observers—political scientists and legal scholars in particular—the event most often singled out as a watershed in the growth of national government is the creation of the Interstate Commerce Commission (ICC) in 1887.[9] The Interstate Commerce Act was a first on several counts. It was the first major venture by the federal government into industrial regulation, though it was anticipated by numerous state regulatory commissions established in the preceding two decades (several New England states created railroad commissions before the Civil War, but they were largely fact-finding agencies for the legislature; their regulatory functions were special and limited). The ICC was the first federal agency to be designed on the model of "expert commissions" whose numbers and staff would be not merely experienced professionals but would be (in time at least) experts in all aspects of the regulated field of commerce. Finally, the ICC was the first independent agency. Histories of the political origins of the Interstate Commerce Act bring to mind the fable of the blind men of Hindustan describing the elephant according to the particular part of its anatomy they felt. So here, the historians have come up with divergent views of the primary political force behind railroad regulation based on where they have looked for evidence. A classic account by Solon Buck identified the principal political force as the Granger movement that was a major impetus for earlier state regulatory initiatives.[10] Later historians have found the primary political force in different shipper interests: one account puts the Pennsylvania oil producers in the forefront, another locates primary responsibility in New York merchants.[11] Yet another, revisionist cum Marxist version, which anticipates later economic theories of regulation generally, finds the primary impetus for regulation came from the railroads themselves, seeking regulatory insulation from aggressive competition.[12] To round out the various interest group accounts there is a synthesis: railroad regulation was the product of different interests—shippers and railroads—which converged on the need for regulation.[13]

These different views of the elephant reflect a common theme in accounts of other regulatory institutions, indeed, of all government. The history of important institutions and government programs is more often one of eclectic confusion than of single-minded purpose. Regulatory programs, in particular, seem to exemplify this pluralism, as a study of the Federal Trade Commission (FTC), the late Civil Aeronautics Board (CAB), and the FCC will reveal. Too, even if the original purpose of an agency or program is simple and straightforward it seldom remains so for long. Political change has a way of forcing alteration in original design while insisting it is only working out the true purposes for which the agency or program was intended; the consequence is that purposes and objectives invariably move in the direction of greater ambiguity.

Some agencies do retain their original purpose better than others. The protypical example is the special-constituency agency or department, of which the Department of Agriculture may be the best exemplar. As the ICC represents the first major venture of the national government into regulatory affairs, the creation of the Department of Agriculture in 1889 represents the premier commitment to clientele government on the national stage.[14] The department was created in 1862 as a minor agency with the responsibility to conduct research and distribute information on farming, marketing, and other agricultural subjects, and to procure and distribute seeds and plants.[15] Giving agriculture cabinet-level recognition made it the model for "representative" bureaucracy designed to serve the distinctive interests of particular interest groups. Pendleton Herring explained the force of reason behind this event:

> When the question of changing the agricultural bureau to a major executive department was being debated in Congress, it was stated that "the creation of a cabinet officer at the head of a great department with numerous clerks will not increase the agricultural productiveness of the country to the extent of a single hill of beans; it will merely create additional offices for politicians to fill." Criticism of the proposed change was refuted not by discussing the merits of the case, but rather by stating blankly that farm organizations all over the country wanted a Department of Agriculture. . . . The very pertinent question was raised: if these farm organizations know exactly what Congress ought to do, why should not other interests be permitted to dictate their wishes to legislators? The issue was scarcely disposed of by the rejoinder given: "Well, sir, the farmers of this country, throughout the length and breadth of the land, are above any other organization on earth."[16]

Such unaffected eloquence disarms mere reason—then and now.

The department's service functions, relatively minor in the beginning, soon expanded into a range of promotional services including extensive financial assistance and subsidies. To these have been added land management functions (managing the national forests and a number of regulatory functions), but its dominant purpose has remained that of promoting the interests of farmers. Indeed, the regulatory tasks are, in significant degree, simply a means of promoting those interests. More important than the services directly distributed to farmers is the fact that the department provides an official representative for their interests. This is the real import of the farmers' demand for a cabinet-level department, and therein is the enduring precedent that Congress set by meeting it.

With the ICC and the Department of Agriculture as models, the national government entered the twentieth century well situated, and well disposed, to confront the demands of different political groups for government assistance and protection. The farmers' success in obtaining their own representative in Washington was immediately followed by pressures on behalf of their industrial counterparts. Organized labor received its own Department of Labor in 1898; like Agriculture, Labor was constructed from a minor bureau previously established (in the Interior Department). The general design and duties of the Department of Labor were to acquire and distribute labor information, especially such information concerning working hours and wages, and the means to promote the general welfare of workers. Thereafter it was industry's turn. In 1903, the Department of Labor became the Department of Commerce and Labor, with duties to foster, promote, and develop foreign and domestic commerce, industrial and labor interests, and transportation. The representatives of organized labor, especially the American Federation of Labor, strenuously opposed the consolidation of the interests of commerce and labor in one department. They continued to press Congress for a separate executive department to represent the interests of wage earners. Congress met their demands in 1913, establishing an executive Department of Labor and transferring to it all labor-related bureaus and divisions from the Department of Commerce and Labor—which then became simply the Department of Commerce. As with Agriculture, both Labor and Commerce later took on some regulatory functions, but for the most part these have been simply extensions of their constituent service and promotional functions.[17]

The quest for institutional status as a means of promoting clientele interests continues: in 1988 Congress created another new cabinet department, Veterans Affairs. The department assumed the functions of the Veterans Administration, an independent (nondepartmental) agency in the executive branch; no new program initiatives were established. The sole purpose in creating the department was to give greater political visibility and clout to veterans' interests.[18] This, in turn, was justified in terms evocative of the eloquent plea made on behalf of the farmers for a Department of Agriculture one hundred years ago. As one veterans' representative put it:

[T]he most compelling reason for passage of this legislation is the contributions and sacrifices our nation's veterans have made for the preservation of our constitution and the principles of freedom, liberty and justice for all our citizens.[19]

With the intelligent use of a thesaurus, there are few groups who cannot claim (and have not claimed) to be special to the American dream. In 1990, President Bush endorsed a proposal to elevate the EPA to cabinet status, an endorsement designed to enhance Bush's electoral claim of aspiring to be the "environmental president." Although such a move would not entail any new programmatic responsibility, as with the Veteran's Department, the idea has been embraced by the relevant constituent interests as a means of increasing their clout. As one environmentalist representative said, it would mean that the head of the EPA would no longer have to stand against the wall at cabinet meetings but would have a seat at the table where he could "initiate discussions and react to harebrained ideas by other Cabinet secretaries."[20]

One must suppose there are limits to how many panjandrums can be accommodated at high table and still be in eyesight of the salt. Certainly there must soon come a time (if it has not already come) when new arrivals will have to recognize the force of the Gilbert and Sullivan line, "when everyone is somebody no one is anybody."

Unlike Agriculture, the ICC model of the expert agency was not immediately initiated. In fact, the national government's next important venture into economic regulation, the Sherman Antitrust Act of 1890, was content to delegate both jurisdiction and the power to define the law to the federal courts.[21] However, the ICC was to become the ideal of Progressive and New Deal regulatory planners—the model for an array of expert agencies whose mandates span an incredible spectrum from central banking (Federal Reserve Board) to labor relations (National Labor Relations Board [NLRB]), communications (FCC), trade and commerce (FTC, ITC, Federal Maritime Commission [FMC]), health, safety, and environment (Occupational Safety and Health Administration [OSHA], Food and Drug Administration [FDA], National Highway Traffic Safety Administration [NHTSA], EPA), to name some of the more salient of the ubiquitous "alphabet agencies." It would be frivolous to say that these diverse regulatory programs are all direct lineal descendants of railroad regulation merely because the organizational form has a family resemblance (more or less) to the ICC.[22] Nevertheless, all share a kindred popular image of "expertise in the service of politics," a phrase used by two modern scholars, Bruce Ackerman and William Hassler, to express the New Deal ideal.[23] I might add that all share the same normative ambiguity that is suggested by the alliance of expertise and politics: *whose* politics does expertise serve? About that more later.

While much of the evolution of national bureaucracy can be related to the two models created by the Department of Agriculture and the ICC, a third part is needed to complete the architecture of the modern government. This is the system of social welfare programs. Introduced by the Social Security Act of 1935 as a tripartite system of income security (federally run compulsory old age insurance; federally assisted, state-operated unemployment insurance; and federally assisted, state-operated public assistance programs),[24] welfare programs became the most durably important legacy of the New Deal—a legacy that has given the modern state its popular name, "the welfare state." The national government's welfare budget—comprising the original income security programs (as expanded), together with medicare and medicaid (added in 1965) and various other benefit and assistance programs (such as veterans benefits and educational assistance) classified as "human services"—is now the largest component of the federal budget (substantially larger than national defense), administered by agencies that, combined (somewhat artificially perhaps), comprise the nation's second largest bureaucracy (behind defense).[25]

It would be rash to predict future trends; in the present political climate one is inclined to doubt a continuation of past growth rates, either in aggregate spending or in institutional expansion. On the other hand, there is no substantial evidence from which one could predict any significant reversal. In the mid-1970s, Herbert Kaufman set out to test the Washington folk wisdom about the survival abilities of government agencies, their ability to survive thhe conditions and circumstances that created them. Surveying the history of 175 executive agencies from 1923 to 1973, he found 85 percent survived the fifty-year period, most of them without substantial change. To the survivors had been added some 246 new agencies.[26]

The situation appears not to have changed materially since 1973. Whatever else it achieved, the "Reagan revolution" did not halt the growth of government, measured either by aggregate expenditures or number and complexity of bureaucratic organizations. True, President Reagan never promised an *absolute* reduction in the size of government (contrary to popular impression) but rather a reduced *growth* rate.[27] However, even that was not accomplished; in fact, the growth rate was slightly higher than it was under President Carter.[28] The continued growth is accounted for by a buildup in defense spending; the growth in spending on nondefense programs was kept essentially at the level of the Carter administration (which had reduced it below earlier levels).[29] However, even domestic program reductions were modest overall. In the area of perhaps greatest concern, entitlement programs, the growth rate was unabated.[30] In an area that had been an early target for cutbacks, environmental and safety regulation, expenditures (in real costs) were greater under Reagan than Carter.[31] Finally, the ultimate irony: despite a promise to eliminate some agencies (notably the Consumer Product and Safety Commission) and departments (Education and Energy), none was eliminated; instead a new department (Veterans Affairs) was created. On the matter of government growth, the judgment of one Reagan advisor, that "there was no Reagan revolution,"[32] must be seen as something of an understatement. More apt, perhaps, is the old joke about the Goldwater-Johnson campaign: a voter complains about being warned that voting for Goldwater would lead to escalation of the war in Vietnam; so he voted for Goldwater, and sure enough the war escalated.

The Imperatives of Political Pluralism

Ronald Reagan had firm beliefs about government, but he was hardly a political philosopher. On the one hand he could assert, with all sincerity, that "government is not the solution to our problem; government is the problem."[33] On the other he could also follow implicitly the edict of one of his predecessors, Grover Cleveland. Cleveland, also not of philosophical nature, is reported to have remarked on the subject of government and its growth: "it is a condition and not a theory which confronts us."[34] Of course, that is the way it typically appears to public officials, including presidents. After their fashion they are correct to perceive it so; after all, they are not elected or appointed to be public philosophers. Nevertheless, conditions do not come neatly labeled with instructions what to do about them. It is necessary to have some notion by which those conditions that are plausible candidates for public choices are to be identified. Without such a notion government becomes a mindless Pavlovian response to whatever stimulates the salivary glands of the body politic.

Probably most people—those who seek public office or vote for those who do—have some rudimentary concept of what it is their government can and ought to do. Unfortunately, it appears that ideas about private and public realms have become vapid and inconsequential as the conditions that generate public responses have increased without limit. Certainly there has been a change in public conceptions of the role of government and correspondingly in the demands made upon it. It is one thing to say, with the framers, that government has a preeminent role in enforcing property rights; it is another to say that these enforceable property rights include the right to income security, medical care, clean air, a safe workplace or . . . the list is as long as the welfare state is broad.

A case can be made for this extension of the government's classic policing function, but it is surely a case that would not have occurred to most Americans until the last half of this century. This is especially true of the extension of property rights to include not only legal protection from harms created by private uses of the workplace or public environment, but security against harms from general social misfortune as well. Income security, health care, and retirement benefits have become part of the "new property," as Charles Reich presciently labeled it, and correspondingly one of our strongest claims on government.[35]

The extent to which all these demands upon government, these claims for "public goods" if you will, have penetrated our society is shown by the extent to which they have transcended ordinary political dialogue. What is striking is the degree to which new welfare and regulatory initiatives have become an established routine that is largely independent of political ideology. It is not simply a matter of preserving New Deal welfare programs or regulatory initiatives. The "New" Deal is old hat. Some particular programs and some agencies created in the New Deal have, mirabile dictu, been terminated; others no doubt will be. But the essential spirit seems to be an enduring one, enduring through liberal and conservative administrations and legislatures. Reviewing the evolution of American bureaucracy, one is not surprised that government activities, and the institutions that sponsor and implement them, should grow under the regimes of Progressive and New Deal activists. What gives one pause is to learn that more new agencies were created in the Nixon years than in the Roosevelt era, and by a considerable margin.[36]

Beginning with President Nixon, five successive presidents actively campaigned on promises to curb the growth of the federal government and bureaucracy, and, over the same period, legislative proposals to accomplish this have become a regular feature of the congressional agenda. Of course, assaults on government and bureaucracy have been a theme of political rhetoric since virtually the founding of the Republic. Meantime, government and bureaucracy have continued to grow in impudent disregard of these professed sentiments. There seems to be a kind of political rachet at work that permits change in one direction only.

The clash between professed political sentiment and observed political practice makes one naturally suspicious of the former: either the political leaders are not sincere, or they have misread the public philosophy. Both inferences are possible but extreme in their assumption of a persistent gap between the behavior of political leaders and their constituents' interests. President Carter's campaign against the Washington bureaucracy may or may not have honestly reflected his personal beliefs; it does not matter. What matters is that obviously he must have supposed his professed opinions and promises coincided sufficiently with public sentiment to get him elected. Once elected he could, of course, renege on the promised performance. It would not be the first time in the annals of politics. And he might even escape political sanction for nonperformance. That, too, is hardly unknown to political history. But over time, and over successive electoral campaigns, a pattern of seriously mistaking or systematically ignoring public opinion is unlikely to persist. If Jimmy Carter had erred in his assessment of public opinion about bureaucracy, it seems unlikely that Ronald Reagan would have pursued his campaign against bureaucracy, or would have been elected and reelected. What holds for presidents holds equally, if not more so, for lesser political figures from whom similar orations against big government appear to be popular but also unavailing.

This apparent conflict between political practice and public sentiment is difficult to explain if one thinks of practice and sentiment in singular or monolithic terms. The puzzle disappears if one takes a closer, disaggregated, look at the "public philosophy" and the "public interest."

It has often been remarked that Americans are not much given to theoretical speculation about government or the respective boundaries of public and private activity. I doubt matters are any different in any other democratic country. Ordinary citizens seldom take to the polls to express a general theory about government, any more than they form political action committees (PACs) to promote a public philosophy. At a level of high generality, it is fair to describe Americans as committed to a philosophy of liberal individualism. But this is balanced by a degree of collective conceptions of public responsibility, as recurrent fascination with civic republicanism in theoretical discourse and the embrace of public welfare schemes in political discourse illustrates.[37] But at this level of generality almost anything goes. In truth there have been rather few times—certainly few in modern times—when a coherent public philosophy could be found amid the babble of ad hoc pragmatism. Thoughtful observers have lamented this indifference to a public interest from time to time. Walter Lippmann was one of them:

> In the prevailing popular culture all philosophies are the instruments of some man's purpose, all truths are self-centered and self-regarding, and all principles are the rationalizations of some special interest. There is no public criterion of the true and the false, of the right and the wrong, beyond that which the preponderant mass of voters, consumers, readers, and listeners happen at the moment to be supposed to want. . . . In order to repair the capacity to believe in the public philosophy, it will be necessary to demonstrate the practical relevance and the productivity of the public philosophy. It is almost impossible to deny its high and broad generalities. The difficulty is to see how they are to be applied to the practical affairs of a modern state.[38]

Unfortunately, Lippmann could not advise how such a philosophy should be defined or implemented in a pluralistic society dominated by self-interest. Indeed, it appears he did not really hold out much hope that it could be within the present political framework.

Modern political theorists are wont to tell us not even to try to define a public philosophy, at least not one with sufficient coherence or focus to have operational significance. By their account, the public interest is not an exogenously defined state of social welfare; it is simply the product of political competition, compromise, and agreement among various segments of the public. The public interest is whatever a successful political coalition can induce the legislature, the executive, the bureaucracy to say it is. This is the perspective of modern interest-group theory, which has come to dominate American political theory in the second half of the twentieth century. Earl Latham, one of the leading political exponents of this perspective in the 1950s, gives a flavor of the style of the theory in its early development. In Latham's depiction, the legislature, seen as a collection of interest groups, "referees the group struggle, ratifies the victories of the successful coalitions, and records the terms of the surrenders, compromises and conquests in the form of statutes"; the bureaucracy and the courts are largely passive instruments. The courts are "instrumentalities for the administration of the agreed rules." The bureaucracy serves to distribute the spoils of legislative victory; the regulatory agency, for example, is "like an army of occupation left in the field to police the rule won by the victorious coalition."[39]

Latham's imagery of the political struggle is arrestingly evocative of Hobbes's natural state of "warre of every man, against every man," except for the detail that Latham's individuals run in political packs (today, PACs). There is, of course, another obvious difference between the Hobbesian struggle and modern group struggle: the latter is subject to some legal constraints. David Truman, the leading interest-group theorist of his and Latham's generation, referred to them as the "rules of the game."[40] However, in Latham's account, as in many modern accounts, the relevant rules are themselves the product of the struggle; they are the prize brought home by the victorious coalition. In the end, Hobbes himself might be hard pressed to distinguish his state of nature scenarios from Latham's accounts of political struggle.

Interest-group theory has undergone some methodological refinement in more recent times. In part, the refinement has come by refracting political theory through the lens of positive economic theory, producing a literature commonly styled as public choice theory.[41] The term *public choice* is anything but precise. In fact, it is a very loose description of a quite varied literature in contemporary political science and economics. There is no accepted convention as to the distinguishing characteristics of the term; indeed, many writers who are identified with public choice often do not use that label to describe their work, and the use of other labels like *rational choice, social choice, positive political science*, or *positive political economy* is fairly common. The range of subjects and analytical styles in the field is striking.[42] Kenneth Arrow's celebrated work, *Social Choice and Individual Values*, is often regarded as the foundation of modern public choice theory.[43] The burden of Arrow's work is to show, mathematically, the impossibility of deriving a social welfare function, assuming certain axioms of individual, democratic pluralism. Arrow's work, with its attention to voting cycles that defeat

coherent majoritarian preferences supposed to be the foundation of democratic principles, undoubtedly inspired many of the modern contributors to
think about the rationalism, the mathematical logic if you will, of group
choice. However, the challenge for future political analysts lay not so much in
extending this abstract inquiry but in analyzing real political behavior from a
perspective of rational choice, including strategic behavior in forming al-
liances, trading votes, preference registration, etc. While much of the subsequent work has been done by political scientists as well as economists, it is
fair to say that it is the latter that have distinguished public choice theory from
the theories of Truman, Latham, and others who, by this time, were in the
mainstream of political science.

Perhaps above all other contributions economists made to the new perspective was an emphasis on the use of formalized models embracing certain
assumptions of human behavior, the central assumption typically being that
individuals are rational (in the sense of a purposive choice of means with
which to pursue desired ends) and self-interested. In conventional microeconomic theory, the rational self-interest model is used to analyze markets;
this has inspired some analysts to analogize choices to market choices. The
use of the market as a descriptive model of political activity, particularly in the
area of economic regulation, is often credited to George Stigler and his
students.[44] The central insights are, however, not original with him; indeed
his specific work on economic regulation as a special benefit for industry had
long been a commonplace of political and economic writing.[45] Stigler essentially refined and generalized conventional political wisdom, framing it in
terms of a market place deal between industry consumers on the one hand and
legislator and bureaucrat suppliers on the other.

As I said, the interest-group/public choice model of demand for publicly
supplied goods is particularistic. Political interest groups seldom seek public
goods the benefits and costs of which will be distributed evenly among all
citizens. Each group rather seeks collective provision of goods from which
they can derive severable benefits disproportionate to their supply costs. Pro-
typically, this distributive strategy of public choice involves an asymmetrical
distribution of benefits and costs; that is, each group pursues publicly provided goods that are characterized by concentrated benefits and diffused costs.
The conventional wisdom behind this strategy is that the concentration of
benefits facilitates effective political organization to obtain such goods that the
diffusion of costs makes it more difficult for those who bear the fiscal burden
of collective goods to organize in opposition.[46]

Notice that any number of groups can play this strategy and still have it
appear that each gains. As each group makes its respective demands on the
public sector, it will appear, incrementally, that the benefits to the group from
making such demands will exceed the costs. Of course, the requisite vote

trading that will be required to secure the support of other groups may redress the imbalance at another time. But given the incremental character of these constantly shifting political bargains, it is difficult to fix an equilibrium point at which the benefits and costs to each group can be measured. The public that bears the lion's share of the costs will always appear to be some remote "other," a nameless, faceless entity with which few will identify as they each proceed to seek their individual vision, their version, of the public interest.

The problem is not one of perception only. Suppose every group correctly evaluates the full costs as ultimately borne by each group. Suppose, further, that on this perception each group recognizes that continuing the process is not a positive-sum game in which everyone gains, but a negative-sum game in which all lose. They may still be unable to act on these presumptions and to refrain from vote trading that yields net losses for all. As William Riker and Steven Brams have shown, the traders face a prisoners' dilemma for they have no means of assuring cooperative action to insure a globally efficient set of trades.[47] The dilemma here is similar to the one used to describe the problem of private market choices involving true public goods, about which more shortly. However, that dilemma has a ready-made institutional solution: in place of private market choice substitute public (political) choice. Unfortunately, there is no comparable institutional mechanism for solving the prisoners' dilemma confronting individuals/groups operating in the public market. In the absence of an enforcement mechanism for ensuring cooperative forbearance by all individuals/groups, each will continue its demands and each will seek vote trades to secure illusory gains.

Nothing has been said of the supply side of the equation beyond the casual observation that politicians, from the president on down, can be expected to respond to their public constituents' manifest wishes. The workings of the supply side are, of course, more complicated than this passive response model suggests. Most modern political theorists describe the supply side in more dynamic terms in which both politicians and bureaucrats play entrepreneurial roles in promoting and shaping constituent demand in order to promote their own respective interests.[48] Students of public choice tend to describe the preferences of politicians and bureaucrats fairly narrowly in terms of personal interests, but ideological preferences obviously can be an element of those interests.[49] Still, however the interests are described, their satisfaction has been often thought to lie in expanding, more than contracting, government expenditures.[50] It is a public sector counterpart to the well-known private market phenomenon that John Kenneth Galbraith labeled the "revised sequence" in which producing firms create a market demand to which they can respond.[51]

Deregulatory trends of the 1970s and 1980s are sometimes cited as an indication of a changing political mood about big government.[52] In a sense they are. Certainly there is no denying that there have been some important deregulatory measures taken—though we will see later that some of these may be less permanent than had been thought. We now have the example of the CAB's demise (interred at the end of 1984, but moribund for several years before that) to prove that not all federal agencies are immortal.[53] And we have other important instances of regulatory rollback to illustrate the possibility of ratchet adjustment. These include a substantial deregulation of telecommunications and of mass communication by the FCC,[54] substantial deregulation of surface transportation (easing of entry and rate controls) by the ICC,[55] some energy deregulation (pricing controls),[56] and cutbacks in antitrust and consumer protection enforcement.[57] The CAB is unique in being officially terminated, but both the Consumer Product Safety Commission (CPSC) and FTC have come very close to being terminated in the 1980s.[58]

It is difficult to say what one should conclude from the recent deregulatory movements. In each case it is possible, in retrospect, to analyze the conditions, both political and social, that produced the changes. From such analysis one can tell a story that somewhat resembles a theory of regulatory change. But it is a theory of such loose generality (as in Grover Cleveland's "it is a condition . . . ") that its usefulness may be doubted.[59] One is tempted to see elements of randomness here—not randomness in the sense that each cannot be described by reference to a set of readily understandable political forces, but randomness in the sense that it would be hard to predict the course of events ex ante on the strength of the received wisdom about politics, government, and bureaucracy. The deregulatory events just cited occurred over a period spanning the Ford, Carter, and Reagan administrations. Ironically, many of the most salient events were inaugurated, even completed, prior to the Reagan administration. More than any other administration in modern times, the Reagan administration defined its agenda in terms of containing and rolling back regulatory and welfare programs. Yet viewing the "Reagan revolution" in retrospect, its contributions in this direction were mostly a consolidation of initiatives begun earlier.

If particular deregulation measures are hard to credit entirely to presidential agendas, they also appear only faintly related to public concerns. Public concern has possibly been more intense on the subject of general government expenditure levels, and particularly deficit spending. The concern has had some effect, most dramatically in the form of the Balanced Budget Act and the Emergency Deficit Control Act of 1985 ("Gramm-Rudman-Hollings"),[60] a statute with an imposing name and an ambition to match, the elimination of the deficit and restoration of a balanced federal budget. What is noteworthy about the Balanced Budget Act for our purpose is the method of enforcement. Overcoming the prisoners' dilemma, as I explained, requires not only information and communication among the parties but a mechanism for enforcing cooperative behavior—in this case cooperative forbearance from pressing their self-defeating demands for government benefits. The different groups can promise to forebear, but some means must be found to enforce the promise. The Balanced Budget Act seeks to do this by setting up a device for automatic spending cuts ("sequestration") in case the parties—Congress, the president, and their varied constituencies—cannot agree on specific sacrifices.

No one would claim that the strategy has worked according to its ambitions. The deficit remains, in part due to unfavorable economic conditions and in part due to accounting manipulations that have allowed Gramm-Rudman-Hollings limits to be evaded.[61] In 1990 Congress took another stab at the problem with a new five-year program that modifies the sequestration mechanism with a new "pay-as-you-go" sequester.[62] Under this new mechanism caps are established for discretionary spending in each of three major categories, defense, domestic, and international programs. Any appropriations bill that exceeds the cap in any of these categories will automatically trigger an offsetting spending reduction in that same category. (There are no trade-offs between categories.) Similarly in the case of entitlement programs any expansion that is not covered by increased revenue sources will trigger a reduction in other entitlement program spending.

Mindful of experience with Gramm-Rudman it would be imprudent, perhaps, to invest much hope in "son of Gramm-Rudman."[63] Still, the basic strategy underlying both Gramm-Rudman and its offspring is noteworthy. The sequestration mechanisms of both are a precommitment strategy by the affected parties. The hope was that the strategy would not need to be implemented, that the political protagonists having interests in programs that were specially vulnerable to automatic program cuts would accept limits in order to achieve a better result through a negotiated budget cut. But barring such argument, the final objective would still be reached, albeit by more drastic means.

The automatic feature of the act has been widely criticized as an abdication of responsibility. It was, in the same sense that Ulysses' having himself bound to the mast was an abdication of self-will, but as with Ulysses so with Congress, one ought at least give credit for recognizing the inherent weakness of the political flesh, in the same way we give ourselves credit for the often ingenious stratagems by which we bind ourselves against succumbing to the siren songs of future temptations.[64] It remains to be seen whether any meaningful principles of restraint can be formulated or whether the boundaries of public action are entirely the product of contingent political convenience such as reducing deficit spending and its attendant economic problems. I broach this subject reluctantly, mindful this is a subject that has occupied political theorists since Plato and Aristotle, whom I have no ambition to emulate in the formulation of grand theory. Nevertheless, some brief observations about political theory are necessary and appropriate to anchor what would otherwise appear to be merely vagrant sentiments about the basis for legal principles in the discussion contained in later chapters.

Public and Private Spheres: Public Goods

Liberal theories of society assume the primacy of individual choices and of free private association over enforced community obligations. Both contractarian and utilitarian philosophy share this common philosophical starting point. The primacy of the individual in society is a distinctly modern idea in political thought as in political practice. In traditional hierarchical societies, notions of individualism were (and still are) suppressed in favor of social stratification and political authority. In classical republican societies (Greek city-states, the Renaissance republics of Italy, and eighteenth-century Swiss cantons are the standard examples; eighteenth-century New England towns might be added to the list as well) individualism was subordinated to ideas of community.[65] Today, of course, the liberal-individualist ideal predominates in Western democracies ("Western" in this context being a shorthand for economically advanced societies without geographic significance); however, its hold on political theory and practice is much less secure than we in liberal societies commonly assume. Though it is not easy to find respectable modern theory in support of hierarchical, authoritarian societies, there is a considerable body of theory supporting communitarian ideals in the context of republican societies.

None of these broad philosophical perspectives—utilitarian, contractarian, or communitarian—offers any unambiguous definition of the respective domains of public and private activity. At the level of general theory, communitarians belittle the public-private distinction. Their basic message is that, in organized society, the public sector has no fixed boundary: all social life is public, and activities conventionally regarded as private are shaped and influenced by social rules and public actions.[66] To be sure, even communitarians do not believe there is no room for private choice, individual determination, and free private associations. As a matter of economic organization, even the most thoroughly socialist regime allows room for private economic choices, for example, among consumer goods. Modern socialist economic theory, while emphasizing the need for public control of basic macroeconomic policies, still values the efficiency and the ethical justice of individual choices at a microeconomic level.[67] However, if there are any ascertainable criteria that mark off the respective boundaries of public and private choice in communitarian theory they are quite obscure.

If communitarians are vague as to the appropriate range of public and private choice, so are most liberals. The individualist premise of liberal theory proves to be almost as indeterminate as the more collectivist premises of communitarian theory. Witness the divergence between the two foremost exponents of liberal political theory, Hobbes and Locke.[68] Hobbes, the father of modern liberal political theory, derives an argument for totalitarianism from individualist premises. For him, the social contract was a means of escaping from the "state of nature" in which individualism and private choice were unconstrained to a collective state in which private choice was entirely controlled. At the other extreme, Locke, who refused to accept Hobbes's dark views of human nature, believed man needed only the guidance and moderate constraint of public authority. For him, the social contract was an instrument of accommodation between the state and the individual. The difference between Hobbes and Locke sets the philosophical extremes of the public-private realms in liberal political thought. However, Locke did not specify the functions of government beyond the obvious function of security and enforcement of individual property rights with any clarity. The exact distinction between the public and private realm is more atmospheric than operational, as befits the highly general character of his social contract theory. The other strand of modern liberal theory argues from utilitarian rather than contractarian premises, but embraces a similar outlook on the public-private distinction. Utilitarian theorists like Hume (a utilitarian in matters of social policy, not in matters of moral principle), Smith, Bentham, Mill, and others in the classical tradition repudiated the contractarian methodology, but their view of the public-private domain is broadly similar to that of Locke.[69]

For liberals, the priority of individual choice over public choice rests on the notion that the latter is inherently coercive, an interference with individual freedom. This conception of freedom, of course, depends on drawing a sharp distinction between "negative liberty," entailing freedom from social interference and "positive liberty," entailing claims to social assistance to promote individual well-being. As a matter of philosophical semantics and political principle, this distinction (at least its political significance) is not beyond challenge, but this is a matter we cannot explore here.[70] No doubt erasing the distinction between negative and affirmative freedoms across the board would call for a rethinking of the priority of private over public as a matter of first principles.[71] But the ultimate liberal defense of the concept of negative liberty, and the priority of private choice that builds on it, is as much an appeal to social experience as it is to abstract principle. Experience teaches that human beings flourish better in social regimes that respect individual autonomy by committing, in principle, to a preference for private over public choice. At least this has been the lesson accepted by Americans, one embedded in our constitutional history and jurisprudence, as I shall argue in chapter 2. This does not deny public choice its role, whether that role is explained in terms of fostering positive liberties or simply promoting the social welfare. It does establish the foundation for setting boundaries on the public realm and requiring justification for public choices that displace private autonomy.

Traditionally, this has meant that public intervention is limited to those functions that require collective action to give recognition to private choices (enforce private laws) or provide services that cannot be practicably obtained through private choice (for example, providing for national defense, police, and various other "public goods"). Unfortunately, neither the classical utilitarians nor contractarians developed, with any degree of clarity or precision, a theory of what these necessary public functions were. Insofar as the contractarian tradition since Locke has tended to stress individual autonomy and the concept of negative rights—freedom from interference by others—it has a natural kinship to the minimalist conception of the public sector, for public choices are inherently coercive of individual choice. Nevertheless, while the rhetoric of individual rights and individual choices may suggest a principle of strict limitation on public choice, it is not difficult to develop contractarian arguments for a very expansive realm of public choice, as John Rawls's theory of social justice demonstrates.[72] In Rawls's social contract, the traditional conception of negative security, protection of rights against interference, is enhanced (though not trumped by) a conception of *affirmative* security against natural disadvantage. The possibility of accommodating greatly divergent views concerning the scope of the public domain reflects the open-endedness of the theory. Or at least it represents the generality of the theory; in fact, none of the contractarian theorists, ancient or modern, have been very intent on developing a clear theory of public/private boundaries.

The classical English utilitarians were more concerned with the limits of government in both the social and the economic sphere, but they, too, failed to develop a coherent theory of the public/private distinction. What emerges from their writings is less a theory than a catalog of particular functions that were thought to be appropriate—national defense, police, postal service, providing roads, maintaining highways, even some redistributive programs. All of these functions are more or less reflections of existing practice in the eighteenth and nineteenth centuries. It is a practice that has been associated with a tradition of laissez-faire, but what is most striking about the English utilitarian political philosophers is their fluid and highly pragmatic conception of the private and public sectors. Adam Smith, the patron saint of laissez-faire, was far from an advocate of the "minimalist" state as we might think of it today. Here is his basic formulation of the functions of the state.

[F]irst, the duty of protecting the society from the violence and invasion of other independent societies; secondly, the duty of protecting, as far as possible, every member of the society from the injustice or oppression of every other member of it; and, thirdly, the duty of erecting and maintaining certain public works and certain public institutions, which it can never be for the interest of any individual, or small number of individuals, to erect and maintain; because the profit could never repay the expense to any individual or small number of individuals, though it may frequently do much more than repay it to a great society.[73]

As Lionel Robbins has pointed out, the last part of Smith's formulation is quite similar in form to one given by John Maynard Keynes, one of the modern apostles of activist government.[74]

Robbins concedes that the parallel between Smith and Keynes is more formal than substantive, but he observes that this itself is important as an indication of the continuity of thought in economic liberalism concerning the relationship of the state and the individual. The presumption in favor of laissez-faire individualism in both economic and social spheres puts the burden of justification on those who argue for any form of public choice. Of course, the critical question is what justifications are sufficient, and here the theory becomes rather unclear. Smith and his followers in the classical tradition were largely content with eclectic examples of activities that the common judgment of the time had accepted as reasonable.[75] These went well beyond the limited functions of national defense, property security, and even the "public works" cited by Smith. They included matters of public health, education, and poor relief programs. How these particular programs are related to a theory of public intervention was never made clear by the classical writers. There was no linkage between the core security-defense functions, which are everywhere uncontroversial, and the more expansive welfare functions such as public health or education. One may imagine that these are functions that the individual cannot do for himself or herself; in Smith's words, "it could never repay the expense to any individual." However, the classical writers did not quite close the theory with the examples because the theory itself had not really been worked out. That remained for later, so-called welfare theorists.

Welfare theory is a theory of the conditions and limitations on private markets, why and where they work efficiently, why and where they do not.[76] It is, by the same token, a theory of public, nonmarket choice insofar as the theory identifies functions (production of goods) that cannot be performed efficiently by the market. A. C. Pigou is often regarded as a pivotal figure for his development of the concept of externalities, social costs and benefits generated by market transactions that are not accounted for by the terms of the transactions and that, in consequence, create a divergence between social and private costs (or benefits), which in turn justifies government intervention to correct the divergence.[77] Traditional welfare theory accepts the individualist premises of liberal political theory that there is no role for public coercion or intervention where private choices made through market transactions are working efficiently. Market efficiency being virtually defined as the promotion of individual welfare, public intervention could only make things worse. Thus, the essential purpose of economic welfare theory is to analyze the comparative advantages of market and nonmarket choices.

Conventional reviews of public goods theory vary somewhat in the presentation of arguments why public choice is necessary to achieve socially efficient results. However, in virtually all of the conventional treatments, public goods are characterized either in terms of *facilitating* private market choices or *correcting* private market failure. In the first category we may put property enforcement generally (although it also, to some extent, belongs in the second category). In liberal theory, enforcement of property rights is one of the most basic of all public responsibilities, second only to protection of personal security, about which more in a moment. I use the term *property* to include enforcement of all laws necessary to a functioning property rights–market system, that is, rules governing the creation of ownership, security of possession, transferability of rights, etc. The need for public rules to facilitate private choice and private transactions is so elementary that it sometimes is given only passing notice in treatments of public goods. There is also a tendency to think of public intervention as market supplanting rather than market enforcing that naturally directs attention more to the second category of rationales for public goods, the correction of market failure. To some extent, one is the mirror image of the other and all of these rationales have in common the facilitation of market-type choices. Thus, elimination of monopoly, removing barriers to information flows, and eliminating abusive practices (fraud and the like) is, in effect, just another way of enforcing the basic rules necessary to ensure that markets work effectively.

However, the market failure label is applied more broadly to encompass a range of public actions designed not to make the market work but to replace it altogether. On the whole, this view of the matter tends toward a more expansive realm of public choice. The classic example is the so-called collective consumption good, sometimes referred to as the "pure public good" although it is not at all clear why it is any purer than any other type. Paul Samuelson's model is now the standard reference, though the basic elements of the theory can be found in earlier economic writings.[78] In his model, pure public goods have two characteristics: one, they are necessarily consumed collectively rather than individually and, two, the marginal cost of supply is zero (or close to zero). Collective consumption arises from the fact that the benefits of the goods are indivisible and, hence, necessarily enjoyed by the relevant community as a whole: because the goods are indivisible they cannot be selectively supplied or allocated on the basis of a willingness to pay. The market cannot be relied on to direct the supply of such goods because individuals in the market will not register their individual demand for the good, expecting to free ride on others' willingness to pay. Of course, if enough people seek to free ride, so that the effective demand is not enough to equal supply costs, the good will not be produced at all. In any case it will be underproduced insofar as the manifest demand for it will not reflect the concealed preferences of free riders. It is necessary, therefore, to have some means for aggregating demand. This is difficult if not impossible to do on a voluntary basis. It is another instance of the prisoners' dilemma. Earlier I noted the same kind of prisoners' dilemma in the political market place; here we see it operating in the private market. Ironically, the solution here is to replace private choice with public choice and thereby to give rise to the kind of phenomenon that can produce another kind of prisoners' dilemma.

Public goods of the collective consumption variety are not many, but they are important. National defense and public law enforcement are the two classic examples of collective consumption goods. It is commonly assumed that the benefits of these two goods are inherently indivisible and, thus, are necessarily enjoyed by the public at large. The criterion of divisibility has been somewhat misperceived in popular discussions of public goods theory, however. It is common to treat indivisibility as a technical characteristic of pure public goods. In certain cases it may be, but even where selective supply is technically feasible it may be so impractical as to warrant treating the good as public.[79] To be sure, many public goods are in fact selectively provided in at least limited ways. Public police forces are supplemented by private police forces. Every university has its own police force, large corporations have their own security forces, airline terminals have private police, and so on. Such examples are sometimes cited as showing that there is no bright-line distinction between even classic public goods and private goods. That is undoubtedly the case if one regards collective consumption as a kind of technical criterion. However, notwithstanding the possibility that virtually all public goods admit some selective supply, there remains the fact that a complete reliance upon private markets would be extraordinarily costly and so impractical as to warrant treating the good as a public good. We could look on it as essentially a problem of economies of scale in production, which introduces the second criterion for classic public goods, the zero marginal-cost element.

In part this can be seen as a mirror image of the indivisibility point. If goods are collectively enjoyed, then the marginal cost of supplying the nth unit must be zero. However, the marginal cost criterion has separate significance. Even where the public good can be divided and selectively supplied, there might still be warrant for public provision if it could be supplied at zero marginal cost. Television broadcasting is a case in point: enjoyment of the program can be supplied selectively through scrambling of the signal, but in the ordinary mode of over-the-air broadcasting the cost of supply for each extra viewer is zero.[80] As has been pointed out, this does not necessarily justify public control and, indeed, public supply produces its own problems. Consider, for example in the case of broadcasting, what mix of programs should be produced, whose program preferences govern, etc.[81] This is not the occasion to pursue those problems but simply to note that, according to the pure theory of public goods, zero marginal cost *may* justify some form of collective supply.

Recall that a central reason for the public provision of collective consumption goods lies in the fact that private markets will not reflect the full benefits of such goods and, hence, they will be undersupplied (if supplied at all). These unrecognized benefits are positive externalities; their flipside is negative externalities where private transactions produce social costs that are unaccounted for by the transacting parties because they are visited upon others. This is a kind of reverse free rider problem, except here the transacting parties free ride on the fact that part of the cost of their market choices are borne by others. Because those costs are not recognized, there is a tendency to overproduce. Externalities have been a standard rationale for public intervention since Pigou argued generally for a system of subsidy and tax incentives to offset skewed market incentives.[82] In more recent times, negative externalities in particular have been the popular rationale for public intervention in environmental, health, and safety areas.

The preceding discussion primarily suggests a concern for allocative programs designed to direct the efficient use of resources—essentially to "expand the pie" of social resources. However, similar arguments can be used to rationalize wealth redistribution as a collective good requiring public intervention.[83] It is at this point, where public goods expands from a theory of production to one of distribution as well, that the elasticity of the concept is fully revealed. Quite plainly, public goods theory is not necessarily a defense of the minimalist state. An illustration is the Supreme Court's affirmance of the use of eminent domain essentially for purposes of wealth redistribution in *Hawaii Housing Authority v. Midkiff*.[84] Hawaii undertook to compel the breakup of large estates by providing that tenants living on residential lots in certain developmental tracts could petition a state agency to condemn the land and sell it to the tenants at prices set by a condemnation trial or negotiation. The Court upheld the condemnation against the claim that the mere redistribution of property rights did not satisfy the public use requirement of the Fifth Amendment (private property shall not be taken "for public use, without just compensation"), applicable to Hawaii via the Fourteenth Amendment. The Court in *Midkiff* interpreted "public use" to be coterminous with the general scope of the police power process and equal protection doctrines. As we will see in the next chapter, the applicable standard here is exceedingly lax. Excepting special cases involving fundamental rights or suspect classifications, social legislation is upheld if it is rationally related to a conceivable public purpose.[85] The Court found sufficient public purpose in the stated object of breaking up an undue concentration of landholding that interfered with the residential land use market "and forced thousands of individual homeowners to lease, rather than buy, the land underneath their homes." In this particular instance, the animating purpose of the scheme was to redistribute ownership of land (specifically fee ownership as distinct from leaseholds) not redistribution of wealth generally. However, it is hard to make sense of the former without reference to some notion of appropriate wealth distribution, and certainly that was the direct effect of the forced transfer.[86] While *Midkiff* has been criticized for its expansive application of the public use requirement, the only substantial basis for criticism is not the Court's general acceptance of redistribution as a possible public good in the abstract, but the slight burden of proof it imposed on the state to demonstrate that there were serious distortions in the market that justified it in this case.[87] The burden of proof problem is a matter to which we shall return in the next chapter.

Quite apart from whether public goods theory provides a focused justification for public action, political realists will object that it does not give an accurate description of the ways and means by which the public goods are actually determined in the political arena. Market-correcting regulation, for instance, is notoriously manipulated to achieve purely private redistributive goals.[88] So, too, is provision of "pure" public goods. We may know that national defense is a public good and, hence, that defense expenditures are, up to a point, in "the public interest." But recognition of its public status tells us little about the level and character of defense expenditures. The operative political choice is less likely to be between public and private goods, than between budget levels and particular types of programs: should defense spending exceed, say, $300 billion; should we invest in more bombers or nuclear submarines? Only to a limited degree is this the old guns and butter trade-off depicted in introductory economics texts. More often, it is a matter of guns and guns trade-offs.

The classic public goods model fails to tell us very much about how those trade-offs ought to be made; neither does it describe how they are made in fact. The political choice between, say, bombers and submarines is influenced less by the contribution each makes to national defense than how much each makes to some particular political constituency. However indivisible national defense may be in some generic sense, the fallout benefits from particular national defense *expenditures* are very divisible in just the way that classic pork barrel is divisible. And the politics of seeking those benefits are precisely analogous to the politics of pork-barreling. This is nowhere better illustrated than in the recent campaign of the Navy to persuade Congress to finance two new aircraft carriers. A key part of the strategy for demonstrating the important contribution the carriers would make to national defense was a fifty-page document showing how much each congressional district would receive of the $7 billion project expenditures.[89] Needless to say, there is a powerful correlation between the divisible benefits received and the enthusiasm for this "vital" public good. We expect the people in Seattle, Washington, and their public representatives to align themselves with air power, just as we expect the folks in Groton, Connecticut, and their representatives to support the virtue of more submarines. (In the carrier episode, it is reported that the ranking Republican on the Armed Services Committee opposed the new carriers as a diversion of expenditures from higher military priorities; his district, incidentally, was slated to receive none of the money to be spent on the carriers.)

Other illustrations to like effect could be recited endlessly but pointlessly. No serious student of American politics denies that the distribution of incidental economic benefits is crucial in determining the level and character of putatively "public" goods. The important question is whether, apart from the distributional aspects that influence public choices, there is anything left to the theory. Is there a core concept of publicness that can provide meaningful guidance for legitimating certain kinds of public decisions, and by the same token delegitimating others? Everything turns on how much specificity is wanted in the theory. If what one wants is a catalog of things that the government should and should not do, it would be almost impossible to prepare such a catalog by consulting public goods theory. Such notions as market imperfections or externalities or joint-supply problems simply do not have the kind of clean boundaries that would allow us to use them with great precision. However, as a framework for critical evaluation of public decisions, the theory is not so wholly indeterminate as to be useless. It may not tell us how much public defense to provide; it may not tell us precisely when and to whom wealth should be redistributed. But it does give us a kind of baseline by which to interrogate those who argue for more submarines for Groton, more subsidies for Wisconsin dairy farmers. The point of the theory is not, after all, to look at the things produced as much as to the character of justification that attends them. The theory starts with a baseline norm of private, market-oriented, consensual activity; the departure from that baseline must be justified within its basic premises. In other words, one must explain why individual choice will be frustrated by its own ultimate objectives. It cannot be sufficient to say that a majority (more realistically, a coalition of interest groups) has chosen, say, to subsidize dairy farmers. One has to have a persuasive story of how promoting their interests promotes the general public interest, and why reliance cannot be placed on private market choices—such as buying their milk at market prices.

At this point public goods theory starts to resemble a process theory, but importantly it is not the kind of process theory associated with modern political pragmatism, whether in the vein of David Truman or George Stigler or any of the modern public choice realists. It is more in an older style of political discourse, one that is now enjoying some revival under the banner of civic republican theory, to which I turn next.

Public Process and Public Values

Welfare theory has always been essentially normative; by contrast, the modern science of politics purports to eschew normative evaluation in favor of a positivist view of how public choice is made. I say "purports to eschew" mindful of the fact that positivist analysis and normative evaluation are not always neatly separated. Too, positivist realism tends to have a certain corrosive effect on normative judgment: it is not easy to hold fast to normative principles that are observed to be ignored in the real world. Modern political realists not only fail to observe any principled theory of public goods (or other theory of public interest broadly defined), they tend to deny its usefulness in public discourse. This has taken its toll on public idealism. When Kenneth Arrow "proved" the impossibility of a democratically derived objective social welfare,[90] he confirmed by mathematical logic what many students of the political process like David Truman were teaching from ordinary observation of the way things were. The combination of logic and observation has been devastating to those idealists who hope for more but who cannot follow Lewis Carroll's White Queen in believing "six impossible things before breakfast."[91]

Nevertheless, it did not always seem impossible to believe the political process might be engineered in ways that could yield a genuine, principled public welfare that was something more than a contingent aggregation of individual preferences. Among modern political realists this view of the political process is identified as naive idealism, of a kind characteristically associated with Wilsonian progressivism. However, the Progressives were not the first nor the last to embrace this persistently popular view of the political process. Indeed, the nation was founded on the assumption that politics was not simply the registration of individual preferences, and it is fair to say that that same assumption was an important element in the framing of the United States Constitution (and state counterparts) as well.

To be sure, the colonialists and the framers were ambiguous in their political theory, which accounts, perhaps, for the differing interpretations that have been offered by historians. The traditional intellectual history of early American thought depicts a strong commitment to Lockean liberalism with its emphasis on the primacy of individual liberty and property rights. On the other hand, more recent historical analysis has shown the strong influence of civic republicanism, with its emphasis on community, public life, and civic duty. Just how deep and sustained civic republican thought was in American political thought is controversial. J. G. A. Pocock, for example, has argued that the republican tradition was pervasive in the revolutionary period and had enduring significance in the constitutional period and beyond.[92] There can be no doubt that republican thought and ideals played an important role in intellectual discourse and popular rhetoric in the colonial period. However, as Bernard Bailyn and Gordon Wood have shown, the discourse was often very shallow and not a little confused in its understanding of the classical principles that writers of the colonial and constitutional period professed to admire.[93] Perhaps confused is the wrong way to express their view; it would be more charitable to say simply that early writers were enthusiastically eclectic in their selection of authorities to reinforce political ideals independently derived.[94] Considering their carefree eclecticism in the blending of different philosophical sources and different intellectual traditions, it is not surprising that they would not discern, or trouble about, the tensions between liberal individualism à la Locke and republicanism à la Rousseau, between the natural rights protection of the individual and the communal demands of civic obligation.[95]

If colonial republicanism was eclectic, it also proved to be quite fragile when put to the test of practical implementation. While republican ideals of civic virtue and public welfare persisted into the later constitutional period and beyond, they lost ground to a more individualistic liberalism that dominated the constitutional era.[96] The enthusiasm for republican principles that had energized at least the rhetoric of the revolution had waned. The republican ideal of a disinterested popular will—a Rousseauan "General Will," if you like—had degenerated into a "factious" majoritarianism. The ideal of public participation and legislative supremacy and corresponding distrust of executive power that had sparked the imagination of revolutionary writers had produced the threat of new tyranny in the form of state legislatures. Localism, an admired characteristic and widely supposed necessary condition of civic virtue, was seen to be a primary course of aggressive self-seeking politics to the endangerment of individual liberties (most notably property rights).

The spirit of republicanism was kept alive in the rhetoric of debate over the Constitution, particularly by the antifederalists who challenged a strong national government as incompatible with the conditions of republicanism. How far this was more than rhetoric can be debated, but there would be no point in debating it here, for it could not alter the central point that the dominant political force and intellectual spirit that produced the Constitution was republican only in the loosest, most qualified sense.[97] This is especially apparent from the defense of the Constitution by its foremost interpreters, Madison and Hamilton, in The Federalist. One has to look hard to see any strong trace of the classical republicanism that had marked political discourse a decade earlier. Madison's celebrated The Federalist No. 10 dealing with the problem of "factions" (today, "special interest groups") is especially noteworthy on this point.[98] Factions cannot be eliminated. They are inherent in the vanity of human interests and passions. To homogenize interests and passions would be futile, and to suppress self-interested behavior would risk a tyranny as great as that posed by factions themselves. Madison's famous solution, of course, lay in a constitutional design that would control the effects of factions. In The Federalist No. 10, the key design is to refer the great and aggregate interests to the national legislature, increasing the number of representatives and making it more difficult for factions to unite into a majority. Too, the larger size of the national arena, Madison thought, would give prominence to representatives who were disposed to take a broad view of the public welfare, as opposed to representatives who were preoccupied with local interests. The "federal strategy" was not the only constitutional mechanism for combating the influence of factions. The separation of powers among the branches of the national government, the different composition of the two houses of Congress, and a limited presidential veto power were coordinate strategies whereby interest would check interest, "ambition . . . made to counteract ambition."[99]

In none of these strategies, and in none of the conditions described in The Federalist, does it appear that republican conceptions of civic virtue played a very important role. In fact, Madison's treatment of factions in The Federalist No. 10 has been interpreted by many modern observers to be an early articulation of interest-group pluralism, the antithesis of republican idealism.[100] The identification of Madison with modern interest-group theory is somewhat misleading. For all his clear-eyed realism about self-interest as a motive force of political action, Madison would not have embraced the modern skepticism about the possibility of pursuing ideals of *public* welfare, nor accepted, as a normative view, the idea of liberalism as purely self-interested individualism. (One may doubt that Locke himself would have accepted such an interpretation of his liberal theory.) Whether or not Madison and the other framers achieved, as Cass Sunstein puts it, a "kind of synthesis of republicanism and the emerging principles of pluralism,"[101] they did not endorse the modern notion that the public interest was the simple product of preference aggregation, or the management of interest-group coalitions. If they were skeptical of the possibility of disinterested civic virtue, they nevertheless had a hope that, within the constitutional constraints they designed, the political process could produce a distinctive, objective public good.[102]

Precisely how that public good can be achieved while adhering to the core tenets of individual, liberal choice—Sunstein's "synthesis of republicanism and pluralism"—is not so readily apparent as the framers' belief that it was possible. For more than a generation now, political scientists and economists have tried to teach us the framers, Madison included, were wrong in their republican faith, and that the political process does not tend toward an exogenous public good either by its own force or by the influence of constitutional constraint.

For instance, Madison's celebrated argument in The Federalist No. 10 notwithstanding, expanding the sphere of political activity in order to diffuse and dissipate the force of faction has not achieved that objective. Indeed, shifting government powers to the larger, national arena has probably increased the problem of factions. It has increased the stakes of the game (the nation's tax base as distinct from that of the state). It has also facilitated the ability to distribute the benefits and costs of political rents asymmetrically. (A more limited jurisdiction narrows the range of cost externalization, making it more difficult for the rent-seeking group to avoid taxing itself for the benefits obtained by public action.)

Separation of powers may have hindered some factious ambitions, but for the most part the kind of checking envisioned by the framers has been modest and largely unprincipled, in any event. The delegation of legislative powers to administrative agencies has allowed Congress to finesse many of the constraints envisioned by Madison. A strong presidency, another promised restraint on factions (see Hamilton's The Federalist No. 70), has also been only modestly successful. Presidential prerogative complicates the organization of political coalitions, but it has not prevented them. In fact, presidential politics is itself often driven by the same rent-seeking politics that are manifest elsewhere.

Which leaves the judiciary—the "least dangerous Branch" as Hamilton called it (in The Federalist No. 78). Consistent with classical republican theory that the legislature was the sole embodiment of popular sovereignty, Madison apparently did not contemplate judicial review of legislation as a check on factious politics.[103] Others, including Hamilton, did envision judicial review of legislative choices as intrinsic to enforcing the rule of law.[104] But the scope of this review was not defined, as indeed the issue received very little attention.[105] Whether such a judicial role can be defended, and how it can be defined, has been the subject of scholarly and political debate since *Marbury v. Madison*.[106] In recent years, conservatives have made it a subject of political controversy of a sustained intensity not seen since the New Deal era.

The next chapter explores this subject. It argues for an activist role for constitutional review that goes beyond mere rights enforcement (at least as traditionally conceived) to embrace a public good conception of public action. I resist describing this public good simply in terms of civic republican ideals, in part because those ideals seem hostile to such a role for courts but more importantly because those ideals are too quick to embrace communal goals over individual interests. However, the republican ideal of deliberative politics, reinforced by the necessity, if not the virtue, of an unrepresentative (in the narrow, agency sense) leadership, is an important element in the conception of constitutional constraint I want to defend. The basic point is that republican theory must be updated and refocused on the core tenets of liberal individualism and market (consensual) choice.

The problem with most contemporary appeals to republican ideals is their refusal to commit to a normative baseline against which public decisions can be evaluated.[107] The tendency is to see anything as proper so long as it is public spirited in some vaguely Rousseauan sense. But to avoid baselines is to eschew any enforceable legal restraint on public action. Without a "default rule" (as modern contract scholars might call it) favoring private ordering, we have no basis for ordering burdens of proof on the question whether a given action is justified. Without such a burden of proof, any attempt to impose legal restraints simply reduces to a feckless wrangle of shapeless arguments among those who support and those who oppose a particular public decision.

CHAPTER 2

Constitutional Limitation on Public Choices

Deriving constitutional principles from political theory is a tricky business; even if there is a significant consensus on broadly stated norms of political action, there is unlikely to be comparable consensus as one moves down the rung of generalization to the level of detail necessary to construct meaningful constitutional jurisprudence. The appropriate level of detail for constitutional principles depends, of course, on what one expects them to accomplish; what I have in mind here is not any particular set of *rules* so much as a set of *principles* concerning the proper ambition of constitutional law. More particularly, it is the principles that should govern judicial implementation and enforcement of constitutional law. This latter point might be debated inasmuch as the courts, including the Supreme Court, are not the sole interpreters of constitutional principle. However, they are the authoritative interpreters. Whatever arguments might be made in principle for coordinate and coequal powers of interpretation among the legislative, executive, and judicial branches, the accepted reality since *Marbury v. Madison* has been that the judicial interpretation is paramount. It is difficult to see how it could have been otherwise for a constitutional system that makes constitutional norms part of its ordinary legal system. Of course, it is this paramount position of the judiciary in constitutional interpretation that makes the attempt to derive constitutional principles from political norms controversial, the common observation being that courts have no comparative advantage over the executive or the legislature in regard to judging political norms. Be that as it may, the courts do have that role and they can hardly perform it by delegating the task of defining its content to the executive or legislative branches.

It has nevertheless been imagined by some that constitutional law does not require adopting any political theory of government; the notion is that constitutional principles should be neutral to political philosophy, at least within the capacious realm allowed by a commitment to "liberal democracy," whatever that may mean. One example of this kind of constitutional argument is associated with the work of John Hart Ely,[1] which imagines the U.S. Constitution as essentially a set of structural and procedural arrangements and principles designed to accommodate diverse and ever-changing political alignments on whatever public choices they wish to make. The structure is supposed to be neutral to any particular substantive outcome, or at least with respect to any theory of social welfare. The only constraint is that there be fair political representation. I will return to Ely's view of constitutionalism. Here, I need only make the point that while his theory may be neutral to particular legislative choices, it is not neutral to political theory. On the contrary, it unambiguously embraces a normative version of the interest-group theory of political behavior that I discussed in the last chapter.

Although Ely occasionally seeks to support the argument by reference to the framers' design, his argument is primarily a direct appeal to democratic pluralism. Another version of neutral principles does seek major support from historical design. It comes to pretty nearly the same result as Ely's theory, but the terms of justification are distinctive and have prompted a nearly endless constitutional debate. The debate over the role of historical understandings, over so-called original intent, warrants at least passing notice. However, it will not occupy us long, for I think most of the debate over original intent is a rhetorical sideshow, designed to influence people who do not want to think about the substance of constitutional principle. I do not say that history has no importance as a guide to constitutional interpretation. Quite apart from the use of precedent as a means of giving determinacy and stability to law, historical understandings in general are an important means of anchoring constitutional values, distinguishing long-term principles from epiphenomenal preferences. In the brief treatment that follows, I shall argue for a distinction between history and evolving historical attitudes as a kind of baseline for a contemporary definition of constitutional principle on the one hand, and original intent as a legal lodestar on the other.

Constitutional Interpretation

It has sometimes been remarked that American constitutionalism is our secular religion.[2] If so, it is an extraordinarily tolerant one, allowing its adherents not only their own choice of patron saints but their own individual catechism as well. Some see the divine spark in the Constitution itself; others see it not in the text but in a disembodied spirit, rather in the fashion of Jean Anouilh's Becket who loved not God but the "honor of God."

The former sect, comprised of political conservatives in the main, insists on anchoring constitutional principles in interpretations of the text and in meanings that may be reasonably ascribed to its creators or, at least, can be discerned in the zeitgeist of the period in which the text was written, explained, and ratified.[3] The latter, more free-spirited sectarians, political liberals for the most part, are disposed to ignore the historic intent of the framers embedded in the text and to appeal directly to "fundamental values" derived from shared social norms. The norms are associated with the principles set forth by the framers two centuries ago. However, they are not identical to such principles; they have a life of their own.[4]

The dichotomy between conservative interpretivists and liberal noninterpretivists, as the two opposing groups have come to be known, is somewhat misleading.[5] Even the most hide-bound interpretivists do not suppose the Constitution can be construed in the manner of any ordinary legal instrument. The "social contract" is not quite an insurance contract, however much the two contracts might be thought to share a Rawlsian philosophical premise of risk sharing. At the other extreme, few proponents of the "living Constitution" suppose that it has a life *wholly* independent of the language of the written text. The differences between interpretivism and noninterpretivism are not so much matters of hermeneutic method as they are constitutional principle. Or to put it more precisely, the respective hermeneutic methods of interpretivists and noninterpretivists reflect their respective philosophies of constitutional principle. If interpretivists tend to give greater weight to historical meaning— "authorial intent" broadly defined—they do so less because they cherish the political wisdom and values of those who wrote the Constitution (though they may, in fact, cherish them) than because they abhor the notion of judicial review of legislation unanchored by textual limitation. For noninterpretivists, on the other hand, the notion of not being tightly bound by text is not so much a negative reaction to historical views (though perhaps they do view them negatively) as it is a reaction to any fixed set of restraints on the power of the courts to intervene where contemporary political fashion calls for them to do so.

If this conflict between liberal and conservative interpretation reflects contemporary political ideology, it is noteworthy that both sides seek support in history whenever they can find it. To some extent this is rhetorical no doubt, but it is also, I think, an important principle of legal argument that serious protagonists, liberals and conservatives, embrace. The use of history as legal precedent is deeply ingrained in law, particularly but not exclusively common law. Precedent has several functional purposes that are somewhat independent of historical continuity.[6] It helps to assure equal treatment of like groups, for example, and this function presupposes only minimal continuity with the past. So too, precedent promotes certainty in the law, and again this objective requires only minimal, short-term historical continuity. However, quite apart from these functional purposes that only marginally implicate the historic sense, law does appeal to historical continuity as means of reinforcing authority. Legal positivists, like John Austin, may insist that, ultimately, law is the force of sovereign authority, but every legal system depends on more than force in the crude sense of physical coercion and threat.[7] As H. L. A. Hart put it, there is a difference between legal obligation and the gunman's threat, "give me your money or your life."[8] Intrinsic to the concept of the force of law is a collective sense on the part of those subject to it that the laws have some claim of legitimacy that transcends raw power.[9] This legitimacy is importantly bound to history. An appeal to the utilitarian value of particular rules of law, or an appeal to basic or fundamental rights and obligations, is almost never sufficient without some further appeal to a tradition in which utility, rights, and duties have withstood the test of time. Certainly this is true of constitutional law. Those who want corroboration of the practical importance of appeals to history as authority have only to scan Supreme Court opinions that constantly appeal to history, even when they have to revise it to make it come out right.[10]

The importance of historical continuity should not, however, be confused with "original intent," that rhetorical beacon of conservative politicians and (some) conservative constitutional scholars. Given that we have an ostensibly written Constitution, it is natural for historical interpretation to take the form of looking for authorial intent, to derive our authority from the text as it was originally intended. It is a misguided strategy, for reasons rehearsed so often they probably do not bear recounting. I will recount them anyway, but only in summary fashion.

To begin with the matter of authorial intent, there is a nontrivial problem of documenting the legislative history surrounding the document. Most of the debate over what the framers' *meant* by certain words and phrases assumes that the contemporary records of the Convention and other relevant records accurately reflect what was *said*. Unfortunately, that assumption turns out to be incorrect.[11] But even if this problem is surmounted, there is the more fundamental problem, familiar to modern legislative glossarists, of how to derive a singular intent from a collective body of authors. We have it from Madison himself that drafting the Constitution was "the work of many heads and many hands,"[12] and manifestly the compromises that were worked out among them provide occasion for ambiguity of intent. And presumably the understanding of the ratifiers must be consulted as well, compounding the problem of reconstructing a coherent intent. All of this is plain enough to anyone who has thought about problems of legislative intent, but it is a problem typically finessed rather than resolved. The finesse commonly takes the form of adverting to evidence of agreement on general principles without the close scrutiny of possibly divergent understandings as to what the agreement means on matters of detail. The fact that the framers were able to reach agreement on constitutional fundamentals has tended to obscure the very different interests and ideological conceptions lying beneath the consensus,[13] interests and conceptions that inevitably produced different views of what the "agreement" meant.[14]

Even if one sets aside these problems, interpretation presents formidable difficulties. A *strict* adherence to the framers' intent would imply not merely fidelity to the constitutional values they embraced but also their own principles of constitutional interpretation. (This may not be a logical necessity; however, one must at least offer a plausible theory justifying adherence to the framers' substantive but not their hermeneutic principles; I am unaware of any attempt to construct such a theory.) However, fidelity to the framers' principles of legal interpretation proves awkward if not simply embarrassing, for the historical evidence indicates that the framers thought of constitutional interpretation as essentially an exercise in textual exegesis on the model of formalist contract construction, not a search for authorial intent in the style of modern legislative purpose analysis.[15]

It requires no argument to demonstrate the unrealism of such a formalist approach today, for I think no serious constitutionalist would assert that we could derive much meaningful contemporary guidance from the text by means of simple textual exegesis alone. Sensible interpretivists themselves allow not only for the use of extrinsic evidence of intent but also contemplate constructions of intent that allow contemporary adaptations, providing those adaptations preserve the original, basic values. No one denies application of the First Amendment to, say, radio and television simply because the framers could not have had any notion of speech by these media. Similarly, it would be considered frivolous to argue that the Fourth Amendment cannot apply to wiretaps and other modern surveillance technology because the framers would have been entirely innocent of such devices.[16] And so on. It is enough, the interpretivist argument goes, that we maintain fidelity to the relevant social values as the framers conceived them. A similar approach underlies the view that the source of constitutional meaning is not strict authorial intent but the general understanding of the time.[17]

But the quest for original values can be highly misleading. Even if one could retrieve an accurate original understanding, in general, or a specific authorial intent, there is still a problem of relevance. The inquiry into intent, for example, cannot be confined to what the framers thought about two hundred years ago. After all, we know they did not think about the lawfulness of television regulation or of aerial surveillance of industrial plants or. . . . The list of contemporary constitutional disputes they did not think about is endless. Plainly we must be a little creative in how we think about original intent. It cannot be simply a matter of what, say, Madison thought but what would Madison think today, for it is only in the latter context that his values can make any sense to us. The same is true for the collective framers, ratifiers, or even general public whose views are supposed to be the basis for an "original understanding."

The problem of reconstruction is not solved simply by extracting the core values from the framers' thought and transporting them to the present, as some originalists appear to suppose. Values are not Kantian noumena lying outside the realm of phenomenal existence; they are the contingent product of our environment and our experience. Consider, for example, the recent emphasis, in historical and constitutional scholarship, of the influence of civic republican thought on the framers.[18] The discovery of civic republicanism provides an important perspective on historical understandings, and thus on original constitutional values. However, quite aside from controversy about the importance of republican thought to the framers,[19] one has to be cautious in interpreting republicanism both in the context of their time and ours. First of all, republicanism was discussed by the framers in the context of debating practical political choices about the basic model of government. Whatever its theoretical attributes, republicanism was first and foremost an alternative to hereditary monarchy and aristocracy. From a distance of two hundred years we often forget that the possibility of monarchial or aristocratic government was a subject of practical concern and normative debate.[20] In that context, discussions of republican ideals—civic virtue and the like—are almost certain to be understood differently than today, where the republican *form* of government is secured and the question is only its philosophical essence. Even aside from that historical difference, the essence of republican theory is hard to fix in a simple, generally accepted and consistent set of principles, legal or political.[21] Celebration of republican ideals is a product of contemporaneous political issues and political rhetoric as much as a studied attempt to construct coherent theory. The framers' admiration for the civic virtues of ancient republics was more the product of eighteenth-century Whiggish politics than of anything to be found in classical Rome, Athens, or Sparta.[22] Indeed, in some instances it is apparent that the conception of traditional republicanism was more the product of romantic imagination than reflective political theory. Samuel Adams's dream of reconstructing a "Christian Sparta" in Boston[23] cannot have been based on an informed understanding of *historic* Spartan or Christian values or on a clear-eyed understanding of the conditions of eighteenth-century America.[24]

So too with contemporary constitutionalism. While the appeal of a republican vision of public life is considerable, one ought not to imagine that its revival today is a simple matter of translating eighteenth-century letters and pamphlets into modern prose and plugging them into contemporary controversies.[25] Even applying an originalist perspective, how can we be sure that the core principles we discern in the framers' world would still be so regarded (by them) if they lived in ours? Would Samuel Adams believe in a Christian Sparta for modern Boston? (The mind reels at the very thought.) Even if the general principles would survive the translation, can we determine the scope of their application? Would the framers have the same view of the value of "freedom of speech and of the press" if they had television? I am not asking whether Madison would think *Friday the 13th* or *Misty Beethoven* are worthy of protection; I am asking how his view of the press function generally might be influenced by exposure to such a radically different sociocultural phenomenon as television.

Some modern philosophers of interpretation have suggested the idea of a dialogue with authors, be they literary or legal, as a means of recovering the contemporary essence of the author's intent. Stanley Cavell, for example, has suggested such an approach to literary interpretation, which Ronald Dworkin has extended to legal interpretation.[26] Something similar has been suggested by Richard Rorty in the context of the history of philosophical thought.[27]

The case for "dialogic reconstruction," if we can call it that, seems especially strong in the case of constitutional interpretation of a text written two hundred years ago. If we are seeking to uncover, in our interpretation, the philosophy, the values Madison sought to embody in the Constitution, Madison must be given a voice we can understand. As a practical matter we cannot go back into his world; he must be brought into ours (by the power of our imagination, not his). Perhaps needless to say, at this point we have come so far from what is conventionally regarded as original intent that its usefulness must be doubted. Strict interpretivists will no doubt agree, though they will derive a different conclusion from the point: an updated Madison is a fiction that only obscures the fact that we are no longer interpreting the Constitution; therefore the historical conversation must be rejected. However, the "therefore" is not logically compelled; if we cannot adhere to a literal rendering of text or a strictly historical account of the framers' intent, what is gained by interpretivism? It really comes down to a choice of fictions.

Interpretivists, as I said, want to fix on original intent out of fear that anything but a fixed reference point will undermine constitutional authority; it will open up constitutional interpretation to free-form judicial lawmaking in accordance with contemporary convenience. The fear of an unconstrained judiciary is reasonable, though much exaggerated in my view. It is important to keep an eye on social purpose. Curbing judicial discretion in matters of social choice is surely not an end in itself; presumably, the reason for constraining judges is to give greater rein to democratic public choice, to "we the people" or at least our political representatives. That preference necessarily assumes the preeminent legitimacy of the political process whatever outcomes it produces; the argument from democracy turns out to be an argument against constitutional judicial review altogether. Originalism, then, becomes simply a strategy for confining judicial review. But, of course, the argument is never pressed all the way: no one argues for a reversal of *Marbury v. Madison*. The effect of the originalist argument, therefore, is to instate as constitutional constraints the values of a small group of eighteenth-century aristocrats ("an assembly of demi-gods" Jefferson called them) who wrote the Constitution.[28] Why? On the instrumentalist version of interpretivism it is simply to curb contemporary judicial discretion. Why? So that "the people" can rule. But then how can we justify limiting "the people" according to the norms of people long gone to their rest?

As an argument for original intent, the appeal to democratic political choice simply cannot be taken seriously. A more substantial argument is that original intent at least preserves the special status of basic constitutional values against the erosion of everyday political convenience. In a sense this is just the reverse of the argument for democracy, and it appeals precisely to the nature of constitutionalism as a means of anchoring basic institutional arrangements and basic public values against the ebb and flow of ordinary political controversy. The argument for stable political arrangements and social norms is intrinsic to any meaningful conception of what constitutionalism is all about. But, again, it is not an argument for original-intent interpretivism. The United States Constitution is now two hundred years old. A lot of history has passed in that time, and with it constitutional meaning has changed in light of contemporary circumstances. We could not recover the constitutional world of the eighteenth century if we wanted to. And we should not want to. Returning to the original understanding, regardless of intermediate glosses, would be disruptive to the very conservative political values that the strict constructionists profess to honor. Leaping over two hundred years of history in order to recapture some original intent, even supposing we can recover that intent, would not promote historical continuity so much as it would historical archaeology.[29]

I do not say that original meanings, original understandings, are of no consequence, either to historians or to constitutional lawyers; I mean to argue only that the appeal to history is not a simple appeal to permanently fixed reference points scattered over time. It is rather an appeal to historic evolution, to an evolving understanding of intent and meaning.

But perhaps I make too much of the argument over history. At root, the central debate among constitutional scholars on the role of constitutional adjudication is concerned less with the relevance of historical meaning than it is with the ambition of judicial review. Let me turn to that directly.

Principles of Limitations and Limitations of Principle

Attempts to articulate a coherent theory of constitutional limitations suitable to a liberal democracy have not been notably successful. A great deal of effort has gone into debating the respective merits of interpretivist and noninterpretivist approaches to constitutional theory, but neither of these perspectives provides a substantive theory of constitutional limitation. The text, even when supplemented (modestly) by historical inquiry as required to divine original intent, is not helpful except to anchor certain constitutional values that claim contemporary adherence. On the other hand, escaping from the text obviously does not solve the problem of standards; it only exacerbates it, just as conservative critics of judicial review have emphasized. What text and history cannot provide must be sought from some political theory of constitutional limitation, and efforts to develop such a theory have foundered on an inability to articulate a coherent basis for defining the boundary between private and public realms or on an unwillingness to recognize such a boundary even if one could be defined.[30]

However, liberal political theory, as I pointed out in the previous chapter, critically depends on conceptualizing such a boundary, and a constitutional jurisprudence that is faithful to basic liberal values must attempt to respond to the task. In critical commentary about the difficulty (or impossibility) of principled constitutional restraint on majoritarian choice—the "countermajoritarian difficulty" as Alexander Bickel called it[31]—it is sometimes forgotten that it is the point of a constitution to enforce limits on transitory majorities in the interest of a basic security for all. (The true Hobbesian "state of nature" is not primitive society but unconstrained majoritarian politics.) Majoritarian constitutionalism is an oxymoron. At least it is if constitutionalism is taken as something more than an ordering of institutional roles—a kind of *Roberts' Rules of Order* by which votes are cast and preferences tabulated, etc.

Ironically, for all of the debate about whether the Supreme Court should review legislative choices, the fact is it has done so since *Marbury* with the persistent approval of a majority of the people and their representatives, whose popular judgements are held in check by it. To be sure, there has been great controversy over particular targets of judicial review. The argument never ceases over the Court's rulings on abortion, religious displays, free speech, school prayer, racial integration, criminal procedure, etc. Interestingly, however, many of the specific rulings that are most controversial are uncontroversially within the purview of judicial review. One can quarrel over the Court's free speech rulings, for instance, but it cannot be seriously debated that the Court has a proper role in reviewing legislation affecting free speech. Nor can it be seriously debated that this role is countermajoritarian and everywhere understood and defended as such.

In principle, the majoritarian public itself accepts this countermajoritarian role. A recent survey showed that while few members of the public could name any Supreme Court justice (over half could name the judge of television's "Peoples Court") over half approved of the job the Court was doing.[32] I do not suggest that this fact necessarily suffices to legitimate judicial review. Inasmuch as it is the burden of my argument to question the unchecked dominance of majoritarian rule, I could hardly be heard to claim that review is privileged by reason of its popular acceptance. Still, it is important to observe that the debate over the institution of constitutional judicial review is sometimes made to appear more threatening to democratic preferences than democratic preferences themselves reveal. When one gets beyond the rather sterile debate over interpretivism and noninterpretivism, the controversy over review essentially reduces itself to the problems of how to determine the criteria for judicial evaluation and how to fix the level of scrutiny (the burden of proof) to be applied to legislative choices—the latter including the question of whether to apply different standards to personal versus economic rights, etc. These are important problems, but they are not quite so fundamental as critics of judicial review want us to believe.

Generalizing about the criteria and the level of judicial scrutiny for all of the varied types of constitutional issues has limited usefulness. An adequate understanding would require us to explore the particulars of various constitutional problems and doctrines, the detail of constitutional law. This would demand an entire treatise. Without undertaking such an ambitious survey, I want to touch on more general matters of principle as they affect judicial review of public (legislative) choices. Setting to one side those special areas of judicial scrutiny under specific constitutional guarantees, like that of free speech, I shall focus on the Court's generic rule for the review of legislation, the so-called minimal rationality test applied under equal protection and (substantive) due process analysis. This will serve my limited aim of examining the basis for constitutional enforcement of public purpose.

We could approach the same task from other constitutional reference points. For instance, one could examine the takings clause of the Fifth Amendment (and, by incorporation, the Fourteenth) on the notion that government interference with individual rights, economic rights at least, is presumptively a taking of property that must be justified by reference to a public use (public good) and be compensated. This is Richard Epstein's approach to protecting economic rights.[33] My own preference for a due process/equal protection framework rests on two considerations. One, the Court has interpreted the public use concept in the takings clause to be coextensive with the minimal rationality test used to evaluate all legislation, whether or not it effects a taking of private property.[34] While this interpretation of public use has been criticized as giving insufficient protection to private property, the strength of the criticism turns on the proper meaning and scope of the rationality requirement.[35] A sufficiently rigorous rationality requirement would make moot concerns about the adequacy of property rights protection. Two, the thrust of takings law is not quite to the point of my present concern. Granted, if government were forced to compensate individuals for economic losses directly inflicted on them, that would be a powerful and often salutary constraint on government action. But, salutary though it may be to require government to pay for injuries inflicted on some for the benefit of others, to require compensation whenever government action significantly impairs individual property would not merely constrain government, but would stop it dead in its tracks. Thus, not every interference with, or injury to, individual economic interests can be regarded as a "taking." How and where the line is drawn is a dark mystery that has long confounded the Court and everyone else.[36] A fine line must be drawn, and is drawn, between legitimate but compensable injury and legitimate, noncompensable injury. I wish to avoid this problem because I am not concerned with whether a particular action constitutes a taking but merely whether it serves a sufficiently public purpose to constitute a legitimate use of government power. This is properly the province of equal protection and due process. Consistent with the Supreme Court's own treatment, I regard the nominal distinction between these two constitutional provisions as inconsequential for the purposes of developing general principles of judicial review.[37]

Searching for *Public* Interests

Turning to the general question of standards of justification under due process and equal protection, we can start with *Williamson v. Lee Optical Co.* in 1955,[38] often cited as an authoritative modern precedent on the minimal rationality standard. *Lee Optical* is not popularly known as one of the great cases of constitutional law. Perhaps that is because it produced no memorable lines of judicial prose, but it may also be because its holding on the standards of substantive review under the due process and equal protection clauses is essentially a reprise of earlier decisions dating back to 1937, when the Court repudiated its aggressive review of economic and social legislation during the "*Lochner* era."[39] Still, *Lee Optical* is an appropriate measure of the Court's current stance toward substantive review precisely because it is not a "great case." If "great cases often make bad law," as Justice Holmes once said, *Lee Optical* attests that great cases do not have a monopoly in that respect.

An Oklahoma statute made it unlawful for any but a licensed optometrist or ophthalmologist to fit optical lenses or even to replace a broken or missing lens except on a written prescription by a licensed optometrist or ophthalmologist. The lower court found that a competent artisan could replace a lost or broken lens without a new prescription (and consequently a new eye examination) as the law demanded. It found the legal requirement was not reasonably related to the ostensible object of protecting consumers and, therefore, violated due process. The Supreme Court, by Justice Douglas, reversed. It accepted the lower court's basic findings; however, it observed that in some cases a written prescription might be necessary to fit the eyeglasses properly to the face and then speculated that the legislature might have thought that "every change in frames and every duplication of a lens should be accompanied by a prescription." The Court conceded that such a legislative conclusion would be illogical inasmuch as the law did not, in fact, require a new examination (if the old prescription were on file the optician could use it). However, the law "need not be in every respect logically consistent with its aims to be constitutional." In short, judgments of necessity, of reasonableness, and of logical consistency were for the legislature alone to make.

Notwithstanding Justice Douglas's indulgent speculations about legislative purposes related to consumer protection—ensuring eyeglass wearers that their glasses would fit correctly, etc.—it does not require eyeglasses to see that the law was not enacted for the welfare of consumers, but for the economic protection of optometrists and ophthalmologists. I doubt that anyone who examined the record of occupational licensure in this field could characterize these particular restrictions as anything other than economic protectionism.[40] I doubt that Justice Douglas had any illusions to the contrary, but, if he did, it would not have changed his or the Court's view. In an earlier case, *Daniel v. Family Security Life Insurance Co.*,[41] the Court had before it a South Carolina statute forbidding life insurance companies from operating an undertaking business or undertakers from selling life insurance. A three-judge district court made explicit findings that funeral insurance was desirable, that respondents' policies were actuarially sound, that any evils of combining insurance and undertaking could be dealt with by existing insurance regulations, and that the statute was enacted in response to lobbying by existing insurance companies who sought to eliminate the plaintiff as a competitor. Finding no legitimate purpose for a flat ban, the district court held the law violated due process. The Supreme Court reversed. Justice Murphy, writing for a unanimous court, refused to give any weight to considerations of legislative motive. At the same time, Murphy made no independent examination of legislative purpose, being content simply to observe that the South Carolina legislature was entitled "to call the funeral insurance business an evil" if it chose to do so.

Although the Court's extreme deference to legislative choice is not without critics,[42] most constitutional theorists, liberals and conservatives alike, have endorsed the general principle of judicial restraint. In part this acceptance rests on a perception that only extreme deference prevents the Court from drifting to the opposite extreme of aggressive interference with democratic choice, as in the infamous *Lochner* era. The underlying political reasons for liberal and conservative distaste for *Lochner* are, I think, different. Somewhat oversimply: liberals object to judicial interference with social welfare legislation; conservatives defend political pluralism. But persons of both political persuasions have found common ground on a point of constitutional principle, namely that there are no objective standards of rationality or public purpose by which the court can evaluate social legislation; hence, only in extreme cases (involving fundamental, personal rights or especially suspect classifications such as race, etc.), is rigorous judicial review warranted.

On this account, then, it is at best futile for courts to second guess the rationality of legislative ends. Nor can it make much sense even to question the rationality of their choice of means since the ends can always be redefined or qualified according to the means chosen. Suppose in *Lee Optical* the statute expressly said, in a preambular clause: the sole purpose of this statute is to ensure that the eyeglass consumer will not suffer serious eye injury from poorly fitted glasses. It then prescribed that such fitting will only be done by licensed ophthalmologists or optometrists who have demonstrated to the appropriate licensing authority the skill required to ensure proper fitting. After thorough investigation, we find the preambular premise to be bogus: there was never any evidence of the possibility of serious eye injury from poorly fitted glasses; in any event, the licensing scheme as established does not require any showing of special skill. The legislative history shows unambiguously that the sole purpose of the statute was to protect optometrists and ophthalmologists from competition from discount retailers (like Lee Optical). In short, our investigation tells us the legislature lied about its purpose. But so what? The argument from political realism suggests courts should not interfere with the legislative purpose even if it be purely economic protectionism.[43]

An argument has been made by Gerald Gunther that courts should nevertheless hold the legislature to its *stated* aims in order to promote at least a modicum of legislative honesty.[44] It is an appealing argument to me, but it must be observed that it is plainly not congruent with the spirit of political realism that underlies the idea of judicial restraint generally. After all, it is precisely the point of realist political theory to show that legislative choices are often not what they profess to be. The realist's blunt response to my hypothetical might go something like this: "Don't be a chump; of course the legislature was not out to protect the consumer (general public) in this case. Maybe next time the public will be better organized to see that *its* interests are served; but maybe not. In any event, such is the political process of democracy."

A variation on this argument is the "long view" of political trade-offs. Essentially, this argument is that one cannot judge legislative choices according to the design of individual statutes; rather, it is the pattern of effects from the legislative activity, across numerous subjects and across time, that determines fairness and rationality. Of course, there is no mechanism for evaluating intertemporal patterns or trade-offs among statutes, so this argument, like the first one, wholly defeats judicial review.[45]

Neither of these arguments for nonintervention quite fits the rhetorical style of the typical defense of judicial deference. Most advocates of restraint prefer to quote Justice Holmes's crisply elegant dissent in *Lochner*.

The Fourteenth Amendment does not enact Mr. Herbert Spencer's Social Statics. . . . [A] constitution is not intended to embody a particular economic theory, whether of paternalism and the organic relation of the citizen to the state or of laissez faire. It is made for people of fundamentally different views, and the accident of our finding certain opinions natural and familiar or novel and even shocking ought not to conclude our judgment upon the question . . . [of constitutionality].[46]

Holmes's restraint was a matter of genuine principle. He was philosophically skeptical of social legislation and more disposed to social Darwinism than his slighting reference to Herbert Spencer might suggest. In private correspondence, Holmes revealed his philosophical and judicial attitudes on the matter. Explaining his agreement with a Court decision absolving the United States Steel Corporation of charges of monopolization in violation of the Sherman Act, Holmes wrote to Harold Laski, this time in terms less elegant than those he chose for his *Lochner* dissent:

I hope and believe that I am not influenced by my opinion that it [the Sherman Act] is a foolish law. I have little doubt that the country likes it and I always say, as you know, that if my fellow citizens want to go to Hell, I will help them. It's my job.[47]

But it wasn't Holmes's "job" to help the public "go to hell," any more than it was Justice Douglas's responsibility to help Oklahoma ophthalmologists and optometrists force discounters from the eyeglass trade or Justice Murphy's job to help South Carolina insurance companies mug a competitor. Whether one assumes the legislative will reflects a genuine popular sentiment or is simply the artifact of a successful coalition of interest groups, it cannot be the constitutional function of courts to ratify it willy-nilly. Such a notion would effectively eliminate constitutional review altogether, or would at the least confine it to the enforcement of a handful of formal constitutional provisions that leave no room for legislative judgment. In their zeal to protect the democratic political process, warts and all, against judicial activism, advocates of judicial deference, à la *Lee Optical*, come perilously close to denying any substantive role for constitutional review.

We seem to be at an impasse. Modern political realists tell us there is no disembodied or principled public interest, no Rousseauan "general will," no Arrowan social welfare function, other than what emerges from the political process. On the other hand, liberal constitutional theory presupposes some constraint on this process and the product of public choice, whether that constraint is articulated in terms of instrumental rationality, as suggested by Gunther, or in terms of a general *public* interest requirement, as other constitutional scholars have argued.[48]

Attempts to reconcile these conflicting demands of liberalism on the one hand and public values/public interest on the other align themselves along two quite different axes. Along one axis are attempts to define some basic public values or principles that are implicit in the social contract that must be respected by political institutions, however organized, and the political process, however conducted. Along the other axis, the attempt is to design a set of procedural or organizational norms to ensure that there is open and fair access to the processes and institutions of public choice.

The idea of fundamental values is deeply embedded in liberal political thought. It was the essence of Whiggish theory that formed the political culture of the framers. The "higher law" of the Constitution as social compact was pervasive in its governance of all political institutions and processes.[49] Although the idea of fundamental principles was not an invention of American constitutionalists, the idea that these principles were legally enforceable was unique, and it was this special attribute of the higher law that generated the liberal tension between constitutionalism and democratic choice that troubled the framers and has vexed American constitutional law ever since. English constitutionalism resolved the conflict through parliamentary supremacy; though English courts can and do enforce constitutional law even in the face of seemingly contrary parliamentary judgment, ultimately Parliament is the sole repository of national sovereignty. For the Americans, a distrust of this legislative supremacy prompted the idea of an independent constitutional role for the courts.

This created an obvious dilemma for the framers. How could the courts enforce constitutional norms over and against the legislature without assuming prerogatives that the people had supposedly reposed in the legislature? In accepted principle, all law, whether embodied in legislation or common law, was subject to the authority of "right reason" and "justice," but how could such a principle be given operational force consistent with the notion that the courts must also be bound by law? If the framers resolved the problem to their satisfaction, they did so largely by finesse. Even the role of judicial review was not clearly defined. It remained for Justice Marshall in *Marbury v. Madison* to articulate that role. But *Marbury* hardly resolved the more basic problem of determining the scope of judicial review. The question was not clearly before the Court, since the constitutional issue (the original jurisdiction of the Supreme Court) required no inquiry beyond the text itself. Where the text was not clearly directive, the question of interpretation inevitably raised the question of fundamental law and this, in turn, the question, What were the sources of such law? There were, of course, some specific textual references to the protection of life, liberty, and property, to freedom of speech, to contract rights, etc. But how were these to be construed?

Consistent with philosophical tenets of the age, there was some early effort to appeal directly to principles of natural justice, illustratively, Justice Chase's opinion in *Calder v. Bull* in 1798, which appealed directly to "the nature and terms of the social compact."[50] However, Chase's opinion is noteworthy not for its invocation of principles of natural justice so much as for its insistence that such principles were directly enforceable as the spirit of the Constitution, even if they were not contained within its explicit terms. Chase's views were challenged by Justice Iredell, who insisted on locating the relevant principles within the written document. Iredell's view is more congenial to the modern legal mind, to which appeals to natural law and social contracts seem somehow quaint. Nevertheless, Chase's argument, or at least his rhetorical appeal to natural justice, was quite in tune with the spirit of his time.

Moreover, if one allows for changes in forensic style and linguistic fashion, Chase's appeal to fundamental norms has survived to modern times. Few contemporary theorists, and virtually no courts, believe in appealing to such fundamental principles wholly independent of constitutional text. But as an aid to interpreting (or "supplementing") the text, the idea that the Constitution embodies both fundamental principles and rights was and remains the dominant conception of the American Constitution. Even Justice Holmes, the last person to appeal to natural law, accepted the idea that there were fundamental principles that could be applied by the courts in reviewing legislative enactments. Despite his extrajudicial remark about allowing the people to go to hell if they wanted, Holmes acknowledged that there were limits set by "fundamental principles . . . understood by our traditions and our law."

Holmes was exceptionally restrained in searching for the sources of such fundamental principles; it is a commonplace of constitutional history that his colleagues at the time were less restrained. That is, indeed, what gave the "*Lochner* era" its bad name. But fair-minded constitutional scholars acknowledge that the active search for fundamental principles by which to contain legislative choices is not special to political conservatives; nor, for that matter, did the search end with the demise of *Lochner*. All that ended was Supreme Court interference with social and economic legislation. That left a large area in which the search for fundamental principles continues.[51]

The now standard, modern example is Justice Douglas's opinion for the Court in *Griswold v. Connecticut*, invalidating a state law criminalizing the use (and advice or assistance furthering the use) of contraceptive devices.[52] Justice Douglas, like Justice Chase nearly 170 years earlier, could find no single provision of the Constitution directly on point. Unlike Chase, he did not explicitly resort to an unwritten social compact or to natural justice; instead he found the requisite principle embodied in the collective spirit of various specific guarantees of the First, Third, Fourth, Fifth, and Ninth Amendments. From "penumbra formed by emanations," from guarantees found in these provisions, Douglas discerned a general right of privacy that protected individuals against government interference with intimate choices such as that involved in the use of contraception.

As the author of the *Lee Optical* opinion a decade earlier, which had emphatically repudiated substantive due process protection of economic liberty, Douglas was loathe to invoke the due process clause. However, his opinion falls quite comfortably within the ambit of *Meyer v. Nebraska*, a *Lochner*-era due process decision that invalidated a state law prohibiting the teaching of a foreign language to school children until they had passed the eighth grade.[53] The Court found the law an unjustified trespass on the "liberty" protected by due process. Of particular importance was the Court's expansive definition of liberty to include

> the right of the individual to contract, to engage in any of the common occupations of life, to acquire useful knowledge, to marry, establish a home and bring up children, to worship God according to the dictates of his own conscience, and generally to enjoy those privileges long recognized at common law are essential to the orderly pursuit of happiness by free men.[54]

Justice Holmes dissented in *Meyer* in an opinion that carries neither the clear conviction nor rhetorical power of his celebrated *Lochner* dissent. Two years later, when the Court in *Pierce v. Society of Sisters* invoked *Meyer* to invalidate a state statute compelling attendance at public schools, no dissent was registered by Holmes or any other member of the Court.[55]

As is well known, some of the rights cataloged by the Court have proved to be more robust than others. *Meyer's* right to pursue an occupation and *Lochner's* right to contract—"economic liberties" generally—became essentially subordinate interests when the Court virtually abandoned substantive review of economic and social legislation.[56] *Lochner*, though never overruled, was discredited; "Lochnerism" became an epithet, a one-word slander of a dishonored era of judicial arrogance. But active judicial review did not die; nor did substantive due process. Among *Meyer's* expansive list of liberties, the Court perceived certain so-called personal liberties, in which areas legislative judgment would not be given the same broad latitude as in the case of economic interests.

In 1965, *Griswold v. Connecticut* became the new model for substantive due process by recognizing a personal right of privacy.[57] Despite an effort by Justice Douglas, writing for the Court, to eschew due process doctrine, the case was generally acknowledged as an application of due process, as was its celebrated offspring in 1973, *Roe v. Wade*, striking down a state law criminalizing abortion.[58] Significant reliance was placed on *Meyer* and *Pierce* in *Roe* and *Griswold*; their authority was untouched by the decline of *Lochner*.

Four years later, in *Moore v. East Cleveland*, the Court provided what is probably the clearest exemplar of modern substantive due process in the course of invalidating a city ordinance that interfered with family living arrangements.[59] The evil of Lochnerian interference with legislative judgments was acknowledged but set aside because of the personal liberty interest in family-living choices.

The Court has been chary about extending *Griswold-Roe-Moore*, however. Indeed, the Court's 1986 decision in *Bowers v. Hardwick*, rejecting a constitutional challenge to a state law criminalizing sodomy, rejected the idea that there is a generic constitutional right of privacy.[60] More recently the Court has signaled a retreat from *Roe*, a signal many observers think will unravel this particular branch of privacy jurisprudence altogether.[61] But whatever the fate of *Roe*, it seems unlikely the Court will retreat entirely from the notion of an enforceable right of privacy of some (unknown) scope.

The right of privacy concept has been the modern focus of debate between interpretivist and noninterpretivist approaches to defining constitutional values, and, despite *Bowers*, I expect it will continue to be so. *Griswold*, *Wade*, and *Moore* are the modern counterparts of *Lochner* and *Meyer*, although most modern noninterpretivists, being somewhat left of center in their political views, deny the implied association between protecting privacy and economic liberty. Both sets of cases place the central problem of discovering the fundamental principles notion in stark relief. Holmes believed there were fundamental principles, but he did not believe economic laissez-faire to be one of them; what about noneconomic laissez-faire? How does one discover fundamental principles or values?

We could, of course, consult contemporary public opinion on the particular subject. This necessarily supposes that there is a body of opinion available to the courts other than that presumed to be reflected in the legislature's judgment. It may be possible to find such a body if one supposes that the legislature is driven by temporary aggregations of different interest groups more often than it is by general public consensus. Nevertheless, judicial resort to contemporary public consensus is tricky, particularly when broad social issues are in issue. For one thing, a consensus on basic values is maddeningly difficult to discern in a heterogeneous society. As Holmes said in his *Lochner* dissent, a constitution is made for "people of fundamentally differing views." And the Court's record in attempting to filter *fundamental* values from the clamor of ephemeral political preferences does not encourage confidence in the feasibility of this approach.[62] Take privacy as an example. Possibly there is some deep consensus about the importance of personal privacy in the abstract, but the widespread, persistent, and strident controversy over the "right to life" versus "pro-choice" demonstrates that any consensus on privacy in general does not extend to abortion in particular.[63]

The appeal to fundamental values suggests something more than contemporary consensus, in any event. Holmes, ever sensitive to the importance of history in shaping legal rules and principles, spoke of "principles as they have been understood by the traditions of our people and our law." The same notion was recently invoked by Justice White in *Bowers* in upholding a state sodomy statute. Again, it is exceedingly difficult to know what to count as a traditional value or principle. In the end, appeals to a Burkean conception of the fundamental principles appear to founder on the same rocks of American pluralism that disable contemporary consensus.

Process and Participation

The difficulty of locating fixed public values, whether in contemporary society or historic tradition, has led some constitutional scholars to dismiss it as futile, rather like the ancient alchemists' search for a philosophers stone with which to transform base metals into gold. Lead is lead. Instead of questing after nonexistent golden values, courts should confine themselves (more or less) to ensuring that the processes by which public choice is made are fair and open to all. John Hart Ely is the contemporary champion of this view.[64] Drawing on a celebrated dictum by Justice Stone in *United States v. Carolene Products Co.*[65] about the need for a special constitutional concern to combat "prejudice against discrete and insular minorities" who are effectively barred from the political process, Ely argues that the Court's constitutional task is to correct and to compensate for such failures in the political process.

Before we examine Ely's argument it is worth pausing to comment on the *Carolene Products* case, the source of the dictum from which Ely derives support. The attention given by Ely and other scholars to Justice Stone's famous footnote as a framework for judicial review of legislative choices is an interesting example of the power of a well-turned phrase to dominate intellectual discourse on the subject of constitutional principles. What is truly remarkable is not Stone's solicitude for protecting discrete and insular minorities from legislative majorities but his evident indifference to the absence of any principled justification for the legislation before the Court.[66]

The subject of the constitutional challenge was a 1923 federal statute banning the sale in interstate commerce of "filled milk," a low-cost, canned milk that was competitive with evaporated and condensed milk. Filled milk is evaporated skimmed milk to which vegetable oil is added in place of the butterfat found in whole milk. The ban on its sale was the product of a sustained campaign by the dairy industry, most notably the producers of evaporated and condensed milk. Three claims were made for banning filled milk: it is unhealthful because it lacks the vitamin A found in the other types of canned milk, customers might confuse it with evaporated milk (that is, evaporated whole milk), its sale injures the dairy industry and thereby injures the public interest. The first two claims had no basis in fact. The only credible basis for complaining about the lack of vitamin A was the concern that it might be used as formula for infants and would crowd out other sources of the vitamin. However, there was no evidence that filled milk was so used. Moreover, on health grounds, the filled milk was almost surely more healthful than condensed milk, inasmuch as the latter used huge quantities of sugar as a preservative. As for the consumer confusion, again there was no basis for this fear; the labels contained full information concerning the content. The last argument reduces simply to an assertion that the economic interests of dairy producers trump those of competing producers denied the right to market their product and those of consumers who were denied the right to purchase a wholesome, low-cost, canned milk. In short, as Geoffrey Miller aptly describes it, the statute was "an utterly unprincipled example of special-interest legislation" garbed in transparently bogus rationalizations, the effect of which was to shut down a lawful and beneficial business and to deprive poor people of a healthful, low-cost food.[67]

For the Court the facts were essentially irrelevant; in the same spirit it later manifested in *Lee Optical* and like-minded decisions, it declared the rational basis test was satisfied. Inasmuch as the producers of filled milk were not a "discrete and insular minority" (in the sense used by the Court at least), virtually any recitation of facts by the legislature suffices, whether or not the facts are relevant or true. This is the kind of result defended by Ely on the ground that judicial interference with legislative choices is only justified when they are shown to be the product of deficiencies in the political process.

Although Ely attempts to ground his theory in the actual structure and content of the Constitution, critics have demonstrated this is a loose if not simply disingenuous characterization of what the document says. It is also quite at odds with what historical evidence shows the framers probably had in mind. As I pointed out earlier, the framers viewed constitutionalism in general, and the Constitution in particular, as reflecting a higher law of rights and limits on government; while it might still be debated how much of this higher law was intended to be embodied into specific clauses like the due process clause, the contract clause, or the first amendment, it is hard to maintain seriously that the framers were content to leave substantive protection of important rights—property, liberty, contract, speech, religion—to the democratic process, subject only to vague moral and limited institutional constraints.

Least plausible of all is the notion that the framers were concerned primarily with enhancing "fair" representation in the political process. It was not the tyranny of unrepresentative minorities that most concerned the framers, but the tyranny of majorities who were all too well represented in the state legislatures. Moreover, the "outs" who were seen as victims were hardly what we would today call "discrete and insular minorities." On the contrary, they were the propertied elite. It may be that the framers looked to structural arrangements such as separation of powers and a strong national government as important political protection against the danger that such popular groups presented to the interests (most notably property) of the few. But to imagine this was the whole of their purpose is to disregard their commitment to the idea that there were fundamental rights that government, representative or not, could not infringe. As I noted in chapter 1, even Madison, whose essay on factions has nourished generations of political realists, believed the public good was more than the contingent product of converging interest groups.

Let us set aside the question of Ely's interpretation of what the Constitution says or meant to the framers. Ely's own criticism of narrow interpretivism (that is, "clause-bound interpretivism") implies that we should not give much weight to his treatment of the original understanding, but should evaluate it in terms of a noninterpretivist perspective. With such a perspective, is Ely's vision of constitutionalism an appealing or persuasive one? The answer, I think, is yes and no. It is appealing in the sense that it not only avoids the vexing problem of defining fundamental values and principles in a pluralistic, conflicted society but also neatly reconciles democratic choice with constitutional constraints. But it is not persuasive. It rests on questionable assumptions about the ability of the unalloyed political process to secure either individual fairness or a fair and efficient public welfare. Ely's argument is that of political process theorists generally In denying an objective public interest, apart from what the political process yields, though it is not clear whether this denial is to be taken as a positive or a nominative theory, or both. The important thing, in any case, is to ensure that the process is fair in being open to all. It is important to emphasize that while Ely's theory is process *based*, it does not prescribe particular political processes, except in the sense of guaranteeing electoral representation and forbidding Congress from delegating broad power to unelected bureaucrats (about which more later). Subject only to these minimal conditions, the internal dynamics of the legislative process are of no concern to Ely, just as they are of no concern to established constitutional doctrine, which imposes no procedural constraints on the legislative process apart from requirements prescribed for the enactment of laws and related institutional constraints.[68]

Ely's central ambition is to ensure that groups are not deprived of effective representation in the political process. But in any given legislative contest, there are winners and losers; the latter, almost by definition, did not have adequate representation for the particular issue on which they lost. Ely does not mean to imply that such losers have been constitutionally wronged; rather it is only those who are *systematically* denied representation that count. But who are they? It is hard to locate any identifiable group that is systematically denied access to political influence. True, some groups may find it easier than others to form effective political coalitions. However, those who are thus relatively disadvantaged are not the "discrete and insular minorities," racial or other, that are the core of Ely's concern. If constitutional solicitude is measured by the ability of groups to join effective political coalitions, it is the diffuse, unorganized general public that is more in need of protection vis à vis the concentrated, tightly organized groups—such as industry or other special lobbies.[69] In fact, as Bruce Ackerman has aptly pointed out, groups that are discrete and insular may often have an edge in political competition against others that are more loosely identified and organized.[70] Their discreteness helps the group overcome the free rider problems that frustrate effective collective action in the case of large groups of diverse membership. Insularity also fosters group cohesiveness and solidifies group preferences.

One can imagine, of course, that everyone can join some group or coalition, and while not all groups or coalitions will always be successful, all will be sometimes: every PAC will have its day. This is the assumption in what I earlier labeled the long-view model of rationality, and it is implicit in some normative versions of interest-group theory. But is it true? What can it mean anyway? How does one go about testing whether, after the struggle is over, there has been a fair distribution of the spoils? Don't we need some basic conception of fair outcome and some standards for defining it (not to mention some idea of an appropriate period of time in which to add up the gains and losses)? Justice Stone's *Carolene Products* dictum itself necessarily appeals to some such notion insofar as it is addressed to protecting minorities against "prejudice." This implies a substantive norm of rationality transcending mere process values and certainly transcending any condition of discreteness or insularity.[71] In order for the political process to claim our loyalty it must appeal to something besides simple nose counts. It must be supposed that, over time, the process yields outcomes that are fair according to some notion of reasonable public purpose.

This is the spirit behind the recent effort by some scholars to revive the concept of republican civic virtue in public law, which I noted earlier. Admittedly, the modern version of republicanism is something of a mixed bag of liberal and communitarian ideas, at least some of which would have flummoxed classical republicans from whom modern writers profess to draw inspiration. However, this is quite consistent with the earlier embrace of republicanism in both the colonial and constitutional eras. As I noted in the last chapter, that was an eclectic kind of republicanism to say the least. What is important to understand about both the earlier version and the present versions is that they all give evidence of normative dissatisfaction with the prevailing school of political realism cum pluralism—pragmatism that preaches the virtue of unfettered democratic choice. If one disassociated civic republican-ism from the intellectual references—from Aristotle to James Harrington—one would be hard pressed to distinguish it from Wilsonian idealism.

Needless to say, this does not give us a lot of substantive guidance about the content of the public interest. In fact, the republican conception is mainly procedural; it gives great weight to public participation in a process of *deliberative* public choice. At the same time its emphasis on disinterested civic virtue, on collective welfare and public values, is at war with the modern pluralist conception of process, even one that is open to all. For this reason it is necessary to get beyond classical formulations of republicanism. If the idea of civic republicanism is to have any usefulness as a constitutional principle, it must embrace some notion of a public good that is not itself wholly contingent on the actual political process. In the classic formulation of republican virtue, the emphasis is on the public good as an open-ended concept, one that is given shape by disinterested deliberation. But to trust the public interest to disin-terested political deliberation requires the kind of faith in virtue that is rare even in church, let alone in the polling place. Even in the best of circum-stances public virtue is not easily distinguished from private interest, and there are no standards for disqualifying citizens for personal bias when they participate in the political process. It follows, I think, that the public good cannot be determined by process alone, at least not process in the conven-tional sense of electoral and related political participation. Something more is required.

Lochner Redux: Public Goods

As I said in chapter 1, it is hopeless to try to define the "something" with precision, as if the public interest could be neatly capsulized in some set list of projects, programs, or "public goods." What is needed is not an arbitrary template to lay down against the varied legislative choices that are subjected to review. What is needed is a baseline conception of public purpose that can serve to focus constitutional inquiry into the legislature's choices and espe-cially into its defense of those choices. In this respect, Cass Sunstein's crit-icism of *Lochner* seems to me unsound. Sunstein criticizes *Lochner* and "Lochner-like understandings" for taking as a baseline from which to decide constitutional cases the unregulated market (the market subject only to the standards of the common law). More generally he criticizes the Court for assuming that the common law was inherently "natural and inviolate," and accepted this status quo as the basis for determining a neutral principle.[72] Of course, the Court took the status quo as a baseline; what else could it take, where should it start if not from the status quo? It is not correct to say the Court took the status quo to be inviolate; it was only a starting point. One must start somewhere. It is impossible to impose a burden of proof without some notion of what it is that must be proved, which cannot be formulated without a further understanding of an accepted baseline. Unless there is some prima facie legitimacy to the status quo, the whole enterprise of judicial review collapses into an aimless wandering through a maze of arguments.

It is not enough to ask the legislature simply to explain and define its choices. Such an open-ended approach too easily leads either to a surrender of constitutional standards or to an arbitrary and unsustainable trumping of legitimate public choices. It is necessary to have a theory of the public welfare which, if not necessarily dispositive of all cases, at least provides a basis for presumptions for and against legislative choices.

At the outset let me put aside cases involving those personal liberties long recognized as calling for special protection, hence strict scrutiny of legislative interference. Free speech, religious liberties, traditional forms of property (I shall have more to say later about nontraditional property rights), racial equality and respect, etc. Without belittling the importance of protecting these rights, they are not my concern here. My concern is rather for a broader concept of constitutional limitation on legislative choices that affect individuals in less direct and, arguably, less substantial ways—the individual as job seeker, or even as taxpayer and citizen.

Classic economic welfare theory offers one such conception. As we saw in chapter 1, it is not a highly determinate theory. Even the most restrictive of the norms for public choice, the "pure" public good, proves to be highly elastic in the hands of creative theorists, and we are constantly reminded how many private purposes have been and continue to be promoted in the name of correcting "market failures." But no idea of the public good is wholly free of ambiguity or is immune from being manipulated to serve other purposes. We can begin with a recognition of that fact, but to end with it would be to give up on the idea of substantive constitutional restraint altogether.

The ambition of constitutional review must be to prevent the ambiguity of public welfare from being exploited by particular interest groups seeking purely private gain at public expense. Regulatory laws ostensibly designed to correct market failures should be judged by whether the legislature has a coherent story, a *theory* in the broad sense of the term, of what the failure is and how its regulatory program will correct it. Incidental benefits to private groups should not defeat a proffered justification of public purpose, *provided they are shown to be ancillary and subordinate*. Submarines have to be produced somewhere, so if the people in Groton get extra spillover benefits from national defense, we need not become too exercised. By the same token, the fact that licensing ophthalmologists might benefit a certain class of specialists by suppressing competition should not itself defeat a valid public health measure. However, a regulatory program that is demonstrably devoted to the economic gain of a particular group is prima facie a candidate for invalidation. *Lee Optical* is illustrative; so is the famous *Carolene Products* case. One could make a respectable argument that even *Lochner* was such a case, despite the abuse that has been heaped on the Court's decision. Notwithstanding the law's professed purpose of protecting the health of bakery workers by limiting their work hours, the overriding purpose (and effect) of the law appears to have been to protect the bakers' unions against competition from nonunion bakers, drawn heavily from the ranks of newly arrived immigrants.[73] I do not say that labor legislation designed to aid union labor against nonunion competition should necessarily be condemned, but it would demand a different defense than the state of New York offered.

Given the elasticity of any theory of public goods, it is only natural to articulate the relevant test in terms of its purpose rather than its congruence to some particular theory of public goods. It is on that premise that some scholars have complained that the existing rationality standard is inappropriate, even if it were enforced. Jerry Mashaw, for instance, has argued that what is needed is a standard of "public regardingness," not rational basis.[74] The distinction between rationality and public regardingness is easily overdrawn, however; essential to any enforceable concept of public purpose is a reasoned justification of both ends and means, a justification that is more than some emotive response to perceived public problems.[75] The point of insisting on rationality is to avoid bootless inquiries into the subjective preferences of individual legislators. It is not dispositive that the statute in *Lochner* mandating maximum hours for bakers was the product of lobbying by the bakers' unions seeking to suppress nonunion competition. What is important, and dispositive, is whether the legislature could devise a convincing justification for a law, the effect and apparent purpose of which was to use the power of the state to promote the interests of one group at the expense of another. Whether one calls such a statute a "naked preference," to use Cass Sunstein's phrase,[76] or a "taking" of property, as Richard Epstein would prefer,[77] or simply an unprivileged exercise of legislative power, as I would argue, is of minor importance. By the same token, I doubt it makes much difference what specific constitutional clause is invoked here, the equal protection clause (Sunstein), the takings clause (Epstein), or the due process clause (my preference). The critical point is the character of the legislation and the nature of the justification required to sustain its constitutionality.

Ultimately, the legislative justification must be judged, undemocratically, by judges (who else?) on the basis of principles that are more than prejudices or preferences about the nature of the public good, which means that judges themselves must defend *their* choices. Subject only to the review of an ultimately unreviewable Supreme Court, their choices and defenses are formally beyond political control; yet the experience of public law suggests, I think, that they are not, in fact, beyond the influence of public and political opinion. In this respect, some constitutional commentators have urged the idea of a kind of public dialogue in which the courts participate along with the public and its representatives in developing some notion of the public welfare.[78]

I shall have a bit more to say about the dialogue idea later in discussing nonconstitutional review of administrative decisions. The basic idea is attractive philosophically though one should be careful not to translate it into a practical program;[79] the fact is, courts and legislatures do not discourse on the same level of principle and cannot be expected to do so. After all, the very occasion for the dialogue arises most urgently precisely when the legislature is animated by nonpublic-regarding purposes that the courts are supposed to constrain. A somewhat more modest notion is captured by seeing the courts as defenders of a kind of Missourian version of republicanism. The reference is suggested by a wonderful critique of constitutionalism as secular religion by Thomas Grey, though the thrust of his point is different.[80] Grey observes that judges are neither priests nor prophets of a secular religion (which some have thought American constitutionalism to be), but public officials who are given an institutional role of viewing problems in a slightly broader perspective than that of the mine-run politician. The image of the judge that fits the American temperament, according to Grey, is not Isaiah but the Wizard of Oz.

> One of our national slogans is the Missourian "show me." We appreciate the story of the emperor's clothes. Perhaps as much as "Over the Rainbow," we like the scene in which the old carnival fortune-teller is revealed turning the crank that makes the Great Oz flash and roar.[81]

For Grey, the part of the Wizard is played by the judges; in my scenario, the Wizard is that other great master of the spectacle, the legislature, while it is the Court that is pulling open the curtain.

It may be useful here to revert to Gerald Gunther's argument for an intermediate form of review, for in part that is what I mean to suggest by the Oz scenario. I suggested earlier that a difficulty with Gunther's proposal was that it did not deal with the situation when the legislature was brutally frank about pursuing particular objectives that were not manifestly public regarding nor public serving. The Court needs to articulate not only standards of instrumental rationality but some conception of ends as well, some idea of what constitutes an adequate justification for the use of public authority, whether those uses affect personal rights or "mere" economic freedoms. The Court need not intervene often to override legislative choice in such cases to give strength and credibility to a lesser, intermediate level of review along the lines suggested by Gunther. No doubt a vigorous substantive review of legislative ends as well as means could disrupt many legislative programs. There would hardly be much point to such review if it were not at least occasionally inconvenient, of course, but critics imagine worse than that. What they fear is that active judicial review of legislative purposes would entail a frontal assault on the modern welfare state à la *Lochner*. In modern folklore, *Lochner* has become the symbol of the arbitrary destruction of democratic choices, rather in the fashion that Robert Browning's Caliban contemplated killing crabs: "Let twenty past, and stone the twenty-first, / Loving not, hating not, just choosing so."[82]

The fear seems to me excessive. Without question, an activist Court would make errors, quite a few. That should not traumatize us. The risk of error is unavoidable; an unwillingness to risk errors of commission entails a risk of errors of omission, the failure to intervene when public welfare and private rights clearly warrant.[83] How to balance those two types of risks is not an easy matter to determine, to be sure, but we should not suppose that a refusal to assess the competing risks allows us to avoid error.

And, in fact, we already recognize the need to incur the risk of errors of commission in judicial review, though they are identified with a different end of the political spectrum. I have in mind not only *Griswold* and its kin, but any number of other decisions involving personal liberties where active review is widely accepted. When the Supreme Court, for instance, applies the First Amendment to strike down a local ordinance prohibiting nude dancing (expressive speech) it may invite criticism, but no one today accuses it of Lochnerism.[84] Why? Somehow we have simply gotten it into our heads that any form of expression is constitutionally more important than the pursuit of an occupation or other economic liberty. For me, it is not important to decide what is properly within the scope of the First Amendment any more than it is to decide what can be canvassed by the Fifth or Fourteenth. The simple point I wish to make is that the tolerance we have learned to bring to judicial review in one area ought to suggest a similar tolerance for review in the other.

It is necessary, of course, to acknowledge the limits of constitutional limitations, particularly inasmuch as my discussion may have suggested an ambition for judicial review that it cannot hope to fulfill. Active judicial scrutiny of legislative purposes—whether in the name of due process, equal protection, limits on governmental takings, or other constitutional guarantees—would not restore Jeffersonian simplicity to public life. In purely macroeconomic terms, the scale of government is fairly impervious to mere judicial incursions even when they are constitutionally grounded. Perhaps, as Robert McCloskey once speculated, the Supreme Court in the *Lochner* era entertained the conceit that it could arrest the rising tide of social and economic legislation that was transforming traditional conceptions of government's role.[85] But I suspect not; I think the Court knew better. In fact, its overall record of reviewing social legislation during the *Lochner* era shows as much; the Court sustained much more of such legislation than it invalidated. And, whether or not it did select just the right targets to strike down, it cannot be fairly said that it was mindlessly arbitrary in doing so. The Court was not so out of touch with contemporary thought as popular history has made it appear. Indeed, the Court's views were quite congruent with a body of social and economic theory that, while no longer dominant, was still an intellectual force in the period.[86] Unfortunately, when the Court thought better of its ambition, it imagined that its prior task had been, pace King Canute, to roll back the tide, and seeing the futility of that endeavor, it capitulated entirely, as if a lesser role of checking legislative excesses was also pointless. Having failed to turn back the waves, the Court backed off even the modest, and quite manageable, task of protecting the harbors against some of the rougher waves.

The metaphor should not be misunderstood. The task is not the containment of big government as such. Macroeconomic welfare effects are not really the object of heightened judicial oversight. There is no concept of public goods so limiting and so inflexible that would necessarily entail a significant reduction in the current national budget. The overall size of the public deficit may be discomfiting, but the discomfiture is largely economic and social, not constitutional. The only thing that transforms government spending into a credible constitutional concern is the absence of a defensible public purpose in programs, particularly government spending programs. One might hope that checking some of the more egregious forms of private rent seeking might contribute to programmatic and fiscal restraint, but this is only a possible by-product of constitutional limitation and I rather doubt it is of large magnitude. Whether or not it is true, as Mancur Olson has provocatively argued, that rent-seeking political coalitions ("distributional coalitions") are a central cause of the economic decline of nations,[87] I would not expect a tighter constitutional scrutiny of the product of such political activity to have a large macroeconomic impact.

For better or worse, the largesse we now dispense to private interest groups in the name of national defense is not at risk from vigorous constitutional review. Ditto the ever growing welfare programs that we loosely call entitlement programs.[88] Nevertheless, if the fiscal benefits of constitutional limitation were zero, the argument for judicial intervention would stand. Think of it this way: coerced wealth transfers are rightly treated by economists as a social waste insofar as they induce the allocation of resources to unproductive purposes, but treating it as *only* waste would miss the point of moral interest.[89] We do not need a course in welfare economics to teach us that theft is wrong. Nor, by the same token, is it a telling objection that despite the law against it, theft remains a vigorous and pervasive activity.

There are, of course, ambiguities when we seek to apply this simple moral intuition to the public realm, and it is probably too provocative to identify legislative wealth transfers as simple theft. But provocative analogies aside, the essential lesson is the same: power that does not seek the justification of principle has no claim to our loyalty or our respect. The purpose of the rule of law is to ensure that some plausible justification is forthcoming.

CHAPTER 3

The Bureaucratization of Public Choices

We examined the bases in political and constitutional theory for restricting public choices by the legislature on the assumption that those choices were, in fact, made by the legislature. For the purpose of considering whether public choices can be bounded by any principled criteria of public need and legitimacy the assumption is appropriate. However, the assumption has a fairly tenuous connection to the reality of modern political practice. Public choices are increasingly made not by the legislature, but by bureaucratic surrogates pursuant to a delegation of power from the legislature. I refer here not to the fact that legislative decisions require executive implementation that entails a degree of executive judgment and discretion. That fact is unremarkable. What is remarkable is the extent to which political responsibility for policy choices is transferred to bureaucratic organizations. The line between policy-making judgments and implementive decisions has always perhaps been an indefinite one; in the modern administrative state it has become increasingly irrelevant as well.

This pervasive feature of modern government is the central foundation of my discussion throughout the remainder of this book, the how and wherefore of bureaucratic public choices, their political environment, and the legal restraints that bind them. Before turning to the subject of bureaucratic activity, however, we need to look briefly at its political and legal foundations. My interest here is specifically focused on legislative-type powers—the power to declare public policy in general terms—as distinct from adjudicative implementation of policy. The distinction between legislation and adjudication may seem a fine one inasmuch as policy can be determined by the latter as well as the former. However, my concern here is not with process; it is with power and prerogative. The delegation issue does not turn importantly on how the agency exercises the power but on how and on what terms and conditions the power was conferred.[1]

Delegation of Power

The delegation of lawmaking power to administrative agencies has always been problematic to the liberal theory of constitutionalism. A central tenet of early American republican theory was the Whiggish idea that the people's sovereignty was not transferred to the legislature; the legislature was a limited agent to whom all powers were entrusted to be exercised as instructed by the people.[2] Derived from this conception was the idea espoused by Locke, also inherent in the English common law concepts of trusteeship, that the entrusted power could not be further delegated to other, subordinate agents.[3] It is a simple notion that requires no elaborate legal or political theory to defend, at least in principle. If the legislature is truly a trustee, any general transfer of entrusted power would seem a plain evasion of responsibility. The irresponsibility is heightened by the transfer of power to a politically unresponsible bureaucracy. The principle restricting delegation of powers received added support from the separation of powers concept articulated by Locke and Montesquieu and embraced by the framers as a central theme of constitutional structure.

Notice that the theory of delegation, more precisely *nondelegation*, does not say that the legislative trustee cannot transfer certain functions and powers to others to aid in carrying out its responsibilities. Indeed, the concept of separation of powers implies just such a transfer of administrative, implemental power to the executive. Only legislative power may not be transferred.

Such is the theory. The reality, as every student of American constitutional law quickly learns, is another matter.[4] In the early years, constitutional doctrine maintained the theory but managed to accommodate the increasing practice of transferring power to the executive by labeling the delegated powers as implemental only, involving no legislative power or discretion, merely fleshing out minor details pertinent to the legislative purpose. Not until the late 1920s did the Supreme Court acknowledge the emerging reality by articulating the legal criteria for sustaining delegations of legislative powers. The seminal case involved a congressional delegation to the president of the power to set tariff rates that would equalize production costs in the United States and competing countries. The Court ruled that it would sustain delegations of legislative power whenever Congress dictates an "intelligible principle" to which an agency must conform; the delegation was found to meet that standard.[5] The delegation sustained by the Court was not troublesome; both the scope of the power and the scope of discretion given to exercise the power were fairly limited. However, the Court's criterion for sustaining the delegation eventually transcended the original context and was soon providing the basis for sustaining far more sweeping delegations of broader powers to regulatory agencies, notably the ICC, the Federal Radio Commission (predecessor to the FCC), and the FTC.[6] The Court's tolerance for broadly expressed delegations of power to agencies was such that it came to appear that the "intelligible principle" principle was purely aspirational in character.

Then, without warning, the Court brought the nondoctrine to life, turning it against congressional efforts to implement the New Deal. The central target was the National Industrial Recovery Act. In two successive cases, the *Panama Refining*[7] and *Schechter*[8] decisions, the Court held that congressional delegations of power to the president were unconstitutionally broad, having no effective statutory limitations. In the third case, *Carter Coal*, the Court struck down the Bituminous Coal Conservation Act that authorized coal companies to set minimum coal prices.[9] The Court invalidated the act as "delegation in its most obnoxious form; for it is not even delegation to an official or an official body, presumptively disinterested, but to private persons whose interests may be and often are adverse to the interests of others in the same business."[10]

The rapid succession of three major decisions invoking the delegation doctrine might have presaged a new life for a moribund constitutional rule. However, just as these decisions had no past, they also had no future. In *Yakus v. United States*, the Court virtually abandoned its prior decisions in sustaining a wartime measure that gave the Office of Price Administration extensive powers to fix commodity prices.[11] The specified purposes were as broad and general as those condemned as standardless in *Schechter*. However, the Court found adequate standards in Congress's direction that the prices must be "fair and reasonable" and, in fixing them, the OPA was to give "due consideration, so far as practicable," to the prevailing prices during a designated base period. Justice Stone, for the Court, wrote:

> The essentials of the legislative function . . . are preserved when Congress has specified the basic conditions of fact upon whose existence or occurrence, ascertained from relevant data by a designated administrative agency, it directs that its statutory command shall be effective. . . . Only if we could say that there is an absence of standards for the guidance of the Administrator's action, so that it would be impossible in a proper proceeding to ascertain whether the will of the Congress has been obeyed, would we be justified in overriding its choice of means for effecting its declared purpose.[12]

Formally, Justice Stone's statement of the rule is congruent with *Schechter*, but the application is not. It implied a judicial tolerance for delegations that left little room for another *Schechter*. Despite repeated occasions for invoking the delegation doctrine, the Supreme Court has not returned to the *Panama-Schechter-Carter* line of decisions.[13]

From time to time, the delegation principle still receives favorable mention in opinions of the Court and in those of individual justices. These do not bear discussion; it is enough merely to observe that, on different occasions, both the liberal and conservative wings of the Court have embraced the notion that there are constitutional limits to broad delegations.[14] By means of such occasional opinions and indirect usages, the delegation doctrine continues to lurk in the shadows of constitutional jurisprudence, a kind of vagrant threat that if Congress goes too far in transferring unguided power, the Court might intervene. But if one looks at the Supreme Court scoreboard, the only safe prediction is that a revival of *Schechter* is not foreseeable. On the several occasions that the Court has confronted delegations on the order of *Schechter*, it has either strained to interpret the statute to imply sufficient standards to avoid the constitutional issue,[15] or it has simply ignored the problem.[16]

This tolerance of delegations is all the more remarkable for its contrast to the Court's intolerance of similar legislative shortcuts across constitutional formality. For example, in *INS v. Chadha* the Court held the legislative veto, whereby Congress reserved a veto of executive determinations made pursuant to delegated legislative authority, was unconstitutional.[17] Specifically, the veto violated the presentment clause of Article I—requiring every bill, and "every order, resolution or vote to which the Concurrence of the Senate and House of Representatives may be necessary" to be presented to the president for approval or disapproval—and, insofar as this case involved a one-house veto, the bicamerality clause requiring the concurrence of both houses before any bill, order, etc., could have legal effect. The Court's opinion in *Chadha* has been rightly criticized as formalistic.[18] It is debatable as a matter of principle and policy whether the legislative veto is a defensible means for Congress to attempt to reserve some control over delegated power, whether, in other words, it conforms to the essential spirit of separation of power concepts. The Court pretermitted any such inquiry, resolving the question by textual exegesis alone. What is more remarkable than the Court's formalist approach, however, is its selectivity in applying it. The question was put to the Court, if the legislative veto violates Article I because it bypasses the prescribed processes for lawmaking, why does it not equally violate Article I when agencies promulgate rules pursuant to delegated power? The Court's answer was that the agency rule maker is not a "lawmaker" but an executor of the law passed by Congress; the constitutionality of delegated rule making authority "involves only a question of delegation doctrine."[19] The Court's semantic manipulation, if not simply silly, is breathtakingly arbitrary.[20] One doubts that the Court itself was taken in by its own distinction of the veto issue from the delegation question; it either saw the veto as a more substantial encroachment on separation of powers than the delegation doctrine, or it believed there was no constitutional corrective for the latter problem that would not wreak havoc on Congress and undermine democratic politics. The ghost of *Schechter*, like the ghost of *Lochner*, is a powerful check on the Court's constitutional imagination.

Not everyone is terrorized by the ghost of *Schechter*. Though the mainstream of academic as well judicial opinion appears to be resolutely opposed to reviving the delegation doctrine, in recent years there has been surprising support for doing so.[21]

In terms of political principle, the case for enforcing limits on delegation rests essentially on the traditional concept of political responsibility, noted earlier. There is, to be sure, a certain antique quality in the Lockean formalism, expressed in some of the early cases, that legislative power is a nondelegable trust. However, the underlying idea of political legitimacy has enduring appeal. We elect legislators to make political choices, not to avoid them by designating others to make them. No one argues that this means legislators must legislate in such detail as to leave no room for executive imagination. What is argued is that the directions and the standards set by the legislature must be meaningfully specific. An agency should not be entrusted with a mandate, say, to prescribe "fair and reasonable" or to proscribe "unfair trade practices" or to regulate "in the public interest," without specifying the content of those terms or at least a limited range of expected applications. As Theodore Lowi, among the foremost supporters of a revitalized principle of restricting the delegation of power, puts it, application of the *Schechter* rule is a "court order for Congress to do its own work."[22]

Appeals to political principle are, as we have already observed, inviting targets for scorn by political realists. Finding little apparent adherence to principle in observed political behavior, the realist is also wont to dismiss such appeals as visionary. Kenneth Davis has argued the point forcefully: first, the courts have not enforced the doctrine; they have not restrained the delegation of discretionary lawmaking power. Second, it would be futile to try to do this because legislators are unable or unwilling to supply the "meaningful" standards that the doctrine supposedly requires. Third, the proper objective is not legislative standards but limits on the reasonable exercise of power by *administrators*, which should be enforced by courts, by requiring them to articulate standards governing their actions.[23]

The first assertion, that courts have not and will not enforce restrictions on delegation, is difficult to challenge. The normative justification that accompanies it is not. To begin with, one should not confuse the question of political legitimacy with the question of nonarbitrariness. Whatever the virtues of nonarbitrariness, they are largely beside the point of the argument for legislative standards. The purpose of insisting that the legislature make meaningfully specific political choices is to ensure political responsibility, not reasonableness or fairness. We may devoutly hope the legislature will be fair and reasonable, and we may even invoke constitutional doctrines of due process and equal protection to enforce these constraints on legislatures. But that is not the office of the principle behind controlling the delegation of power; that principle is political legitimacy. Davis's realist critique allows no room for the question of legitimacy. Even if the courts sought to enforce legislative standards, Davis thinks legislators are "often unable or unwilling to supply them." He here touches on (though he does not explore) the affirmative case for broad delegation. The case for delegation consists of two sets of arguments, both of which are essentially pragmatic in character. One set of arguments centers on what we may call managerial efficiency, the other on political expedience.

In its most extreme form, the efficiency argument evokes Wilson's faith in technocratic government.

> Self government does not consist of having a hand in everything, any more than housekeeping consists necessarily in cooking dinner with one's own hands. The cook must be trusted with a large discretion as to the management of the fires and the ovens.[24]

The argument from managerial efficiency need not embrace Wilson's deep faith in technocratic decision making; a more modest argument simply emphasizes the comparative advantage of legislatures and executive agencies. Relative to executive agencies, the legislature has neither the time nor the expertise necessary to legislate detailed prescriptions into every law. Nor would it be efficient for it to use its resources in this manner. The comparative advantage in specification lies with the executive, which has both greater resources and more expertise that it can turn to the task. Congress's comparative advantage is to develop and to register political choices on broad government programs—the general character of public goods, leaving their precise definition and distribution to executive bureaucrats. For Congress to devote its energies to precise standards for implementation would only make matters worse.[25]

Superficially, the efficiency argument seems sensible, but a closer inspection reveals deep flaws. The first part of it, dealing with resources and skills, confuses research with choice, information with judgment. No one asks, no one expects, Congress to assume the burden of developing, in-house so to speak, all of the requisite information and analysis necessary to make informed decisions. From the beginning of the Republic, American legislatures have depended on the executive to do most of the basic information gathering and analysis, and to make recommendations as to what legislative actions (if any) are required. There is no need, and no point, to Congress replicating the executive bureaucracy in order to gain the advantages of bureaucratic resources and skills. What is required is that legislators and their staffs devote sufficient time and energies to understanding the relevant issues to make meaningfully specific political judgments about the policy issues.

Ultimately, the question of managerial efficiency is one of priorities and not resources; at bottom, the question is what legislators and their staffs should do with their time. We can ask this somewhat differently: what do congressmen do with their time that is more important than exercising legislative judgment? We do know, in fact, that most congressmen, or at least their staffs, spend huge amounts of time on constituent services—"casework."[26] Can it be that casework is more important than legislative homework? It is always fair to ask, of course, whether it would be time well spent for congressmen to worry about the details of legislative programs. The question implicates a matter of political philosophy at a fairly deep level: what is the business of legislators? Is the House of Representatives, for example, a forum for constituent services or for making decisions about public choices for the nation as a whole? The very notion of efficiency now becomes problematical. It may be more efficient, in some factory production sense, to have important public choices made by executive bureaucrats. However, if that kind of efficiency is what we want, we should perhaps make the legislature merely an advisory body or, alternatively, move toward some form of integration of the legislature and executive along the lines of European parliamentary systems.

Efficiency arguments for legislative delegation ultimately fade into arguments of political expedience. Delegation is a means of avoiding the political stymie that stands in the way of legislative resolution of public problems. So the argument goes. Of course, this argument, like the argument from efficiency, finesses the question of ultimate political purpose. It is a natural bias of Americans that we tend to value legislative productivity according to the number of laws passed. Casework and distributed special benefits may be more important to voters' evaluation of individual legislators but, even here, lawmaking—successful sponsorship of laws—is an important criterion by which legislative *leaders* are distinguished. It is an understandable sentiment; legislators work hard to persuade us that the problems they confront are important and require legislative attention. It is only natural for us to ask them, in turn, what they have done about the problems, and to be disappointed if they cannot produce some tangible evidence of that attention. Translating this popular sentiment into a judgmental norm is, however, subversive of the deeper conception of political responsibility that promoted the framers to develop a set of constitutional constraints on legislative activity. It is part of the constitutional structure of both Congress and state legislatures that legislation should not be produced in the most expeditious manner, according to the demands of the immediate occasion. The legislative process was not designed by the framers (and by the early legislators in promulgating their own internal rules) to *minimize* political stymie. The reverse is more nearly true. This was, it will be recalled, part of the Madisonian strategy for controlling "factious" majorities.

I do not suggest we glory in impeding legislative "progress." I argue simply that legislation based on facile consensus, made possible only by delegating hard choices concerning policy details, is unlikely to be real progress, at least if progress is defined in terms of public-regarding legislation. Bypassing the need for a deeper consensus may be a cheaper, more efficient way of producing legislative output, but more output is an artificial, even mischievous, measure of public need, using the term public here in the admittedly idealistic sense of something more than the mere sum total of interest groups.

The political argument against the political case for delegation does not, however, depend on an idealistic view of how the political process works. Quite the contrary, the case against delegation draws on the realist's model of interest-group politics; it simply refuses to give that model normative weight. Consider, from the realist's view, why congressmen would seek delegation of legislative authority. The received wisdom is that delegation is a means for enacting a legislative program where a consensus exists on general features (the need for regulation) but not on details (the shape or content of the rules). However, this traditional account glosses over the question of why individual congressmen holding opposing views with regard to the content (hence impact) of legislation want to avoid impasse, why they specifically choose delegation of power to agencies as a means around it.

Members of Congress have several alternatives in formulating a legislative response to a perceived problem. They can do nothing, which allows existing common law or statutory arrangements to continue. They can regulate by statute but provide for direct judicial enforcement at the instance of private parties. Or they can provide for agency enforcement of the statute, but with no agency discretion to affect legislative policy (except by the use of inherent prosecutorial discretion). Finally, they can delegate power to the agency to "write" the statute and to resolve political questions (and to bypass legislative conflicts). What governs the choice among these options? More specifically, why is the last option often chosen? Several explanations are possible. One obvious answer is that the last option is the most "efficient" in maximizing legislative output; essentially it reduces the cost of enacting legislation and, assuming constant demand for legislation, yields more of it. But in the context of broad delegations of power, we have to ask what, and why, is the "it" being produced? What needs to be explained is why a congressman would prefer the uncertainty attendant on delegation of legislative power to an agency, rather than press for immediate legislative resolution of the substantive policy content desired. One obvious answer is that legislators may not know what the desired content is, either because of the present complexity of the problem or because changes in circumstances over the life of the legislative program will require changes in solutions devised today. I think a more important answer is that legislators may be ambivalent because of conflicts among their constituents. If, of course, there is an obvious net advantage to favoring one set of constituents over another, a legislator will presumably take a decisive position where he or she can, accepting both credit and blame on the assumption that the former will outweigh the latter. But it may not be obvious whether, on net, credit will exceed blame. Such a situation calls for a strategy of ambiguity in which the legislator can seek credit for doing something while shifting blame for outcomes that cause unexpected political harm.[27]

The delegation of broad power to an agency, the actions of which are indeterminate, can be seen as such a strategy. One might suppose that, given an alert, intelligent constituency, a legislator would not be able to do both. But the credit claiming and blame shifting do not occur simultaneously or with respect to the same action. Credit is claimed for the creation of a "responsible" agency to study the problem and act on it. Granted, constituents are not so stupid as to give full credit for responding to their particular problems; nevertheless, there is some credit for taking action, even if it is incomplete. No one likes a do-nothing legislator, but everyone understands the need to seek the "assistance" of expert agents in resolving "tough" problems. If, when the agent takes action years later, the results prove to be injurious to constituents, the legislator may receive some blame for her earlier delegation (if constituents have good memories), but this can be offset by the legislator's claiming that the agent abused its discretion and by offering to intervene on behalf of the constituent. Anyone who thinks this scenario does not describe real life is invited to examine the action of legislators in oversight committees.

It has even been suggested that the creation of administrative agencies with delegated power enhances the legislator's opportunity for vote-winning casework.[28] Casework must here be defined rather broadly to cover not merely securing particular benefits for constituents, but also assuming a role as an overseer of the bureaucracy. Fighting the bureaucrat is an eternally popular strategy. However, legislators who merely vote against the creation of agencies seldom get much credit for fighting the bureaucracy in the abstract. Credit is far more likely to be given when one confronts a particular agency with regard to a specific problem. What this suggests is a strategy of approving the delegation of general power to the agency and the subsequent pursuit of influence over agency choices as they appear to present discrete matters of interest to constituents. At this point, no doubt, it is timely to ask, so what? Assume the dynamics of delegation choices are, as represented, the consequences of strategies of credit claiming and blame shifting. Legislators act to maximize their net credit, which means that they seek to shift blame when they can, which also means that they frequently seek ambiguity where it will enable them to be all things to their constituents. Why is this of any special relevance to the creation of agencies, or the delegation of power? It may not be *special* to the delegation of power as distinct from other legislative activities, but it is relevant to the question if delegation ought to be assessed as a matter of constitutional concern. The constitutional concern is not simply a matter of process formality; it is also a matter of public purpose. For those who believe that there ought to be some further constitutional enforcement of public purpose in all legislation, that is, some restraint on the use of public power to obtain rents or private interests, the delegation of power raises a special concern. The very nature of the strategy of ambiguity and responsibility shifting that underlies delegation is, I think, designed to favor the production of private-interest legislation. Responsibility shifting is preeminently a strategy encountered when legislators are engaged in dispensing benefits to particular interest groups at the expense of others (in most instances, a more diffuse, less well-organized constituency).[29] Of course, such legislative distributions do not need to take this form. Anyone familiar with rivers and harbor legislation, defense appropriations, or tax legislation knows that pork barrel distribution often takes direct forms. But my argument for enforcing responsibility for public choices does not rest on any claim that it will eliminate all such distributions. Concededly, some of the force of the argument would be lost if it turned out that Congress simply increased the amount of direct distributions through other forms of legislation. But we have no reason to think this would happen.

The transfer of political power to the bureaucracy also influences the distribution of political power among constituent groups in a way that encourages private interests at the expense of the broad public. In the abstract, delegation of legislative power is not biased toward any particular political interest group; however, it seems plausible that broad delegations favor concentrated groups relative to those more diffusely organized. The logic of this assumption is straightforward. Obtaining legislation is an occasional thing. It may require a strong political effort, but for a limited period of time. By contrast, influencing agency legislation is a sustained, continuing thing in which well-organized, concentrated, and well-financed interest groups have a comparative advantage over looser political coalitions that may be strong for a time but whose energies dissipate over the long run.

In particular, the agency rule-making forum is probably superior to the legislative forum for those well-organized groups that seek active government intervention simply because it is cheaper and easier to obtain effective results. For example, the broadcast industry has very strong political support in Congress, but there is no way it could have obtained from that body what it obtained from the FCC in the 1960s and 1970s. (The FCC's cable television rules between roughly 1968 and 1978 are a case in point, but other examples can be readily supplied.[30]) So too, I think labor unions could not have obtained from Congress what they procured from the OSHA.[31] And the food industry could never have obtained the cartel-facilitating food standards-of-identity regulations from Congress that it did from the FDA.[32] I should emphasize that my argument here does not assert that bureaucrats are inherently more susceptible to special-interest influence than are legislatures. I very much doubt that individual bureaucrats are more easily "captured" than legislators. What the agency offers the interest group is a more effect forum for action, one with fewer institutional impediments, than the legislature. Indeed, it is precisely the institutional constraints on legislative action that provide the common justification for delegating broad policy-making powers to the agency. Of course, in either forum the influence by one group is subject to a check by that of an opposing group. But in the legislature, the influence of one group is not only constrained by opposing groups, it is constrained by other groups that compete for legislative attention. The myriad groups vying for a place on the legislative agenda, coupled with the structural and procedural obstacles (e.g., the committee structure rules that must be navigated), can frustrate groups in their quest for legislative action even when there is relatively weak opposition. It is small wonder that agency forums have become the premier locus of interest-group activity in modern times.

Concededly, one must be cautious in making predictions about probable outcomes under a legal regime with which we have no sustained experience. Contrary to the thrust of my argument that delegation facilitates the private-interest "capture" of regulatory policy, others have argued precisely the opposite. Jerry Mashaw, for example, has argued that the delegation of legislative power to agencies forces interest-group politics to be filtered by the screen of the administrative process, subject to constraints of rationalistic judicial review as well as the additional political check of executive oversight.[33] From this it follows, according to Mashaw, that delegation dampens the effect of interest groups and promotes a more general *public* welfare.

No doubt delegation of power to agencies does subject the ultimate policy choices to constraints that do not bind Congress itself. This is mostly a function of judicial review. The scope of review has always been recognized to be greater for agency rules than congressional rules. The conventional constitutional standard demands only minimal rationality of legislation. By contrast, agency rules, promulgated pursuant to delegated power, are reviewable under a statutory test of rationality that is more demanding.[34] This does not mean that judicial review of agency rule making is, in an absolute sense, very exacting. It is not, as we shall see later. But, relative to the review of congressional enactments, there is no question that the courts have a more expansive role in the review of agency rule making. Insofar as delegations promote private-interest "legislation" (rule making), the greater degree of judicial review can counter that effect by demanding rational justification in terms of a public purpose.

Implicit in this argument, however, is the assumption that enforcement of the delegation doctrine would not significantly constrain legislative coalitions. In other words, the assumption underlying Mashaw's argument is that the same type of legislation would be enacted in a different form; special-interest distributions would be made without being screened by administrative discretion, in turn overseen by judicial review. It is, more or less, an assumption of political homeostasis in which there is a constant amount of private-interest legislation and the only variable is the form it will take. Of course, if that assumption is true, if political action is a bowl of Jell-O that responds to pressure in one direction simply by displacing space in another, then the argument for restraints on delegation of power become purely formalistic. I think the bowl-of-Jell-O assumption is incorrect, however; political choices, no less than market choices, are sensitive to cost. Legislators favor delegation as a vehicle for policy choices either because it is more beneficial or less costly than other alternatives. Indeed, as I suggested earlier, it is often the case that other alternatives are so costly (in broad, political terms) that they are virtually nonexistent options.

At this point I must emphasize that an effective delegation doctrine would require fairly rigorous judicial scrutiny of a kind that would not be satisfied with empty verbalisms of the kind too often found in legislative preambles. It is, of course, precisely this kind of scrutiny that makes the Court and most commentators anxious about revisiting *Schechter*. As I said earlier, the ghost of *Schechter* is kith if not kin to the ghost of *Lochner*. The pairing of *Lochner* and *Schechter* need not be intimidating, however. As I noted in the preceding chapter, the Court still has had no difficulty applying *Lochner*-style review in selective areas. The central controversy over the judicial review of legislative purpose is less a matter of first principles than of political convenience as to where to draw the line. So too with separation of powers. The Court recently has shown respect for the principle in *Chadha* and other cases; what remains is for it to give that respect a meaningful scope.[35]

One need not imagine that a revitalized restraint on the delegation of power would reproduce the republic of virtue envisioned by eighteenth-century idealists to believe that it might partly arrest the erosion of public values that has been the legacy of modern political realism. In the end, of course, our expectations here must depend on an understanding of how delegated power is exercised, or, more precisely, by whom it is exercised and how their judgments are influenced and controlled. I turn next to a brief sketch of the bureaucracy and its political and institutional environment.

The Bureaucrat

Bureaucrat is a term few bureaucrats choose to describe themselves. For good reason; in common usage the word has been heavily freighted with connotations that most normally sensitive persons (bureaucrats included) find offensive. The redoubtable William Borah expressed common sentiment with uncommon eloquence in a senatorial election campaign in 1934 when he declared that "of all the forms of government which have ever been permitted to torture the human family, the most burdensome, the most expensive, the most demoralizing, the most devastating of human happiness and the most destructive of human values is a bureaucracy."[36] People may work in bureaucracies without necessarily being tagged with the characteristics ascribed to bureaucrats, because the characteristics tend to be associated with a group, rather than individuals, and group characteristics can be the product of an institutional environment and functions. Nevertheless, it is a sure sign of self-deprecation for a bureaucrat to adopt the label willingly. Much of the classic writing on bureaucracy is oriented more to the institutional environment and the dynamics of a group of persons in that environment than to individuals. Noteworthy examples are the sociological work of Max Weber and Herbert Simon.[37] Some modern writers have attempted to "de-reify" this group-institution approach by looking at the bureaucrat as an individual, and analyzing his or her individual behavior. This approach is typical of economists and political scientists who work with public choice models of behavior that are essentially individualistic. The work of Anthony Downs is fairly representative.[38]

Viewing bureaucrats as individuals has the great virtue of recognizing the fact that bureaucrats are, after all, real people with more or less the full range of characteristics as ordinary folks, the same appetites (utility functions in the argot of economics) and basic intellectual abilities to fulfill those appetites. If we assume that bureaucrats reflect most of the common traits of individuals in society, we should then expect similar behavior. To the extent utility maximizing—or, pace Herbert Simon, satisficing[39]—is an objective of ordinary individuals, we should expect similar behavior from bureaucrats, other things being equal. Of course, other things are not in fact equal; to understand bureaucratic behavior is to understand the ways in which the bureaucratic institutions shape individual goals, attitudes, and opportunities. Searching for the distinctive ways in which this occurs returns us to an institutional perspective, but with this caveat: we are not looking for a group psyche so much as for the set of institutional, functional, and environmental influences that make up what we might call (unscientifically, of course) the "bureaucratic experience."

We can begin by considering what are the distinctive institutional characteristics of bureaucracy. Anthony Downs, one of the pioneers in developing modern rationalistic models of political activity in general and bureaucratic behavior in particular, offers the following definition of bureaucratic organization.

1. It is large. . . .
2. A majority of its members are full-time workers who depend upon their employment in the organization for most of their income. As a result, most of the members have a serious commitment to the bureau; they are not dilettantes. . . .
3. The initial hiring of personnel, their promotion within the bureau, and their retention therein are based at least partly upon some type of assessment of the way in which they have performed or can be expected to perform their organizational roles, rather than solely upon either ascribed characteristics (such as religion, race, social class, family connections, age) or periodic election to office by some constituency outside of the bureau.
4. The major portion of its output is not directly or indirectly evaluated in any markets external to the organization by means of voluntary *quid pro quo* transactions. . . . The above list of essential traits does not include several characteristics that Max Weber set forth as intrinsic to bureaucracy in his famous treatise. The omitted traits are hierarchical organization, impersonality of operations, extensive use of rules, complexity of administrative tasks, secrecy, and employment of specially trained personnel on a career basis. Most bureaus evidence most of these traits, but almost all of them can be logically derived from the four primary characteristics set forth above.[40]

One might perhaps quibble with particular aspects of Downs's or Weber's list of distinguishing characteristics, but in general they convey the central features of bureaucracy: it is rationalistic, complex, impersonal, professionalized, and autonomous. While all these characteristics typify bureaucracy, some are equally applicable to other organizations, a factory assembly line for example. However, two characteristics especially stand out as distinctively bureaucratic: professionalism and political autonomy.

The first characterization is largely uncontroversial. One can debate the degree to which professionalism is the governing force of administrative activity, but the concept of a professional cadre of technocrats is central to modern civil service systems.[41] The second characteristic, political autonomy, is somewhat more problematic. Students of the school of "scientific" public administration will probably object that the modern bureaucrat is not autonomous because he or she is constrained by the professional imperatives of rational pursuit of the objectives defined by political officials acting on instructions from the people.[42] As I observed earlier, this view is part of a general conception of the public sector that is very idealized. Its depiction of bureaucrats pursuing social welfare objectives within defined legal and professional constraints does not account for the modern reality of delegated power. Within the often capacious boundaries of that delegated power, bureaucrats are able to implement their own preferences about social welfare or, as Ludwig Von Mises would have put it, they produce and distribute goods free of the disciplining effect of the market.[43]

Bureaucrats' political autonomy is reinforced by the fact that their activities, their "output" if you will, is not easily evaluated. We saw that, for Downs, one of the definitional characteristics of bureaucratic activity was that it is not subject to market evaluation. For Von Mises, this was not only the central characteristic, but the central vice of bureaucratic choice. Since the bureaucrat does not sell public goods in the market, there can be no objective measurement of the value of bureaucratic output. Of course, the absence of economic market measures is not unique to bureaucratic organization but applies with equal force to all political choice. At bottom, Von Mises is not arguing against bureaucracy so much as he is against all public, nonmarket choice. To evaluate the arrangement in those terms requires a comprehensive analysis of the comparative efficiencies of market and nonmarket choices. We have already examined these more basic questions about as fully as the present occasion allows. It needs only to be said that Von Mises's concern about the absence of market measurements must presuppose the measures the private market offers are the correct ones. If one assumes that public choice is only justified where market alternatives are inadequate, for example where there is a market failure, then it seems a poor objection that the choice is not strictly governed by market criteria.

Von Mises's insight nonetheless does serve as a useful reminder of the obvious point that the substitution of public choice for market choice creates a problem of objectively evaluating the product, which obviously thereby compounds the monitoring problem. In private markets, the monitoring problem is simply a function of product valuation to great extent. The consumer need not monitor General Motors's production function; he need only evaluate the end product. Assuming a reasonably efficient market exists (and, of course, this can be a tricky assumption but one we can make here), the market will assist in this evaluation by providing information on relevant product features. Imagine now that General Motors did not produce an automobile but regulations governing automobile design; assume, in other words, that GM is now the National Highway Transportation Safety Administration (NHTSA) in the Department of Transportation. The task of evaluation becomes immeasurably more complex. One can examine the product in the pages of the *Federal Register* and evaluate it by a careful analysis of the expected benefits matched against the costs (both the costs of the bureaucratic input and that of conforming the manufacturing process to the design specification). But no one who has had the mind-bending experience of consulting the *Federal Register* will think this a simple task, or one the normal taxpayer or automobile consumer would lightly take on.

To be sure, the taxpayer and the consumer are not wholly without monitoring resources. They can call on the assistance of interested surrogates, for example the manufacturers or other special representatives (Ralph Nader et al.), and they, in turn, can ask the courts to enforce their valuation. This is, however, a poor substitute for direct consumer monitoring. As we will see, the process by which courts enforce the standard set by administrative agencies is primarily directed at input, not output. If the process of generating the product is fair and reasonable, the product is deemed acceptable. Monitoring by other institutions, such as Congress, is largely similar. It is, roughly, like saying that if GM's production process is efficiently designed, we will not look at the Buicks that come off the assembly line to see if they really run.

The reason for this indirect form of monitoring of bureaucratic activity is easy to appreciate; there are few objective measures available for evaluating an end product directly. Even if we had some kind of objective performance measure, it often takes many years of experience to gain the requisite data for judgments. GM's automobile failures will (usually, not invariably) reveal themselves in a matter of months or a year. It may be a decade or more before we can get comparable data on, say, NHTSA's passive restraint regulations and, even then, evaluation of the data is subject to unusual measurement difficulties, given the complexity of social and economic variables that affect results. Hence, the standard of immediate evaluation is effectively limited to the only material at hand, the inputs. It is obviously a second-best type of monitoring. Too, the standards themselves are not the same. The rationality standard applied to administrative agencies allows a rather broad tolerance for discretionary choices, that is, for the implementation of bureaucratic preferences that do not necessarily reflect preferences of public "consumers."

That bureaucratic preferences often diverge from those of the public or the public's elected representatives—about which more later—is a commonplace. This is but one aspect of the ubiquitous principal-agent problem that is observed in both the private and the public sector.[44] But it is very difficult to arrive at a consensus about the direction or degree of divergence. The common hypothesis among students of public choice is that bureaucrats, like politicians, like everyone else, seek to promote their own utility where they can. (This is sometimes expressed as a *shirking* problem, but that term has misleading connotations of merely failing to work; the problem of agent deviation is more subtle than that.) This hypothesis does not tell us much. It gets us beyond Wilsonian naïveté, but not much beyond. If we assume that bureaucrats have utility functions similar to those of ordinary folks, we must assume an indeterminate range of preference orderings. How, then, can we predict what choices a bureaucrat will make? This question is really just a particularization of one asked by critics of rational choice models generally when they complain that rationalistic assumptions are too indeterminate to have predictive value, or at least the predictive value ascribed to them by rational choice modelers.[45] I will not pause to address that complaint in general terms, but it cannot be denied that the assumption of rational pursuit of utility is very loose in its specification of what constitutes utility. Almost invariably the utility is identified ex post, looking at what individuals do, judging this to be a revelation of their preferences and concluding that their actions were a rational pursuit thereof. Unfortunately for the cause of science, the revealed preferences turn out to be quite varied and complex.

Attempts to model bureaucratic behavior along rationalistic lines do not necessarily deny that individuals have complex and multifaceted utility functions, but they hypothesize that, in the bureaucratic environment, individual preferences converge on a singular utility maximand. Among public choice theories, William Niskanen's budget maximizing hypothesis is popular among public choice theorists. Niskanen explains that the bureaucrat's utility—broadly including such variables as salary, perquisites of the office, public reputation, power, patronage, and ease of work—is a function of the total budget of the bureau during the bureaucrat's tenure in office. Niskanen does not deny that bureaucrats may also have a genuine desire to serve the public interest, but he argues that the constraints of bureaucratic organization channel the bureaucrat into specialized roles that (by Niskanen's assumption) preclude discretionary pursuit of general public interest objectives.[46] The bureaucrat's budget-maximizing incentives are, moreover, shared by the bureau's lower echelon staff who share the rewards that come from budgetary expansion, greater opportunity for promotion, job security, etc. Finally, executive and legislative officers who oversee the bureaucracy also have an interest in bureau budget expansion for somewhat different and more complex reasons (very broadly, it facilitates their monitoring of agency priorities and performance).

We can set aside, for the moment, the interests of executive and legislative officers. What we need to consider is the plausibility of the model of bureaucratic incentives. The budget expansion model invites comparison with models of rational business behavior. In fact, Niskanen's bureaucratic budget maximizer somewhat resembles William Baumol's model of managerial behavior in which private business managers are assumed to seek maximum sales (subject to a certain profit constraint).[47] However, one could also analogize Niskanen's model to the more conventional profit-maximizing model of business behavior. As with the private manager pursuing sales growth or profit, Niskanen bureaucrats sell tangible rewards and obtain them only as a function of positive output. This market model of bureaucratic behavior supposes that bureaucrats seek tangible rewards of the same kind sought by private managers. We might ponder that assumption for a moment. Since the bureaucrat does not, in fact, operate in a market environment, why should we look to market models of behavior? Can we not, with equal plausibility, hypothesize that at least some bureaucrats will display the same set of preferences as other persons who are not guided by the market? Why do we not suppose that at least some bureaucrats have the same utility preferences as priests, university teachers, or bums? Casual observation tells us that most bureaucrats do not follow the contemplative life, religious or academic; and, popular caricatures notwithstanding, most bureaucrats do not behave like bums. Still, these alternative models do suggest the possibility that individuals seek profit in ways that we would not always associate with maximizing the production of tangible output. A more detailed model of the bureaucrat's utility function would presumably recognize the variety of bureaucratic preferences.[48] For instance, except to the extent that external market forces demand positive output, both public and private managers might prefer leisure to positive production. Or they might simply take satisfaction from promoting their own idea of the social good.[49]

The pursuit of personal preferences, whether self-interested or altruistic (public spirited), presupposes a degree of bureaucratic discretion or slack in the principal-agent relationship. In Niskanen's model there is little slack; bureaucrats are driven by external as well as internal imperatives to pursue budgetary expansion. Recalling the story of public sector growth outlined in chapter 1, it is hard to deny the historical force of this argument. One must allow, of course, for recent deregulatory movements that, in some instances, have been a principal initiative of the regulatory bureau itself, in apparent defiance of the budget growth model. How Niskanen would handle such cases is not clear. I presume he would argue along the line that bureaucratic retrenchment reflects a change in the external political signals that ultimately control the bureaucrat's reward structure. This is not a very satisfying explanation. It reduces the model to the following rather unhelpful proposition: bureaucrats will seek rationally to advance their preferences in conformity with the reward system that prevails in the political environment in which they operate; the political environment normally (i.e., historically) has rewarded growth in output, but sometimes it has not.

It is yet too early to say that the recent trends in deregulation are a serious embarrassment to the Niskanen model. The assumption of public sector expansion still retains credibility based not only on historic trends, but based on what is known and observed about the natural tendencies of the political process that were noted in chapter 1. However, even if we retain the basic growth model, there are some things yet to be explained about the ways and means by which these "natural tendencies" work their way into the administrative agenda. This requires us to take a closer look at the institutional and political environs of the agency, specifically its relationship to its principal clientele interests, its relationship to the legislature and to the executive.

Which of these relationships should be presented first is a matter of perspective. From a formal, legal perspective, administrative agencies are creatures of the legislature that some have supposed gives the legislature pride of first place. On the other hand, most agencies are an integral part of the executive establishment, broadly defined; even the federal independent agencies are more a part of the executive branch than they are part of the Congress.[50] Overshadowing both of these claims to priority of consideration is the fact that most of the contacts between the agency and either the executive or the legislature concern the agency's treatment of its public clientele, its interest groups if you will. Moreover, as a matter of routine business, it is the interested clientele groups that most immediately influence and shape the administrative agenda. This does not imply that executive or legislative directives and influence are inconsequential. It suggests only that they are secondary; they are, for the most part, constraints rather than the immediate motive force of agency action.

Clientele: The Public versus "The Interests"

Following Von Mises and Downs, we may take it as a distinctive characteristic of bureaucrats that their output is not directed by market signals. That does not mean, of course, that bureaucrats are unresponsive to external demands for their services; it is just such demands that keep them in business, for whatever reasons they wish to do business. In a sense, then, bureaucrats do face a "market" for their services; it is merely one in which demand is not monetized. (I exclude here not only the case of simply monetary bribes but also future monetary gain from employment in the private sector—what Ralph Nader once called, in his inimitable fashion, the "deferred bribe.")

The distinction between monetized and nonmonetized demand captures one important difference between political votes and market votes. Of particular significance in the context of analyzing bureaucratic behavior is the fact that nonmonetary demand makes it critically important to look at *who* is demanding. In a commercial market, the identity of a buyer is ordinarily a matter of no consequence (putting aside credit considerations). The doctor's money is no better or worse than his or her patient's. Plainly, this is not true of the market in which the bureaucrat trades. For the bureaucrat to evaluate the demand, and to respond to it according to his or her habit or interest, he or she must know who makes it: patients are not the same as doctors; the old are not the same as the young; grocery clerks are not business executives, and so on. The permutations are as endless as the ability to discriminate for whatever reason commends itself to the advantage of the bureaucrat.

This discrimination works most sharply against the undifferentiated assembly of John and Jane Does that comprise the "general public." In an economic market, the public is influential in registering its demands. Preferences are easily expressed, easily aggregated, and have power commensurate with large numbers. In the bureaucratic marketplace, without the money denominator, individual citizen preferences are less easily organized into an effective unit of demand. Being unelected, bureaucrats are not compelled to be responsive to mere numbers. For precisely this reason, there is almost no way for the general public to express itself effectively on matters of bureaucratic choice. When citizens do go to the polls it is typically to express preferences of the most general character that are largely irrelevant to bureaucratic choice. Even if the public were able to express specific preferences on matters relevant to bureaucratic choice, the bureaucrat gains no tangible reward for being responsive. The psychic rewards of being publicly "responsible" may or may not align with publicly expressed sentiment. Being a democrat does not necessarily imply being a populist. Thus, it should come as no surprise that, as Woodrow Wilson put it, "the real voice of the great people of America sometimes sounds faint and distant in that strange city [Washington]."[51] And if it was faint to Wilson, who was directly elected by "the great people," imagine how faint it is to bureaucratic gnomes who labor in the remote recesses of the Department of Health and Human Services, or even to the chief of a highly visible regulatory agency. In contrast to the faint voice of Wilson's "great people," the sound of the interest groups is loud and clear.[52]

There remains a great ambiguity in the term *interest groups*. In popular usage the label is most often used for organized industry (including labor) groups seeking economic rents for their members, but there is no compelling reason to limit it to profit-seeking groups. Consumer groups, environmental groups, religious groups, and other special-issue groups (antiabortionists, school prayer groups, reform groups) can be similarly classified. This is the essential message of interest-group political theory, as we saw. From this perspective, every organized political group is, potentially at least, an interest group, and all groups are, more or less, of equal dignity in the forum of politics; that is, none can claim any special right to speak as representative of the public interest. David Truman's comments are fairly representative of interest-group theorists in this respect:

> [E]fforts to distinguish among interest groups on the basis of personal preference, that is, subjective judgments as to their "public" or "private" character, may be an unavoidable part of a citizen's functions, but they have nothing to do with the methods of scientific analysis. They contribute little to a systematic understanding of the political process by whatever methods such knowledge is pursued. The basis of such judg-

ments cannot be reliably communicated, and the results are therefore useless in analysis.[53]

This refusal to make distinctions among groups based on labels embodies a proper skepticism toward the promotional claims of groups. At the same time, the refusal to make distinctions among groups based on differences in the nature of the interests they seek to represent seems to me too nihilistic. For purposes of normative evaluation and positive analysis, there is some advantage in distinguishing among interest groups based on the breadth and flexibility with which they define their (own) interests. It may be that, say, environmentalists like the Sierra Club or the Natural Resources Defense Council are no less "interest groups" than the National Coal Association. I am prepared to concede to the interest-group theorists that, as partial elements of the public, an agency is properly suspicious about either group's claims or demands. But the interest-group theorists who decline to make even tentative, rough distinctions between such groups do so because they reject the possibility of any objective definition of a public interest (hence no group can be identified with it). For reasons explored earlier, I am not prepared to concede that.

Normative assessments aside, a blurring of distinctions among interest groups obscures analysis of political effectiveness, particularly in influencing bureaucratic decisions. David Truman was surely correct that the adjectives *public* and *private* that qualify interest groups are popular, not scientific terms. But mere rejection of unscientific terms does not establish a scientific methodology, and we ought not to delude ourselves by thinking that an artificial leveling of all interest groups is somehow inherently scientific.

In truth, the entire "science" of interest groups leaves something to be desired. There are a few general principles that appear to work enough of the time to warrant their cautious approval, but all have enough exceptions to make one hesitate to state them boldly. Consider, for example, the notorious "industry capture" thesis applied particularly (though not necessarily) to administrative regulatory agencies.[54] The classic version is the "life cycle" theory (or "fall from grace" theory) articulated most forcefully in the 1950s by Marver Bernstein.[55] According to this view the dynamics of administrative regulation operate as follows. When a social or economic problem arises, the legislature creates a regulatory agency to solve it. Because the legislature is unable or unwilling to give detailed guidance about how to handle, or even how to define, the problem, the agency is given broad, ill-defined powers. Initially, the agency attacks the problem with innovative zeal, but eventually the zeal wanes. In time, the agency develops not only a familiarity with the industry it regulates but also an identity with industry interests. In short, the agency becomes captured by the industry it is supposed to regulate.

This conventional wisdom about the regulatory process takes a few liberties with readily observable facts.[56] For one thing, industry capture is at best an awkward explanation for regulatory behavior in dealing with competing industry interests. It would be difficult for the FCC to be captured simultaneously by long-distance and local exchange telecommunications carriers on matters affecting the boundaries of their respective markets or by broadcast and cable interests on matters affecting competition between them. The ICC, at various times, may have been captive to both trucking and railroad interests whenever the policy choices it faced involved conflicts between their joint interests and outside interests, for example, when both transport modes faced external competition from unregulated transportation or from airlines. But in general, this external conflict has been less common than the internal conflict within the regulated "family." In the context of such conflict, the capture explanation would appear to have limited value as a guide to agency behavior. The most one could say is that the agency has a strong incentive to compromise in order to accommodate the conflicting interests.

The capture theory is not meaningless. Though it cannot always explain how the agency will choose among competing industry interests, the theory does suggest how the agency will typically choose between industry and nonindustry interests or between regulated and unregulated interests or, by extension, between highly concentrated interest groups and more diffusely organized groups. The "fall from grace" version of the capture thesis is nevertheless quite misleading. A history of most regulatory schemes suggests the presumed initial state of agency purity is exaggerated: there was never any grace from which to fall. The agency was captured from the very beginning, captured by virtue of the legislative mandate itself. Those who have perceived industry protectionism instead of industry control as a product of the *agency* succumbing to industry pressure too often ignore the fact that the protectionism inheres in the scheme Congress enacted. This is the central point of George Stigler's economic theory of regulation, which is essentially a theoretical refinement of earlier interest-group political theorists like David Truman, Earl Latham, and others whose views on regulation, and government in general, I noted in chapter 1.[57]

This is not to say that Congress *explicitly* mandates protectionism or in so many words directs the agency to establish and maintain industry cartels; though this is not unknown, it is not the usual pattern. More often, as we have seen, regulatory statutes are drafted in deliberately ambiguous language that resists any simple generalization as to purpose. (At the very least, the ambiguity usually denotes a plurality of purposes, many of which conflict.) Even so, the structure of regulation is almost inevitably protectionist to the extent that it requires a suppression of market forces in favor of administrative choice. This is most obvious in the case of economic regulatory statutes involving entry and rate controls that directly and necessarily restrict competition and promote a conservative regulatory style that resists uncontrolled change in the economic or social environment. It is precisely this resistance to unregulated change that promotes protectionism in the existing industry patterns. It is not necessary, and in some instances it is not plausible, to see in this a conscious conspiracy between administrators, industry, and legislators—the infamous "iron triangle" of which so much is written. Such a triangle exists more as a pattern that reflects the convergence of the three distinct forces than as the product of concerted design.

Perhaps there is no difference between a convergence and a conspiracy. My preference for the former is an attempt to emphasize a degree of autonomy for each of the three groups and the possibility of their diverging interests. At the very least it is necessary to allow for some indeterminism in the pattern of their relationships in order to account for some of the modern trends toward deregulation. I noted earlier that deregulation is something of an embarrassment to political theories of regulation as industry protectionism. Deregulation also introduces some confusing complexity into widely accepted learning about the driving force of legislation and the preferences of bureaucrats. The traditional interest-group theory of legislation and its modern refinement by public choice theorists are hard-pressed to explain both the rise and the fall of airline regulation. One could always treat the CAB as the proverbial exception that proves the rule; unfortunately, as we have noted, similar patterns have emerged in other areas, most notably in surface transportation and in communications.

The case of cable television regulation and deregulation is especially interesting in this respect because it rather dramatically illustrates both the strength and the weakness of both interest-group and public choice theories of regulation.[58] Cable television played no part in the FCC's 1952 national television allocation plan, which provides the basic framework for television channel assignments and related regulatory policies to this day. Cable was, in those early years, a minor, auxiliary service similar to various broadcast auxiliary services whose purpose was merely to "fill in the gaps" of regular television service, that is, to extend service to areas where, because of geographic remoteness or terrain obstacles, regular television service was unavailable. But, along with the growth of regular television in the 1950s, cable television also expanded. By the early 1960s it had begun to emerge from its auxiliary service role into a service that was potentially competitive with regular television broadcasting. Broadcast stations, concerned about the potential economic impact of cable, sought the FCC's protection.

Initially, the commission declined to take action on the ground that the threatened economic impact was not sufficient to justify regulation; it also professed to be uncertain of its jurisdiction over cable systems insofar as they did not fit the conventional definitions of radio stations subject to licensure and related regulation under title III of the Communications Act nor of wireline carriers subject to common carrier regulation under title II of the Communications Act (even if they were common carriers, being largely intrastate carriers, cable systems would have been within the jurisdiction of the states, not the FCC). But the commission's self-restraint was short-lived in the face of continued pleading by broadcasters complaining of dire consequences from this unregulated medium. Beginning in 1962, the commission asserted jurisdiction over cable systems and evolved a complex set of regulations designed to protect local broadcast stations against economic harm from cable. The protectionist regulations were justified on the twin grounds of preserving the existing system of local, over-the-air broadcasting and ensuring a measure of "fair competition." The first argument was a composite of several concerns centered around the scenario of unrestricted competition from cable threatening to supplant or greatly reduce the viability of local broadcast stations. The second argument stressed the fact that cable did not pay for the product it delivered, the mere retransmission of broadcast signals not being a "use" of the program for purposes of the copyright law.

By the mid-1970s, the political and legal climate had changed significantly, however; cable had expanded operations substantially and had become an important, and politically potent, industry. The commission began to consider deregulatory measures. It had some help. For example, a court of appeals decision in 1977 wiped out special regulations restricting "pay cable" services (programs sold on a per channel or per program basis). In 1979, the Supreme Court invalidated certain other regulations requiring cable systems to have certain channel capacity and to provide free public access, education, and government channels. (Such requirements exceeded the boundaries of the "ancillary jurisdiction.") And Congress finally adopted a copyright law requiring cable systems to pay a prescribed royalty fee for the use of copyrighted programs, thereby supposedly meeting the "fairness" objection to an unregulated cable industry. However, most of the initiative came from a "new" FCC that was more sympathetic to market forces and less concerned about protecting broadcast stations. In the late 1970s, the FCC eliminated what were generally regarded as the two most significant restraints on cable operations. When the agency's decision was affirmed in 1981, it marked the end of an era and the completion of a remarkable cycle of bureaucratic activity. (However, as will be noted, a fresh cycle of reregulation may be in the making as this is being written.)

In retrospect, the FCC's crusade against cable seems a quixotic one. It is child's play to show that most of the FCC's fears were the product of an overactive imagination. Projections of cable's probable adverse economic impact on broadcasting never had a solid factual basis, as the commission itself later had to admit.[59] Even if the threat of economic harm had been more credible, the commission's forebodings about the effect on viewers would not have been. For example, its concern over possible loss of local broadcast programming as a consequence of cable systems importing programs from distant markets was hopelessly at odds with the long-prevailing reality that made three New York–based networks, supplied by Hollywood-based film producers, the dominant force in commercial television. If the FCC was not concerned with programs from New York and Hollywood being "imported" to Peoria, Illinois, by the broadcast networks—and for the most part it was not[60]—how could it become excited over cable systems importation of distant signals? As to the fair competition question, the agency overlooked the obvious fact that, while cable might not pay for its programs, broadcast stations did not pay for their transmission medium. More basically, the fair competition argument simply did not answer the question of why this was a matter for the FCC, given that the Supreme Court had denied copyright protection against retransmission of broadcast signals by cable.

To say that the FCC was wrong in its experiment with cable regulation presupposes, of course, that its public interest explanations be taken at face value. The modern analyst of bureaucratic behavior will want to probe deeper into the individual motives or the political forces or the institutional imperatives that produced the result. Unfortunately, the story told in full is difficult to reduce to any single law of bureaucratic behavior. The first thing that comes to mind about the FCC's initial regulatory adventure is William Niskanen's observations about the proclivity of bureaucrats to expand their domain. The commission's cable actions from the early 1960s until the late 1970s seem admirably obedient to Niskanen's law, particularly if one defines that law broadly to include not merely budgetary growth but other forms of enhanced agency power that may not have large budgetary consequences. (The agency's budgetary increases for cable regulation were, in fact, quite trivial compared to the enormous expansion in jurisdictional reach and legal power.)[61] The agency's initiatives were also a perfect fit with industry capture theory insofar as they responded to the agency's oldest and most-loved client, the broadcast industry. But if these explanations fit the first phase of cable regulation, they are seemingly at odds with the second phase of deregulation. Here we have not growth but retrenchment, not control but decontrol, not clientele solicitude but indifference (more or less). The "natural law" of bureaucratic growth must be more complex, apparently, than is suggested by Niskanen's model. So, too, the political economy of regulatory supply and demand evidently needs more embellishment than we can coax out of capture models.

One possible explanation is the FCC's own public interest version, which holds that the rules were a response to economic and social factors—threatened harm to local service and fairness—that changed over time. But the rationales of preserving local service and fair competition were always a bit disingenuous; in any event, there is no evidence of significant change over the relevant time period. It is more plausible that FCC officials and staff simply became more enlightened; a simple comparison of the later product with the earlier reveals substantial evidence of positive learning (largely a product of new staff, so the "learning" is more institutional than personal). This explanation also seems a reasonable account of the agency's activities in other areas, such as telecommunications, that involved a different set of external circumstances and political constituents. A similar explanation has been offered for deregulation moves outside the communications field, particularly in transportation.[62] Notice that this explanation presupposes a greater degree of slack in the principal-agent relationship (viewing the interest groups rather than the general public as the principal) than has been traditionally seen by students of public choice.[63]

An alternative explanation might be that there was a change not in the agent but in the principal, either a change in the principals' preferences or a new set of principals. The cable communications case plausibly fits this explanation as well as the changed-agent theory. I mentioned that the economic conditions of the broadcast industry did not change all that much over the period in question. But the economics of the cable industry did. Despite the regulatory restraints under which it labored, the cable industry gained in economic strength, and, as it gained in economic strength, it gained political influence accordingly, in Congress and at the FCC itself. In Stigler's terms we might say that the cable industry was now in a position to buy a little agency protection for itself. Perhaps as important as "raw" political influence was that cable gained status. With regulation, the cable industry itself became an agency client and a member of the regulated "establishment." Following the 1972 decision, the FCC gave more than token recognition to this new status by creating a separate bureau to oversee its cable rules. The effect was a subtle transformation in agency attitudes as the cable bureau became the industry's inside contact and representative. (In the late 1970s with the abandonment of most of its regulatory program, the FCC merged the cable bureau back into the broadcast bureau whence it came, the merged bureaus now being called the "mass media bureau.") With its new status as a regular (regulated) client, cable not only received freedom from restrictive regulations but also sought (and in part obtained) protection against others—in particular protection against state and local regulators. The denouement came when Congress finally stirred itself to action by enacting the Cable Communications Policy Act of 1984, the central thrust of which was to affirm the FCC's basic policies and regulations (those still in effect) that set limits on local regulatory prerogatives with regard to such matters as franchise terms and rates.

While the alternating cycle of regulation and deregulation in cable television confounds the simple ratchet theory of regulation, recent events in the field suggest the continuing relevance of regulatory protectionism cum bureaucratic expansionism. Partly in response to prodding from Congress but ultimately in response to successful lobbying from broadcasting and film industry interests, the commission, in 1988, revived a significant part of the restrictions on cable transmission of syndicated programs that it had abandoned a decade earlier (while Congress itself has considered repealing its 1984 restrictions on local regulatory prerogatives).[64] In itself these moves are too marginal to signal a wholesale reentry into federal regulation, and on that account one must be cautious not to base huge generalizations on it. In other fields, notably the regulation of telephone service, the FCC has continued the deregulatory moves it began in the 1970s with remarkable consistency—and this in the face of considerable political hostility from Congress, from state regulators (who continue to resist deregulation within their sphere of intrastate service), and from some segments of the industry (notably the new competitors such as MCI, who continue to seek the benefits of regulatory handicapping).[65] The new regulatory moves in cable do nevertheless give evidence of the relentless pressure of political forces, within and outside agencies such as the FCC, to slip back into the comfortable security of regulation whenever the "undisciplined" marketplace creates too much disruption of established economic interests. The volatility of competition, with its constant threat to the economic fortunes of established firms, is frightful to the conventional bureaucratic mentality. Apparently there is no reform so successful that it cannot be reversed by a combination of political interest and ignorance. In regulation as in baseball, to quote the philosopher Yogi Berra, "it ain't over 'til it's over."

Political Overseers: Congress and the President

One of the more noteworthy points of the story of cable regulation and deregulation is the character of involvement by political officials outside the FCC, in either the Congress or the executive branch. Over a period of twenty years, regulation ran a full cycle of evolution—from no regulation, to a stage of comprehensive and mind-numbingly complex regulation, to virtually no regulation—without formal congressional action. When the cycle of regulation ran its course, Congress finally acted, largely to confirm what the FCC had done and to impose certain restraints on the local regulation of cable. Involvement by executive officials in the regulatory history was somewhat greater. The Office of Telecommunications Policy, an agency within the White House (since reorganized as a bureau within the Department of Commerce), helped to develop a so-called consensus agreement among the major industry groups concerned with regulation (the cable, broadcast, and program production interests) that provided the basis for a comprehensive set of regulations adopted by the agency in 1972. A few years later, White House and other officials influenced the move toward deregulation. In general, however, executive influence was indirect and fitful. For both the legislature and the executive, the role played in this particular regulatory story was obviously something different from that assigned by formal constitutional theory: Congress did not enact laws (relevant to the policy issues as they emerged) and the president (or his subordinates acting under his general direction) did not execute them. This is not to say that there was *no* executive or legislative influence, merely to say that it was indirect and rather subtle at best.

The problem is not one of insufficient legal power. Congress's power, it goes without saying, is virtually plenary. There are, to be sure, constitutional limits on how it exercises its power over the bureaucracy, as the Supreme Court has warned in several recent cases. For instance, the attempt to control administrative action by reserving for itself the power to appoint enforcement officers was held unconstitutional in *Buckley v. Valeo*;[66] an attempt to control administrative implementation by placing executive functions in a congressional agent, one not subject to presidential removal, was held invalid in *Bowsher v. Synar*;[67] and Congress's attempt to reserve a veto over administrative implementation of its statutory delegations of power was held unlawful in *INS v. Chadha*.[68] These separation of powers cases do not, however, prevent Congress from controlling administrative discretion by the simple, if often ignored, technique of enacting specific laws telling the agencies what to do and how to do it.

The president's legal powers over the bureaucracy are more constrained. He has a constitutional mandate, and prerogative, to see that the laws are faithfully executed, but, of course, Congress is the source of those laws. As the source of the law, Congress has the power both to define the substantive policies and to specify the ways and means by which they are to be enforced, thereby binding presidential discretion (subject perhaps to some undefined constraint by virtue of the president's own constitutional prerogative to execute the law).[69] Nevertheless, the practical political reality is that legislative enactments leave ample room for administrative discretion and for executive control of that discretion in numerous ways: political appointments to the agency and, except for the independent agencies, removal of appointees; budgetary controls; direct and indirect oversight of major policy making.[70]

These respective legal powers of Congress and the president are, however, only faintly relevant to the way in which legislative and executive influence of administrative policy is exercised. The effective influence tends to be both informal and widely diffused in ways that defy simple description. The descriptions that follow are, therefore, highly stylized.

Congress

Congress's habit of authorizing agency action in broad terms has made agencies virtually coordinate lawmaking bodies in many instances. As lawmaking power has shifted to the administrative bureaucracy, the traditional lawmaking role of Congress has been transformed into one of directing or controlling bureaucratic lawmaking. The ways and means by which this new role is exercised is the subject of considerable scholarly speculation and debate in the political science literature. Underlying the different perceptions of congressional influence of agency policy are different models of respective legislative-administrative powers and how they interact.

At one extreme is the "monopoly bureau" model embraced by William Niskanen, among others. It postulates that, so far from being in control of the agencies, Congress is actually subordinated to them by being dependent on the administrative specification of budget and production levels. In Niskanen's model, agencies are assumed to have superior information about the relevant costs of alternative outputs and also full information about preferences (specifically, those of the relevant committees controlling the agency's budget and agenda) and are able to exploit this information in the form of take-it-or-leave-it proposals to the Congress. Congressional committees are assumed to be unable to formulate alternative positive options and unwilling to accept a zero output, hence they acquiesce.[71] Niskanen's model focuses on general spending initiatives that require Congress's approval. Of course, the agency's power is even greater to the extent of its existing authority to initiate and implement policy *without* prior congressional approval. In such a case, Congress must muster at least a majority of its members to countermand it. However, if the agency's policy initiative is backed by a credible threat of presidential veto, even a congressional majority cannot defeat it. By strategically selecting initiatives that satisfy the preferences of one-third of Congress, the agency can dominate the policy agenda.[72]

At the opposite extreme, observations of congressional-agency interaction have led some to formulate models of congressional dominance. One version, developed by Matthew McCubbins, Roger Noll, and Barry Weingast, sees Congress prescribing a combination of organizational structures and procedural constraints designed to channel agency policy choices along the right tracks, in particular to "stack the deck" of policy outcomes in favor of Congress's preferred constituent interests.[73] As a descriptive account (which it purports to be), the theory is not persuasive.[74] It hypothesizes that Congress is unable to formulate or agree on particular policy choices and hence delegates them to agencies, but at the same time supposes Congress is able to agree on structural and procedural arrangements that are sufficiently specific as to direct policy choices. If the first condition is true, it is hard to see how the second condition is possible. How does Congress define a process or structure that will yield particular policy outcomes if it cannot define (or agree on) what those outcomes are? Second, even if Congress would manage this difficult feat of directing the agency to make the "correct" policy outcomes without being able to define them, there is very little evidence of it doing so. In fact, the structural and procedural features of most federal agencies are very broad and more or less confirm, across such a wide variety of programs and constituent interests, that it is impossible to see them as designed to "stack the deck" toward any particular set of policy choices. About the most one could claim is that Congress from time to time seeks to empower certain political interests by procedural devices such as broadened judicial review of agency choices.

A somewhat more plausible and more widely held account of congressional control is one that sees such control being exercised not through general, preformulated constraints on agencies, but through more ad hoc pressures. This mode of control is distinctively a function of committee oversight and, as such, it is the product of a very small number of individuals in key committee positions. Barry Weingast and Mark Moran in particular have developed a general model of such control, based on a study of the FTC.[75] Similar, but less theoretically formal, accounts have been given of other agencies, such as the FCC.[76] It is not difficult to find evidence of such influence. The *Washington Post* and other national journals offer routine coverage of episodes of agency bashing by congressional committees, and the usual report includes appropriately deferential responses from the administrators intended to suggest that the oversight is effective. And it may be in some instances, though one should be cautious not to give too much credence to what the administrators say. After all, being stubborn does not necessarily entail being stupid about it. The FDA commissioner who has just been berated for his failings by Congressman John Dingell may or may not change his ways, but he is unlikely to make a public show of defiance that would only prolong the confrontation and possibly force the congressman to take more drastic measures. The true test of agency responsiveness can only be judged over a longer period than the typical news story covers, and here the evidence is rather more ambiguous. Let me cite two examples, selected only because they involve agencies that are frequently cited in reports of the effectiveness of congressional committee oversight; they are the two agencies used in the Weingast and Moran study. The FCC is frequently mentioned in this connection; yet even a cursory scan of recent controversies between it and the House and Senate oversight committees shows more stubbornness than compliance. The agency's defiance of the expressed views of a majority of both houses of Congress in eliminating its fairness doctrine (long a favorite of Congress) is only the most dramatic of many contemporary instances.[77] The FTC is a second case in point. Despite its often noted responsiveness to committee oversight, even the FTC has shown considerable resistance to congressional influence. Its refusal to acquiesce in congressional committee desires to go slow in implementing its unfairness doctrine (no relation to the FCC's fairness doctrine) in the 1970s reached the point of forcing Congress to respond with legislation specifically curbing the agency's enforcement program.[78]

Between the opposing models of agency dominance and congressional dominance an intermediate account has been formulated in which the emphasis is not on opposing powers but on mutually advantageous interaction, a positive-sum rather than a zero-sum game between an agency and Congress. According to one version, to which I alluded earlier, Congress structures administrative programs in such a way as to create a continuing opportunity for its members to intervene on behalf of their constituents, particularly to facilitate distribution of some special benefit to the constituency.[79] In this model, oversight is an essential element of the congressional casework, the objective of which is not influencing public policy so much as it is obtaining benefits, or serving as a kind of ombudsman, for individual constituents. It may not even be necessary to obtain a benefit, in fact; it is enough to create the appearance of doing so. Insofar as members of Congress are moved by the desire to be reelected, what matters is the ability to claim appropriate credit for actions valued by their constituents.[80] The agency, too, can benefit by promoting the appearance of effective influence by congressional members. Particularly if no major policy initiative is at stake, it will pay the agency to be solicitous to casework demands insofar as doing so builds congressional support for more agency activity that, in turn, creates more casework. The congressional-bureaucratic relationship is, in short, symbiotic—as with the tick bird and the rhinoceros or the pilot fish and the shark.

The positive-sum interpretation of the congressional-bureaucratic relationship does not convincingly account for many instances where one of the two sides is plainly the loser. (The FCC and FTC examples just cited are illustrative.) Still, the theory is helpful in showing how, contrary to appearance, the relationship between legislator and bureaucrat may be mutually beneficial. It may be somewhat misleading to describe this relationship in terms of legislative casework insofar as that conveys the image of rather trivial constituent services interceding with the bureaucracy on disputes over social security checks, licenses, or other such routine tasks. If one extends the casework to include larger constituent benefits, for example, pork barrel distributions controlled by bureaucrats, the pattern of interdependency between legislators and bureaucrats is more apparent.[81] One should not suppose that this relationship entails explicit bargaining or trades over individual initiatives. The basic model presupposes only that each party perceives long-term advantages in cooperation over a range of programmatic or policy choices and

that they have sufficient countervailing power to block unilateral preferences.[82] Needless to say, this bargain model confounds simple predictions;
insofar as it supposes a kind of bilateral monopoly between agencies and
Congress, the outcome for any given set of trades is indeterminate.

The model is also normatively ambiguous. In support of this relationship, one might say that an interactive model permits a desirable blending of
professional agency expertise with political influence and responsibility. This
supposes, of course, that the agency contributes expert judgement and the
congressional contribution is politically responsible. Probably most modern
proponents of the model do not imagine such a convergence of favorable
assumptions; it is too Wilsonian. I too am skeptical, at least enough so as not
to repose any large trust on this bargaining as a means of advancing a genuine
public welfare, as distinct from a mere coalition of active interest groups. We
have no reason to think an agency's professional expertise, such as it may be,
will reliably trump political criteria, and the political criteria are too often
simply those of concentrated interest groups with effective access to the
agencies. Congressional oversight is supposed to correct this problem, but the
oversight process is itself largely driven by the same narrow interest-
perspective that created the problem in the first place. The possibility of
conflicting interest groups in administrative and legislative arenas does open
up the possibility that the conflict will force a somewhat broader coalition to
emerge, although those looking for a more publicly oriented vision of public
policy probably will not take much comfort in the chance that such will
emerge serendipitously from the mere clash of interest groups. Congressional
oversight is subject to all the frailties of pluralistic democracy that afflict
legislative politics generally. The same tendency of Madisonian factions combining to secure from the legislature private benefits at the expense of an ill-
organized (less well-represented) general public repeats itself in the oversight
process. If Wilson's "voice of the great people" is faint when legislators
deliberate among themselves over new laws, we have no reason to think it will
be any louder when legislators confront bureaucrats over administrative rules.

In fact, the oversight process arguably enhances the private interest–
factional dispositions of Congress. The fact that the oversight process is
specially dominated by committees and prominent individual committee
members almost wholly unmonitored by Congress at large reduces the constraints that operate on legislators when they can act only with the active
consent of other members. If the incentives of a legislator are the same for
oversight and for lawmaking roles, the opportunities are not. Following conventional wisdom, I assume these incentives are shaped primarily by the
interests of those constituents who are able to monitor and respond actively
(with reward or sanction) to the member's actions. As a lawmaker, however, a
member's abilities to serve those interests are constricted. Even members with

extensive influence over their colleagues can seldom expect to have much influence as lawmakers without forming coalitions, which reduce the member's control over choices and require sharing the rewards of successful action. As the chairman of a committee or subcommittee, the member is frequently able to retain greater control and to reduce sharing the benefits from legislative influence since an effective coalition usually need not exceed a majority of the committee or subcommittee exercising oversight functions. Increasingly, the effective influence of individual members, or of small coalitions, enhances the likelihood of an outcome favoring special-interest groups insofar as these are the natural objects of the legislator's bounty.

I conclude from this assessment that one should not look to oversight by congressional committees or by individual congressmen to enhance the general public responsibility of bureaucratic activities. Conceivably, oversight might provide an opportunity for more public-regarding groups to influence decision making in ways not otherwise open to them at the agency level alone. This supposes, of course, that the congressional oversight process is more open to such groups than is the agency's decision-making process. No doubt it is possible for virtually any group to find someone in Congress to represent its claims or arguments in regard to some agency initiative. The question is whether oversight, in general, is an important mechanism for giving voice to groups, individuals, or interests that are otherwise "too faint to be heard," in Woodrow Wilson's phrase. In the ordinary course of events, we have reason to be skeptical.

The President

Reference to the president in discussing the executive role is conventional but somewhat misleading for the same reason it is misleading to refer to Congress's role. Although the Constitution formally lodges the executive power in the president, the executive power is institutionally diverse and diffuse. No one supposes the president can or should personally attempt to direct bureaucratic decision making, even on matters of important public policy. President Reagan gave us a new appreciation of just how removed a president can be from hands-on control, but for the most part he only dramatized the inevitable drift toward an amorphous and anonymous executive persona.[83] If the head of an agency such as OSHA or EPA receives a call from "the White House," she can bet her pension that the caller is not the president but a staff member, probably of middling rank in the White House hierarchy. And most interventions into agency affairs will not come from the White House at all, at least not directly; the executive influence will be filtered through multiple layers of departmental organization. Interventions into one agency's affairs may come directly from another agency, such as the Department of Justice's

Antitrust Division, which routinely performs a kind of monitoring role for regulatory agencies, or OMB, which performs a more general managerial oversight role for the executive branch.

These are important forms of policy influence and direction, to be sure, but one should not suppose that, individually or collectively, these interveners are simply representatives of the president. In fact, these executive interveners are themselves part of the administrative bureaucracy and, as such, present the same type of monitoring and control problems ("agency cost" problems in the vernacular of public choice theory) as the agencies they seek to influence. For instance, when the OMB seeks to influence NHTSA (Department of Transportation) to alter certain safety standards, how do we know which set of executive officers and bureaucrats speaks for the president? If the Justice Department declines to support an EPA decision on appeal, which agency represents *the* executive branch? The problem is not hypothetical. One former White House staff member, Bradley Patterson, reports a particularly vivid illustration involving a conflict between the Department of Justice and the Department of Interior over native American rights.[84] The former was defending an appeal of a Tax Court conviction for tax evasion. The prosecution rested on rejection of a claim of tax exemption for Indian trust land, which claim was supported by the Department of Interior, based on a recent policy pronouncement by President Nixon. When the Justice Department refused to recognize any basis for changing its support of the prosecution, which it defended as routine, the president's counsel (Leonard Garment) convened a meeting of representatives of Justice, Interior, and the IRS. His solution to the problem was ingenious, if unorthodox: the Justice Department was to go ahead and file its brief in support of the prosecution, but was to include in the brief the Interior Department's defense of the Indian claim. So much for the notion of presidential, or even White House staff, direction of executive policy!

Patterson reports the incident as unique in that the government was presenting *both* sides of the case. In fact it sometimes happens, in the case of independent regulatory agencies, that the Justice Department will oppose, or at least withhold support for, an agency decision on appeal. However, this is not the important point; what is important is what the illustrative case suggests about the problems of monitoring when the monitors are large bureaucratic institutions. The Department of Justice normally speaks for the federal government on all legal matters. Moreover, it has been known to resist White House intervention in its legal decisions.[85] (In the Indian claims case this was finessed by putting the government on both sides; it is noteworthy that Garment did not simply overrule Justice.) The problem is obviously greater in proportion to the distance (in organizational, if not physical, space) between the monitoring office and the White House. But even within the White House itself the growth of the staff has created a bureaucracy that has increasingly attenuated links to the president. The White House office staff assigned in direct support of the president (exclusive of separate organizational staffs within the executive office of the president, such as OMB) was reported as over 550 in 1987.[86] Executive surveillance of the bureaucracy is therefore often circular, one bureaucratic unit watching another. Classical political theory supposes this institutional oversight is structured hierarchically, pyramidally, with power and control focusing ultimately in the president. Ordinary observation reveals a more complex geometry. Indeed, it is perhaps misleading to describe the reality as a geometry at all, for the pattern of control is not sharply defined nor is it constant, varying as it does from one presidential administration to another.[87]

The tenuousness of presidential control is partly a matter of sheer managerial complexity. It just is not possible for the president to deal with more than a small fraction of the major policy choices that must be made, at least deal with them in a manner that is meaningful to the low echelon political official or career bureaucrat responsible for their implementation. The problem here, I should emphasize, is not one of technical competence or expertise of the kind that led Max Weber to despair of the possibility of effective political control of bureaucracy.[88] Weber perceived the difficulty of political control in terms of the disparate training and experience of the political officer (or public representative) and bureaucrat. It is the dilettante trying to tell the expert how to pave a road, regulate utility rates, regulate the money supply, or allocate radio frequencies.

Weber's view is obsolete to the extent that it puts the problem of control in terms of an allocation of power over *technocratic* choices when the important modern question is control over *political* choices. It is not so much a question of deciding whether railroads should receive a rate increase of 10 percent or 15 percent, whether AM radio channels should be 10 kilohertz or 9, whether M1 or M2 or M3 should be the relevant indicator for measuring the money supply. It is more one of deciding whether to allow rate increases or even whether to regulate them, whether to put time and effort into reconfiguring the radio bandwidths, and whether to increase or decrease the money supply. These larger questions are the real stakes in the contest of control, and their resolution requires surprisingly modest expertise. It is not relative technocratic competence that gives the bureaucrat the edge so much as political will and time. The real advantage the bureaucrat enjoys is an ability, one, to give more sustained attention to a given problem and, two, to extend the time horizon of decision making. If routine bureau time-horizons are measured in months and years, the average political officer's is measured in hours. It stands to reason that the average politician, who is likely to be in office for only a few years, would have a more compressed sense of time than the bureaucrat, for whom tenure is a career.[89]

Consider as one example the case of OSHA. OSHA provides a particularly interesting case for examining high-level executive oversight on a couple of counts. First, because it is an executive agency (within the Department of Labor) in contrast to an independent regulatory agency, there cannot be any serious doubt as to the legitimacy of executive direction and control—within, of course, the legal boundaries set by Congress in creating the agency. Whatever legal arguments may be made for limiting presidential influence in the case of independent agencies they have no force here.[90] Second, since its inception, OSHA has been politically controversial and a salient target for conservatives, making it a prime candidate for presidential interest, particularly for conservative Republican administrations. Yet a study of OSHA rule making during the Nixon and Ford administrations, both ideologically disposed to curb regulation generally and OSHA regulation in particular, found no significant intervention in OSHA rule making by White House staff during the period of these administrations. The explanation is simple: there was simply not world enough and time, as they say, for this level of monitoring. It is reported, for example, that of the two Ford administration staff members who had nominal responsibility for OSHA, as part of a general portfolio that covered all regulatory matters, one had no acquaintance with pending agency rule makings, and the other had very little acquaintance with them.[91]

The low political visibility of routine bureaucratic action makes it particularly difficult to obtain and maintain presidential attention to the task of directing or controlling it. Sad to say, there is relatively little political credit to be obtained from sustained involvement. Credit can be obtained from occasional efforts on behalf of some important political constituency but, of course, it is just that kind of involvement that is most difficult to justify in terms of the president's wider obligations to the public. I noted earlier the common belief that the president's broad-based, national constituency puts him in a special position to constrain the rent-seeking behavior of narrow interest groups.[92] This is true, in some degree at least. Unfortunately, it is also true that the very same position diminishes the president's political incentives to become deeply involved, and to sustain his involvement long enough to have effect. Except when the benefits of presidential involvement are highly visible to the general public or intensely enjoyed by a powerful constituency they are unlikely to exceed the costs of intervening in an agency policy controversy in which contending interest groups have intense or at least well-defined preferences. As Harold Bruff aptly puts it, since the president bears only attenuated responsibility for decisions made in the agencies, "intervention is likely to be a zero-sum game from his standpoint—he trades the pleasure of one constituency for the hostility of another."[93] The political problem is compounded by complaints from Congress about presidential intervention. Some of the complaints reflect legitimate concern over political influences that encroach on legal mandates or formal decision-making processes specified by Congress (about which more in the next chapter) though Congress tends to regard all presidential intervention as contrary to congressionally specified criteria or processes, while ignoring all similar interventions by congressional committees, individual members of Congress, or their staffs. Be that as it may, congressional hostility to executive influence is a fact of political life the president and his aides must weigh in deciding whether to invest the time and effort to influence a particular decision or policy.

What these considerations suggest is a very selective intervention strategy or one in which the president can control agency action without becoming deeply entangled in policy controversies. It is in the nature of such intervention strategies that they tend to be negative rather than affirmative, a quick entry into and exit out of a particular controversy, probably at the eleventh hour, under conditions where the political forces that supported the agency initiative cannot effectively regroup after the president has intervened. Presidents who come into office with aspirations to control bureaucratic decision making more systematically, whether with a view toward greater political accountability or greater managerial rationality, have had to abandon the ambition after the political costs of doing so were seen to exceed the gains. Richard Nixon's ambitious efforts to assert control through reorganization and strategic appointments were interred after Watergate, though by most accounts they were effectively dead long before, a casualty of Congress's fear that its own oversight prerogatives would be curtailed.[94] Jimmy Carter's similar ambitions to reorganize the executive branch in order to facilitate control were also frustrated, in part sabotaged by his own officers and in part done in by Congress.[95]

Some have seen promise in the more focused regulatory review programs, pursued with varying degrees of rigor since the Nixon administration, to control regulatory policy initiatives through the mechanism of OMB clearance or review.[96] Formally, the review program (perhaps plural would be more accurate in light of important changes in the program over the course of five administrations) is designed to require cost-benefit efficiency justifications for major regulatory initiatives (other than those of independent agencies). Of course, no cost-benefit evaluation can ever be so pure as to exclude political interests, and the review process has been no exception. This is not said in criticism; quite the contrary, it is what we should expect. At the same time, the more such elements of political interest intrude, the greater the potential clash between an agency's mandate from Congress and its mandate from OMB. Unsurprisingly, the perception of an increased politicization of the process under President Reagan fueled congressional opposition that has persisted under President Bush. The survival of the entire program is now in question as Congress has threatened to cut off funds for it.

Termination of the program would be a setback to responsible executive governance, but a fairly modest one. There are some success stories, to be sure, but one cannot credibly claim the program has effectively controlled the regulatory enterprise within the executive branch. Moreover, at best, this kind of institutionalized review program does not quite solve the bureaucratic control problem, for it involves the circular problem of one bureaucracy monitoring another. I do not doubt that some form of regulatory review, by OMB and by other agencies, can be a useful tool of good policy making, but the more it becomes bureaucratized the more it risks compounding the very monitoring problem it was created to correct. *Quis custodiet ipso custodes?*

I have thus far considered the oversight role solely in terms of giving directives to agencies on more or less specific issues of policy. Of course, influence and control is often more subtle and indirect. It is now a commonplace of modern political commentary that the president is not, and cannot be, the chief manager; he is, rather, the chief political officer. Following Richard Neustadt, it is now part of the received wisdom that the president's primary power is that of persuasion not command,[97] and the power of persuasion is exercised frequently by indirection, by setting general policy ideals and goals that loyal aides transmit successively through the executive establishment.

Ronald Reagan showed us how this model works, but he also showed us its limitations.[98] Reagan's hands-off style decentralized executive power to such a degree as to permit his officers (and their subordinates) to pursue their own agenda without political accountability. We have the scandal of the Department of Housing and Urban Development (HUD) as a reminder of how far out of control such untethered discretion can get.[99] The HUD case may be an extreme example of irresponsibility, an unusual instance in which presidential laissez-faire is accompanied by a vacuum of responsible control in the White House and departmental hierarchies. But the extreme case still illustrates the pervasive problem of maintaining control. In the best of circumstances, central control by leadership example is a sometime thing. Even clear and resonant pronouncements on general goals (for instance, "deregulate the economy," or even more specifically, "ease the burden of environmental regulation") are subject to rapid dissipation as they are transmitted through successive levels of implementers and decision makers, each the recipient of competing messages—from interest groups, Congress, and peer groups within the bureaucracy.

Even assuming strong personal loyalties to the president's political program on the part of bureaucratic implementers, the effectiveness of a few occasional expressions of principle by the president or his top aides is often overwhelmed by the centrifugal force of the bureaucrat's "local" constituents. Nature abhors a vacuum. So does politics. If the president cannot find the time to engage himself, through top aides if not personally, in the bureaucrat's concerns, others will.[100] The tendency of executive officers at the highest level to be captured by their immediate constituency, or at least become absorbed in "local" concerns to the neglect of central (White House) policy, has been the bane of presidents from time immemorial. One does not counter such tendencies by a few simple directions issued episodically from the Oval Office. It is not enough to be a "great communicator," it is also necessary to be a great nag. Henry Kissinger reports his vexation as National Security Affairs Assistant attempting to ensure fidelity to White House policy decisions on East-West trade: "No sooner were these instructions issued than the departments began to nibble away at them. Departments accept decisions which go against them only if vigilantly supervised. Otherwise the lower-level exegesis can be breathtaking in its effrontery."[101]

A lot depends obviously on who the individual bureaucrats are and where their general loyalties—let's call them residual loyalties to mark them off from the shifting obligations that arise on particular policy issues—lie. Herein lies the president's most powerful means of suasion and influence: appointment of the right people to the agencies. Without question this is where presidents have had their greatest impact on administrative policy making. It is fair to say, for example, that the deregulation movement of the 1970s and 1980s, such as it was, was driven by the appointment to the regulatory agencies and bureaus of deregulation-minded individuals who were sufficiently strong minded and competent to effect, pace Thomas Kuhn, a paradigm shift in then prevailing public policy in the teeth of powerful political opposition, including (in some cases) opposition by many regulated industries reluctant to trade regulatory protection for competition.

Unfortunately, the power of appointment has been too often squandered in the case of administrative officers at operational management levels. It is not irrelevant that the more than 4,000 full-time, nonjudicial positions that are subject to presidential appointment are listed in a so-called plum book and commonly labeled "patronage."[102] The regulatory agencies in particular have been treated as dumping grounds for assorted patronage payoffs.[103] One might think that political patronage would at least secure loyalty to the president; sometimes it does. Often, however, the premier loyalty is to someone other than the president—an interest group, perhaps—who secured the appointment. Moreover, loyalty only goes so far, particularly in the absence of any clear and direct guidelines about what appointees are supposed to do in order to be loyal. As important as loyalty—in the abstract sense of being a "true" Democrat or Republican, liberal or conservative—is competence and a strong, even independent sense of mission. The absence of competence and strength of purpose makes appointees vulnerable to the political pulls of the interest groups and peer-group bureaucrats that they confront regularly in their workaday environment.

The Courts

We have scanned the political environment of the bureaucrat, the direct and indirect influence of interest groups and public political officials. It remains to say something about the courts and the influence of the rule of law. The specific content of the rule of law, as embodied in both procedural and substantive constraints, will be explored in detail in the next chapters. Here I anticipate that discussion with some brief observations on the general legal environment.

To describe the typical bureaucratic environment as a legal one can be misleading. That agency members and their staffs often determine legal issues in a fashion similar to that of judges should not obscure the more salient fact that, for most administrative decision makers in most agencies, adjudication is neither a large nor a very important occupation. Even when the decision maker is engaged in activities that might involve "legal" principles, his or her involvement is more commonly as a legislator than as a judge. In such a legislative capacity, the official is more exposed to political influence than the judge, and generally freer to respond to it in ways that accommodate personal preferences. Even setting aside the greater room for accommodating narrow self-interest motivation in the form of, say, economic or social advantage (for example, subsequent private employment with an agency client), there is a much greater scope for making pure policy choices free of the constraints of legal principle and precedent. I do not mean to say that agency officials cannot be, and are not in fact, constrained by the rule of law or by judicial enforcement thereof. The point is simply that, for most policy issues, the rule of law is not routinely internalized as a major desideratum of agency choices. Under the best of circumstances judicial review tends to be rather fitful, and the results of any given decision ambiguous.

There has been very little analysis of the effects of judicial oversight, of the degree to which agencies internalize judicial precedent. We have a few collections of affirmance and reversal rates, but these "box score" counts do not reveal much about the effects of judicial review.[104] What one wants is a measure of the real impact on particular agency policies or bureaucratic behavior. For this we need a great deal more information about the pattern of judicial intervention, and, more important, how agencies have responded to it. For this purpose probably nothing but a detailed study of particular agencies and programs can supply the information. We have few such studies.[105]

It is difficult to make generalizations without inviting scorn from those who berate social scientists for thinking "data" is the plural form of anecdote (a quip I first heard from an economist, Roger Noll). Unfortunately, the task of systematically gathering relevant information on effects is so large that no one has been bold enough to try it. In some respects the problem of determining the effects of judicial review here is the same as determining the effect of any adjudication. In ordinary common law adjudication of private disputes, a legal decision has two effects: one, it settles the dispute between the parties (or settles the legal terms on which the parties will settle *inter se*); two, as precedent, it has at least an incremental effect in shaping a general rule supposed to guide future decisions and, by the same assumption, the future behavior of the parties. In administrative cases, where review involves a particularized "dispute" between an agency and one party—for example, review of a disability determination—we can regard judicial review essentially the same as a common law adjudication. In other cases involving larger, less particularized issues of public policy, however, the effects of judicial review will be far less clear.

For one thing, the immediate mandate of the court itself is more likely to be indeterminate. Where agency action is disapproved, the court's mandate will typically be open ended as to the permissible range of agency responses. Thus, the usual remand for further agency findings or clearer articulation of agency reasons typically leaves the agency some legitimate discretion in choosing further actions. It also leaves some room for evasive or strategic actions to avoid the intended thrust of the court's decision.[106]

We might expect judicial approval of agency action to have a more determinate effect; affirming the rationality of agency decisions signals their acceptability and provides positive incentives for the agency to proceed further. Of course, the signaling effect depends importantly on how the court articulates its affirmance with respect to the agency's power and the character of the legal issue. In all events, judicial intervention is most likely to be successful in influencing policy choices when it conforms generally to criteria that the agency itself accepts, at least in principle, when the court does not frontally assault the agency agenda, the particular "life-style" of the affected bureaucrats, or the political environment in which they operate.[107] This might seem to entail a very limited oversight role for the courts, but that inference follows only if one conceives of judicial oversight as authoritarian censorship of agency choices. Viewing the rule of law in more flexible terms, as nudging agencies in the direction of greater attention to rational public purposes and coherent relationships in making policy choices, the potential for effective judicial oversight is substantial.

I view such a potential as not only benign but as necessary to establish any significant role for a rule-of-law constraint on bureaucratic discretion.

That view is quite widely embraced by political liberals but not by many contemporary conservatives, even those critical of bureaucratic government generally. In part, the conservative hostility to active judicial review reflects a skepticism about courts as effective monitors and judges of public policy, but it also reflects cynicism about the rule of law itself as a meaningful principle apart from the vicissitudes of interest-group politics. In this latter aspect it reflects a normative acceptance of modern positivist analysis, which I noted earlier. I reject both the skepticism and the cynicism. What follows in the next chapters is based on the assumption that it is possible to formulate workable principles (though hardly precise guidelines) for enforcing rule-of-law restraints on agency action.

One final point on a matter of semantics: administrative law is sometimes said to be composed of an "internal" and an "external" law, the former referring to agency due process and standards, the latter to judicial enforcement. This conventional classification of the two "laws" is convenient but a bit misleading insofar as it obscures the interdependency of the internal and external law. An internal law without externally defined norms and enforcement would not be meaningless, perhaps, but would be largely inconsequential. Such externally imposed norms are not likely to have a sustained effect unless they become incorporated into the process and standards of the agency. It is not possible for courts to monitor the vast apparatus of the bureaucracy routinely, and it is seldom possible to insure control of determinedly deviant behavior over the long term. The efficacy of external norms is thus ultimately dependent on an agency's acceptance of the legitimacy of external norms, even if it does not agree with them in all particulars. On this account, then, both the internal and the external law should be seen as two sides of the same coin.

CHAPTER 4

Administrative Due Process

The demise of any meaningful limitation on the delegation of power to agencies has virtually removed from constitutional dispute the legitimacy of discretionary administrative power in general terms. Legitimacy has come to be defined largely in terms of procedural "due process."[1] To be sure questions of substantive authority arise and, to a degree, these implicate issues of substantive principle. However, questions of substantive principle tend to be subordinated to a scrutiny of the processes that shaped the agency's decision or rules.

Early concern with legal process was more a matter of defining limitations on the substantive powers of government than defining a set of internal procedural requisites for administrative action. However, the limits on judicial scrutiny of an ever-expanding bureaucracy made it impossible for courts themselves to provide a legal forum of first resort to enforce those limitations and to ensure the protection of individual rights. The early rules were grounded in basic constitutional requirements under the Fifth and Fourteenth Amendments. A body of nonconstitutional law appeared later as part of particular regulatory schemes, which in turn provided the basis for more general requirements in the form of state and federal administrative procedure acts. Preliminarily, I shall consider constitutional principles, but these serve largely to define the boundaries of expedient policy, the realm of what I shall label "ordinary process."

Constitutional Due Process

Constitutional due process has been traditionally framed by two dichotomies that in turn have provided the models on which most nonconstitutional administrative law is based. The first dichotomy is between "legislative" determinations involving the promulgation of rules of general application and "adjudicative" determinations involving the settlement of discrete controversies directly affecting individual interests.[2] Legislative determinations have traditionally not been thought to be *procedurally* constrained by constitutional due process requirements, at least where they are made, in fact, by a legislature as opposed to an agency exercising legislative power.[3] There are constitutional directions for how laws are enacted, and there are some other constitutional limitations such as the prohibition of unduly vague legislation or bills of attainder that might be characterized as broadly procedural. Indeed, the basic requirement of rationality in legislation could be understood to be procedural, insofar as it is a requirement of due process (as well as equal protection). Nevertheless, it is more useful to interpret this as a substantive, not a process, constraint.

Adjudicative determinations are subject to due process requirements depending on the individual interests at stake. The special condition applicable to the protection of adjudicative determinations incorporates the second classical dichotomy in due process analysis, the distinction between protected and unprotected interests. Until quite recently, the unprotected interests were labeled mere *privileges*, but the term had no real descriptive power since one could not know whether an interest was a privilege until the court decided whether it was worthy of constitutional recognition. While modern law has purported to do away with the privilege notion, it has not eliminated the basic dichotomy. The distinction is now between protected *property rights* and *liberty interests* on the one hand and unprotected *unilateral expectancy* interests on the other. As we will see, it is not clear that the change in terminology has materially altered legal doctrine; it remains mired in confusion about how protected rights are identified.

Rules and Adjudications

The constitutional jurisprudence on the first dichotomy, between legislative and adjudicative action, is fairly thin. The governing precedents are two Supreme Court decisions in 1908 and 1915, both involving taxation of property owners. The first involved a tax assessment by the City of Denver for the cost of paving a street; the tax was assessed on abutting property owners in proportion to their frontage along the street.[4] The Court ruled that the owners were entitled to a hearing on the assessment; it was a bit vague about the requisite formalities, though it noted that many of the elements "essential in strictly judicial proceedings" (whatever they are) could be dispensed with. The second decision involved an order by a state agency increasing the valuation of all taxable property in Denver, again challenged for want of a hearing on the valuation.[5] The Court rejected the challenge. In a characteristically brief opinion by Justice Holmes, the Court found "hard to believe" the argument that the Fourteenth Amendment required a hearing for individuals affected by a general order of this kind: "Where a rule of conduct applies to more than a few people it is impracticable that every one should have a direct voice in its adoption."[6] The Court distinguished its earlier decision on the ground that, in that case, "a relatively small number of persons was concerned, who were exceptionally affected, in each case upon individual grounds."

Although neither case specifically uses the terms *adjudicative* and *legislative*, those are the conventional labels used to describe the dichotomy. Unfortunately, neither label is self-defining and the decisions themselves are not as clear on this matter as one might wish. Note, first of all, that the nature of the institution cannot be helpful here. The distinction between legislative and adjudicative action is clear enough where the former is taken by a legislature and the latter by a regular court. However, both cases involved action by an administrative body. Indeed, the problem only arises in the context of rule-making action by administrative agencies since there are no procedural due process constraints on legislators.

The constitutional range of the distinction between adjudication and rule making has remained unsettled probably because the general statutory prescription of certain process requirements has more or less occupied the field. The federal Administrative Procedure Act requirements of general notice to the public and opportunity to file written commentary presumably satisfy all constitutional due process expectations for rule making affecting general classes. On that assumption, the Supreme Court has affirmed the use of general agency rule making to determine specific issues and foreclose them from contest in future individual hearing prescribed by statute.[7] Nevertheless, the anxiety that fixed rules may not do full justice to the infinite variety of circumstances can still be found in Court opinions dealing with administrative rules.[8] The question of whether due process compels individualized treatment pushes us back to the earlier question of whether there are *constitutional* process constraints on administrative rule making that would not apply to the legislature. Though there is no decisive precedent on this point, it appears to be a common assumption that some minimal process requirements such as those prescribed by the Administrative Procedure Act reflect an underlying constitutional command.[9]

Perhaps. Certainly one is numbed by the thought that administrative rule makers could be allowed the same procedural latitude given legislators. But this numbness may simply reflect a conflation of positive law norms into constitutional *grund norms*. To put the matter in a concrete context, imagine that Congress, after struggling to enact statutory safety standards for diesel locomotives (never mind why they might want to do this), delegates to the Interstate Commerce Commission authority to develop such standards by rule making. Believing that the process of rule making in this instance should be as unconstrained as possible (giving full rein to the ICC's expertise), Congress exempts the rule making from any formal process requirements. In order to avoid complexities introduced by the availability of judicial review, suppose further that Congress specifies that the rules shall be reviewed only on the same terms of substantive rationality applied to an act of Congress. Rules are promulgated, without public notice or opportunity for public comment, although the ICC staff and commissioners consult with assorted industry and congressional representatives. While the rules are intelligible and capable of being implemented, no explanation is given as to how they were developed, or the specific factual assumptions underlying them. If the same rules promulgated by Congress would not be vulnerable to challenge for lack of (procedural) due process, are they any more so when promulgated by the agency pursuant to valid legislative delegation? It is hard to see why they would be, unless one incorporates a due process component into the delegation doctrine along lines such as the following: the delegation of legislative power is valid only when it incorporates due process protection for persons affected. Some delegation opinions contain hints of such a notion,[10] but due process procedures have never been made a constitutional prerequisite of delegation.[11]

If due process in rule making is not a specific component of the delegation doctrine, it nevertheless might be derived from notions of political legitimacy. The absence of due process constraints on legislators is grounded in the premise that democratic political processes are sufficient to ensure fairness and, after a fashion, public rationality. By contrast, bureaucrats are not politically accountable; enter due process as a surrogate for ensuring fairness and rationality. The argument is somewhat disingenuous for, as I argued earlier, the political process is, at best, incomplete in its assurance of either fairness or rationality. This is precisely the argument for a more aggressive conception of substantive due process. However, we do, in fact, make a sharp distinction between the legitimacy of the political process in the electoral and legislative arena on the one hand and in the bureaucratic arena on the other. In the latter, political power is, after all, one step further removed from democratic controls, and this might call for imposing constitutional due process limits on administrative rule making. This assumes, of course, that the kind of procedures that might be required for rule making would effectively promote fairness and rationality. We must defer pursuing this question. It is necessary, first, to consider some other elements of constitutional doctrine that are critical to a determination of when due process principles apply. We have been considering only legislative due process, the assumption being that if the choices were adjudicative in character, constitutional due process would apply. That assumption is incorrect. A finding that agency action is adjudicative is merely the occasion for making another threshold determination.

Due Process Thresholds: Rights and Interests

If agency action is classified as adjudicative, it must still be shown that the interests affected by it are protected interests before due process claims will be honored. The history of constitutional doctrine on this point is a history of confusion. Much of the confusion arises because of the propensity to resort to labels or elliptical expressions in place of a careful exposition of the source of rights and the nature of the protection required by constitutional norms such as due process (and/or substantive constitutional limitations). A notorious case in point is the once common reference to "rights" versus "privilege" to describe protected and unprotected constitutional interests.[12] The right-privilege notion was closely related to another controversial notion of conditioned rights, the idea being that individual rights could be limited, or even terminated, as a condition of receiving government benefits that are dispensed at the discretion of the government (and hence are mere privileges).[13] Both the right-privilege notion and that of conditioned rights (or, as it has been more commonly but misleadingly labeled, *unconstitutional conditions*) have had a rather checkered history and there remains considerable confusion over both the scope and the purposes of these concepts. The contradictions and confusions in the twin concepts of conditional rights and right versus privilege dichotomy have been fully explored by others.[14] Here it is necessary only to explore briefly one aspect of the issue as it bears on due process. This is the problem of defining rights, which is foundational to the right-privilege conundrum.

The immediate source of the problem is the constitutional language of the due process clauses in the Fifth and Fourteenth Amendments, which specify the "rights" protected by due process as "life, liberty or property." None of these terms is defined by the constitutional text. *Life* is straightforward for the most part; anyway the meaning of life (literal not figurative) does not figure in disputes about administrative proceedings. Despite continued provocation, no one has yet proposed that we deal with the shortcomings of public employees by shooting them; hardship though it may be to have one's welfare payments terminated, the case has not yet arisen where termination threatened a life. However, *liberty* and *property* are full of ambiguities that canonical interpretation cannot resolve.

The interpretive problem is nevertheless quite modern. There are a number of pre–Civil War state decisions construing the terms (most notably property) in similar state constitutions, but the United States Supreme Court had no occasion to consider the definition of due process rights until quite late in the nineteenth century. Even then, the Court's approach to the problem was not a matter of textual interpretation so much as a matter of free-form constitutional principle.[15] For instance, it was not thought to be particularly important to decide whether some interest was property or liberty; it was enough to determine that it was worthy of constitutional protection.[16] This approach is, I think, quite consistent with the sense of the phrase "life, liberty or property," as used by the framers. Although some modern interpretivists have sought to pin the framers down to specific and rather narrow historical meanings,[17] we have good reason to think the phrase itself was mostly atmospheric and the terms property and liberty were not understood to refer to any set of historical legal precedents.[18]

This is not to suggest that there were no limits to the scope of the due process clause. Quite the contrary; that is what the dispute over the right-privilege dichotomy was (and is still) all about. Some interests were regarded as too insubstantial to claim protection as rights; they were mere privileges. Dissatisfaction with this particular way of viewing the due process issue led the Court to abandon the terminology of privilege. For a time it appeared the Court might even abandon altogether the idea that due process was dependent on an antecedent determination of rights, and might instead apply a kind of fluid, functional test in which due process would be applicable to all important interests, the specific requirements of due process being calibrated according to the nature of the interest, the circumstances, etc.

In 1970, *Goldberg v. Kelly* appeared to embrace just such a notion, though, technically, the Court did find a property right by reason of statutory entitlement.[19] *Goldberg* involved a due process challenge to state and city regulations establishing procedures for terminating financial aid payments (AFDC payments) to ineligible recipients. Under the regulations, local officials proposing to discontinue or suspend aid on grounds of ineligibility were required to give notice to the recipient of the reasons for the determination and an opportunity to seek review of the determination. While no personal appearance or oral hearing was provided prior to termination, provision was made for a full hearing after termination of aid. The Court held these procedures were inadequate. A pretermination hearing was required; welfare recipients' dire financial need for financial assistance outweighed the government interest in conserving fiscal and administrative resources by stopping payments promptly on discovering reasons to believe recipients were no longer eligible. Though the general applicability of due process to the case was not challenged, Justice Brennan nevertheless took the occasion to elaborate on some broad principles for the application of due process in the modern welfare state. Noting, first, that the particular benefits at stake in this case were a matter of statutory entitlement, he suggested that all such welfare entitlements might be regarded, as Charles Reich had proposed, as property—to which, of course, the due process clause expressly applies.[20] Whether the entitlements are labeled property appears to be only a matter of formalism for Justice Brennan, since the real criterion of due process applicability lies not in labels, "right" or "privilege," but in the practical importance of the individual interest weighed against that of the government.

The expansive promise of *Goldberg* turned out to be short-lived. Only two years later, in *Board of Regents v. Roth*, the Court declined to follow the path that Justice Brennan had charted for it in *Goldberg*.[21] In *Roth*, an untenured public university teacher claimed due process entitled him to a hearing on the university's refusal to rehire him at the end of his one-year appointment. Under state law, an untenured teacher had no procedural protection in case of a simple refusal to rehire, and Roth had been given no reason for, nor any opportunity to contest, the university's decision. Applying a simple balancing test, in the manner of *Goldberg*, the district court found a violation of due process, a finding affirmed by the court of appeals. However, the Supreme Court, through Justice Stewart, rejected simple interest balancing as the dispositive criterion of due process. For *any* due process protection to apply, the Court ruled it must first be shown that there was a deprivation of property and liberty. Roth had shown no such protected interest in this case. His liberty was not impaired, since Roth's ability to be employed elsewhere had not been impaired. No property right was implicated, because Roth had no "legitimate claim of entitlement." The state law gave untenured teachers no such entitlement by contract or otherwise; at most Roth had a mere "unilateral expectation," which was insufficient. *Goldberg* was distinguished by the fact that the benefits in that case were a matter of expressed statutory entitlement.[22]

Although the Court purported to reject the old right-privilege distinction in *Roth*, critics have claimed it did no such thing.[23] And in fact, although *Roth* eschewed the simplistic and question-begging term *privilege*, it adhered to the operative part of the right-privilege distinction. Under *Roth* it is still necessary to locate an independent right to which due process can attach. Where such a right does not exist, it matters not whether we call the individual's unprotected interests a privilege or a nothing—as in the ancient argot of contract interpretation where the absence of the conditions of an unenforceable contract was described as *nudum pactum*. *Goldberg v. Kelly* expanded protection for important claims against the state—claims that had heretofore been subject to necessary treatment as mere privileges. That was its obvious virtue. Its apparent vice was, in the pertinent words of Macaulay's impertinent quip about the original American Constitution, "it is all sail and no anchor." If we thought the old concepts of property and liberty were vague, what must be said of the new ones—especially property? At least with the older ideas we could appeal to some fundamental norms that were thought to be embedded in the ideas of individual freedoms vis-à-vis state interference. Even in its most expansive conception, the social contract does not embrace the totality of all social actions. What was the domain of this "new property" and of the due process that attends it?

Nor did *Roth* offer much by way of additional precision to improve on the older jurisprudence. The Court said that a property right entails more than a "unilateral expectation of it"; it requires a "legitimate claim of entitlement." This was elaborated slightly in the companion *Sindermann* case: a person has a property interest in a benefit "if there are such rules or mutually explicit understandings that support this claim of entitlement."[24] It requires no great analytical sophistication to see that this formulation is almost entirely question begging. What does support a "legitimate claim" of entitlement? The language suggests either a contractual or quasi-contractual approach: property arises out of mutual understandings or, at least, an implied promise by the state on which the individual justifiably relies. This theory of legitimate expectations parallels Bentham's theory of property, which also rested on expectations "founded on the laws."[25] However, Bentham viewed those expectations as grounded in broad social consensus. The modern version of expectations arising out of specific legal rules is circular. As one due process scholar (now judge) observes: "Insofar as promises, expectations and reliance are the bases of a property or liberty interest, the statute or rule which generates the expectation or reliance is its proper measure."[26]

The problem of defining property according to expectations is especially problematic, given the modern conception of property. Thanks to American legal realists, every beginning law student is taught that property is not a singular construct, but, according to a now clichéd metaphor, a "bundle-of-sticks," a collection of distinctive powers and remedies.[27] The powers and remedies are not uniform across all property. For example, conventional property—sometimes called common law property (reflecting the fact that it is largely the creation of common law doctrine rather than statutes)—is usually characterized by two major elements, the right to exclusive possession/use and free transferability. However, these elements are subject to various legal conditions that limit their realization or their enforcement. For example, the right of exclusive possession/use is limited by the enforcement remedies provided: it may be protected by injunctive relief against interference or only by an award for damages. In some cases it may not be enforceable at all against certain persons, those who have special easements or use privileges. In functional terms, then, the property right describes—is functionally the same as—the set of legal attributes that are protected and how they are protected.

This is elementary as far as common property law is concerned. However, when this elementary idea is transposed to due process property concepts, it has been the subject of sharp controversy on and off the Court.[28] At bottom, I think the controversy is really more over the propriety of a positivist view of constitutional due process than it is over conceptions of property. Despite arguments by Justice Brennan that property has a constitutional dimension, the rest of the Court has repeatedly emphasized that the definition of property is a matter of positive (nonconstitutional) law, whereas liberty has both constitutional and nonconstitutional origins.[29] This dichotomy between liberty and property is anything but compelling, but the Court has adhered to it.[30] In *Cleveland Board of Education v. Loudermill*,[31] involving the discharge of public employees without a pretermination hearing, is was argued that employees had only such property as the state legislature conferred and that such property was "defined by, and conditioned on, the legislature's choice of procedures for its deprivation." In speaking for the majority, Justice White rejected the argument. Justice Rehnquist dissented, arguing essentially that the greater power of the state to define the substantive terms of employment embraced a lesser power to specify procedural rights—essentially a variant of the old conditional rights argument. Justice White asserted:

> The categories of substance and procedure are distinct. Were the rule otherwise, the Clause would be reduced to a mere tautology. "Property" cannot be defined by the procedures provided for its deprivation any more than can life or liberty. The right to due process "is conferred, not by legislative grace, but by constitutional guarantee."[32]

Justice White's argument about "reducing the Clause . . . to a mere tautology" is unanswerable. If the legislative definition is dispositive as to both the existence *and* the content of property, the due process clause has no function. This is the famous "positivist trap" about which too much has been written. However, so long as the Court eschews a *constitutional* definition of what constitutes property, it has no warrant in manipulating the statutory or common law definition of property so as to take only part of it. Recalling the bundle concept, if the state law confers a set of rights, X, Y and Z, and calls this bundle property, the Court has no basis on which to say X and Y alone constitute the property right. Only if it is willing to assume the responsibility for defining the *substantive* right is it justified in unbundling the states' aggregation of sticks so that it can include its own procedural stick.

Critics of the positivist approach, both on and off the Court, have seen it as a return to the argument underlying the conditioned benefits jurisprudence that the greater power includes the lesser: the power of the states to create (or not create) property carries with it the power to define all the attributes thereof, procedural and substantive. The language of Justice Rehnquist's dissent in *Loudermill* lends support to that interpretation. But it is incorrect as an interpretation of the positivist theory. Whether or not a positivist conception of rights provides an appropriate ground for due process, it misses the point to relate it to the greater-includes-the-lesser notion, which is an argument from power. The positivist concept is not one of power, but of interpretation. To the extent that property (or, equally, liberty) is a predicate of due process, it is necessary to have a definition, a means of identifying what property is.

For most conventional property interests in things, the definitional problem is essentially nonproblematic. At the very least we can fall back on more or less accepted common law conceptions that will identify the existence of the property right and specify its content. But it has been recognized from time immemorial that property rights extend beyond interests in things to an array of legal relationships and obligations. The Court has recognized the extension of property, but has ignored its underlying functional meaning. Put it this way: in *Loudermill* the Court found that the state had created a property right. But how did it know this? The statute did not say that public employees had a property right. What it said was that employees had a right to certain discharge procedures, which did not include a pretermination hearing and were thereby thought deficient. Respondents probably put the case badly by arguing that the statute created a conditional right. Suppose, instead, they argued that the statute created *no* property right to employment, but did create a property right to specific discharge procedures? How can the Court say otherwise, if it is the statute that is the source of the right? What it could do, of course, is to define the existence as well as the content of property independent of positive law. That is, it could simply treat the Constitution itself as the source of property. In fact, despite the Court's steadfast refusal to accept the Constitution as creating property, that is what the Court's creative interpretation of positive law property has done. In essence, the Supreme Court has created a functional property right to the extent of its application of due process.

Balancing the Interests in Due Process

The vexing search for a coherent theory of property or liberty has obscured what is ultimately at stake. In general terms what is at stake, of course, are processes for the protection of the right in question. But what does that mean in specific terms? When the Constitution mandates due process, *what* process does it mandate? The Supreme Court's not very illuminating answer has been, "it all depends." What it depends on and how it depends on it has not been precisely specified, but the Court has articulated general formulas, currently the most authoritative being that of *Mathews v. Eldridge* in 1976, a case strikingly similar in its facts to *Goldberg v. Kelly*, but with a dramatically different result.[33] *Eldridge* involved termination of disability benefits under the Social Security Act (*Goldberg*, recall, involved termination of welfare benefits, AFDC payments). As in *Goldberg*, the recipient was accorded notice of the proposed termination and an opportunity to respond in writing and, if the benefits were terminated, recipient could demand a full evidentiary hearing. These procedures were attacked on the ground that *Goldberg* compelled a full evidentiary hearing before termination of benefits. The Court held, *Goldberg* notwithstanding, that the existing procedures were adequate. It formulated three factors to be balanced in determining what process is due:

First, the private interest that will be affected by the official action; second, the risk of an erroneous deprivation of such interest through the procedures used and the probable value, if any, of additional or substitute procedural safeguards, and finally, the government's interest, including the function involved and the fiscal and administrative burdens that the additional or substitute procedural requirement would entail.[34]

The Court's interest balancing test was not new with *Eldridge*; it was essentially a refinement of a general balancing test employed by the Court for more than a decade.

To say that this balancing test can yield a range of specific procedures is an understatement, rather like saying a kaleidoscope produces a lot of patterns. At one end of the range the process due is truly minimal. For example, a year before *Eldridge*, the Court in *Goss v. Lopez* held that a high school student who was briefly suspended for disruptive conduct "must be given *some* kind of notice and afforded *some* kind of hearing"; however, the emphasis was on "some": it would be sufficient to discuss with the student the basis for official actions, with "opportunity to explain his version of the facts at the discussion."[35] A year after *Eldridge*, in a second student disciplinary case, *Ingraham v. Wright*, involving an impromptu "paddling" of an unruly student, the Court ruled that due process was satisfied by an opportunity to pursue, after the fact, a civil damage action for excessive punishment.[36] At the other end of the process range, *Goldberg* required a full evidentiary hearing before the government action in question. In *Eldridge*, the Court essentially limited *Goldberg* to the particular facts; however, the exceptional character probably was more in the timing than the content of the hearing.

We can forego examination of all the variations that run through Supreme Court decisions on point. It would not add much further understanding of how the balancing test has been implemented. The Court's application of *Eldridge* has been criticized as erratic, even incoherent. Jerry Mashaw, for example, argues that "although promising transparency and generality, it has produced instead an opaque and Balkanized jurisprudence that can only hope to be understood within the particular context of specific programs or substantive fields of activity (education, public employment, or the like)."[37] Mashaw may be right, though his criticism appears to expect a lot from what is intended to be only a general formula. It is the nature of such a formula that it will not yield a clear set of outcomes, particularly where it is designed to give liberal room for administrative variation in different contexts. To expect more is to demand a closer judicial surveillance of agencies than the Court itself appears to intend, or it assumes a greater degree of uniformity among administrative situations than exists with respect to relevant due process criteria.

It is on this latter point that Mashaw's stronger criticism rests. It is not the Court's enforcement of *Eldridge* criteria so much as the criteria themselves that are the target of Mashaw's criticism. Or rather it is the normative basis of the criteria, for Mashaw challenges the basic utilitarian model (which, in somewhat Pickwickian fashion, he calls a "model of competence"). While important on some practical level of legislative policy judgment, he argues the model is inappropriate to constitutional adjudication precisely because there is no basis for preferring the Court's utilitarian determinations over those made by the legislature.[38] Mashaw is cautious about embracing a rights-based approach to due process to the extent it might suggest a kind of absolutism that would override, or at least obscure, the need to balance competing claims of right. At bottom, however, his conception of due process is one of individual rights, defined essentially in terms of dignitary values such as autonomy, self-respect, and equality. What is needed is to translate these general values into a set of operational standards to be used in determining a set of appropriate processes.[39] These processes would not only not turn on utilitarian calculus, they would be independent of any threshold finding of a liberty or property interest. The "positivist trap" that has plagued due process at least since *Roth* would be circumvented by a conception of due process that derives wholly from constitutional protection of dignitary values, whatever their status under positive law.[40] In this respect as in others, Mashaw joins a number of others who have argued either for abolition of the thresholds or for a constitutional definition of the threshold property and liberty interests that would essentially achieve the same end.[41]

We can quickly put aside Mashaw's critique of judicial utilitarianism. It seems a bit overdone to me. If the Court can claim no special competence to override a legislature's utilitarian calculus supposedly based on majoritarian preferences, where does it derive its prerogative to override legislative/ majoritarian preferences on other grounds? It is by no means obvious that courts cannot, in fact, make "better" utilitarian calculations than legislatures if one is willing to assume the possibility of a general public interest that is other than what the political process generates. The discussion of this point in chapter 1 is directly pertinent here. Nevertheless, assuming the courts are unqualified to define the public interest on utilitarian grounds, are they more qualified to do so on other grounds? It is not at all obvious that judges are better as moral theorists than as political or social engineers.[42] In fact, the experience of most judges prior to their appointment equips them to be the latter more than the former. Most judges come to the bench from active participation in the same political world wherein legislators dwell. (Indeed, their political activism is often the motive force behind judges' appointment to the bench.)

Fortunately, Mashaw's proposal for bypassing the threshold requirement of a property right or liberty interest does not depend on his critique of utilitarianism and is, in fact, quite sensible. The argument for an independent due process right unanchored to antecedently defined property or liberty is slightly embarrassed by having no obvious textual support in the written Constitution. But it is a commonplace that constitutional law has not been greatly handicapped by want of clear textual support. Inventing an autonomous due process, for example, does no more violence to the written Constitution than the Court's invention of a right of privacy.[43] In any case one could, with only modest creativity, resolve the problem by interpreting liberty to include freedom from arbitrary government power, that is, power expressed without due process.[44] A due process unanchored to any specific right or interest would presumably closely resemble the English concept of "natural justice" which, being derived from England's unwritten constitution, is purely a common law creature of protean shape, tailored to the circumstances of each situation.[45]

To those who are discomfited by the already protean character of due process, the English precedent will no doubt seem a nightmare. However, the protean character of natural justice already inheres in American due process. The Supreme Court is constantly reminding us that the process is a flexible concept whose particular procedural requirements must be responsive to the different circumstances and interests involved. Indeed, flexibility is the essence of *Eldridge*. The threshold requirements of property or liberty do not, in fact, give much firmness or clarity to the present law. What these thresholds do supposedly give is some baseline for determining when courts must intervene in the administrative process. The real fear is not that unanchored due process would lack specificity and clarity but that it would lack restraint: without a property or liberty anchor, the courts would be invited to intervene in situations where the nature of the interests at stake simply does not call for judicial surveillance.

This has been a concern since *Goldberg v. Kelly* brought due process to the welfare state. The courts have been asked to intervene in what seems to be an ever-increasing number and variety of disputes that involve areas as diverse as welfare benefits, public employment, student discipline, and prison administration. The Supreme Court's growing hostility to being asked to formulate due process rules for such disputes is evident in numerous recent opinions, most notably in student discipline and public employee disputes.[46] On the assumption that the Constitution should not be interpreted to constitute the Supreme Court as a roving superintendent of schools or a chief personnel manager (etc.), the Court's fear of being dragged into everyday conflicts in the name of ensuring individual dignity or fairness or what have you is surely a legitimate reason to place some limitations on the reach of due process.

Even Mashaw, despite his vigorous attack on the Court's due process jurisprudence, appears sympathetic to the Court's concern. The question is whether the requirement of threshold rights or entitlements serves this purpose. Mashaw and other critics think not. I agree. Insistence on such thresholds neither screens out the trivial, nor serves as a useful guide to ensure wise and restrained judicial intervention. Given the elastic, expansive definition given to property entitlements in contemporary jurisprudence, these concepts cannot be used to mark the boundary between important and unimportant cases for judicial intervention. The two school disciplinary cases mentioned earlier will illustrate the point.

Recall that in the first, *Goss v. Lopez*, the Court held that public high school students were entitled to "some kind of notice" and "some kind of hearing" before being suspended from school. The threshold requirement of an entitlement to public education was found in relevant state law; the Court also found a liberty interest to have been affected by virtue of the fact that disciplinary suspension affected the students' "good name, reputation, honor, or integrity." Given the definitions of property entitlements and liberty interests by the Court at least since *Goldberg*, the Court's finding of such interests here is unexceptionable. What is debatable—and four dissenting justices did debate it—is whether the nature of the dispute really warranted judicial intervention by way of the due process clause. The Court essentially abandoned *Goss* two years later in *Ingraham v. Wright*. By a shift in one vote, the *Goss* dissenters became a majority and the *Goss* majority became dissenters. In *Ingraham*, the discipline took the form of corporal punishment rather than suspension, but in practical effect the educational deprivation was the same (one student suffered physical injuries that kept him out of school 11 days— one more than the suspension period in *Roth*). The Court could not distinguish *Goss* on the issue of threshold interests; it found a liberty interest in being free of punishment (oddly, it found no deprivation of a property interest in public education because the punishment was not intended to disrupt his education even though, in fact, it did keep him out of school). Conceding that the requisite threshold interest was present, the Court nevertheless held that due process required no special procedural prerequisites to punishment. Purporting to apply *Eldridge* (which had intervened in the years between *Goss* and *Ingraham*), the Court found that the student's interests were adequately protected by a common law tort suit, in case punishment proved excessive or unwarranted, and that special administrative procedures were not warranted.

Whether the Court was correct in *Ingraham* or in *Goss* in its assessment of the need for judicial surveillance of school discipline, it seems plain that such an assessment cannot turn on whether the student's interests constitute property or liberty. At least it cannot turn importantly on present conceptions of property and liberty. Where then shall we look for limiting standards to mark the boundary of constitutional importance? We seem to be brought back to an open-ended balancing formula as a means of setting some limits on judicial oversight. It is not much of a limitation; the *Eldridge* formula, for example, has been employed by the Court more as a convenient metaphor than an operational test. In *Ingraham*, for example, the Court's majority was less concerned with the balance of costs and benefits of due process with respect to the particular public action before it than with setting a general limitation on judicial review. To the extent the Court was interested in the balance of utility, it was for a very general level of activity, in effect deciding that judicially enforced due process was unwarranted for school discipline generally. On the example of *Ingraham* (among other cases), it is thus possible to set general limits on judicial intervention in ordinary public affairs without engaging in a detailed cost-benefit analysis.

Building on *Ingraham*, one can conceive of the Court attempting to formulate general choices of public action where it will and, anent *Ingraham*, where it will *not* apply constitutional due process norms. The question is whether there is any definable set of cases in which it can be said, categorically, that constitutional due process never applies. I am skeptical. I think any attempt to fix the metes and bounds of due process by such classifications is likely either to break down into the kind of ad hoc evaluations we now see in applications of the balancing formula, or to produce the highly artificial distinctions that have come to characterize the determination of threshold rights test. We would be better off adhering to a simple *Eldridge* formula that, for all its manipulability, at least allows the Court to accommodate an extraordinarily diverse set of situations and to adapt to changes in the values that implicate due process concerns.

Ordinary Process

The offices of constitutional due process are limited. It is not wise or practicable to constitutionalize large areas of administrative activity by devising a due process code of procedures for all agencies and administrative functions. This is the proper realm of the legislature and of the agencies themselves in the reasonable exercise of discretion.

We can describe this realm as that of "ordinary process." It is not an altogether apt phrase;[47] in some cases, the basic requirement of nonconstitutional due process are indistinguishable from constitutional elements. Be that as it may, I want to concentrate on certain elements of ordinary process without regard to whether they rest on a constitutional foundation, whether or not they affect constitutionally protected rights for example. I shall focus on two very basic features of administrative process: participation by "interested" parties and "formalized" decision making, that is, the degree to which decision makers are bound by matters formally raised and tested in the processes prescribed. I will argue for a conception of administrative process that is open to public participation on matters of general public interest, in the way that legislatures are supposed to be, and yet also constrained by decision-making formalities, in the way that legislatures are decidedly not. There is an apparent conflict here between open participation on the one hand and formal deliberation on the other. One may well ask, is the administrative process like the legislative process or not? Pressed to that binary choice I would take the latter, but the issue cannot be reduced to that simple choice. It is true that, when it comes to policy decisions, the administrative process resembles the legislative process, but it is also true that we have different expectations for agency policy choices, and the kind of unconstrained informality of political influence in the legislative process is unacceptable in the administrative process— is inconsistent with the rule of law as it has been defined by statute (for instance, the Administrative Procedure Act) and common law standards of judicial review. However open the administrative process may be to different persons and groups, it is still subject to standards of rational justification that effectively preclude certain motives and modes of influence. Such, at least, is the premise of the following discussion that attempts to describe, in very general terms, what the purpose and the scope of participation and decision-making formalities should be.

Participation

Participation can cover a wide range of involvement in diverse settings. At its most basic level it may involve nothing more than an opportunity to file a written comment on proposed agency action in which the participant has some interest. Such a minimal form of participation is required in informal ("notice and comment") rule-making proceedings, which are the norm for all but an insignificant number of federal rule-making proceedings under the Administrative Procedure Act. At the other end of the range is the full hearing with all of the features attendant on trial-type proceedings—oral evidence, cross-examination, representation by counsel, formal findings, etc.—that are the norm for most adjudications.

Traditionally, participation in adjudicatory proceedings involved particular persons (including entities) having distinctive rights at stake. However, in recent years, persons not having such rights have been allowed to participate in agency hearings in order to represent other affected interests—public interests broadly conceived. The development of broader participation in agency adjudications by persons other than those with legally protected rights at stake is related to a parallel development in the law of standing to seek judicial review of agency action that I will examine in more detail in the next chapter. Such intervention by interested persons other than those with legally protected interests directly in issue is not, of course, a novelty of modern administrative law. It is common to permit intervention by a range of persons or groups who have interests that will be affected by the outcome of the suit in much civil litigation. In the administrative context, however, the scope of intervention has become much broader, and its character is somewhat different. Liberal participation in agency hearings has emerged not primarily to recognize third party interests or to economize litigation costs by bringing all affected parties into the same proceeding. The dominant purpose of expanded administrative participation (and standing to seek review) has been to recognize the supposed public character of the agency's actions and to permit third persons to be heard as "public interest representatives."

In this respect the traditional distinction between adjudication and rule making in administrative law has broken down, at least as to those cases in which there are matters of general public interest in controversy. This does not mean that there are no differences in the two processes that might affect the practical scope and character of participation, about which more later. However, as a matter of first-order principle, we can regard the argument for public participation to be essentially indifferent to the particular form of the proceeding, whether in the form of rule making or adjudication. For this reason, I want to discuss participation in broad terms without distinguishing sharply between adjudicatory and rule-making proceedings.

Office of Communication of the United Church of Christ v. FCC, one of the leading early (1966) cases on pubic intervention in agency adjudication, provides a useful introduction.[48] The FCC granted a one-year renewal of the license of a television broadcast station. It refused to renew the license for the statutory term because of doubts about whether the station had presented programming advocating racial segregation without affording opportunity for presentation of the other side, and had otherwise failed to give fair and balanced presentations of controversial public issues. Two church groups and two individual residents of the area served by the station sought standing before the FCC to argue for an outright denial of renewal of the license for the station. The FCC denied standing to intervene on grounds that the groups and individuals had asserted no invasion of a legally protected interest or direct and substantial injury and that they could therefore assert "no greater interest or claim of injury than members of the general public." The court of appeals reversed.

The court held that, as representatives of the public legitimately concerned with and affected by the outcome of the agency's decision, they should have "standing." The court's rationale relied heavily on earlier *judicial* standing cases, notably the Supreme Court's seminal decision in *FCC v. Sanders Bros. Radio Station*, which had granted standing to seek review of the grant of a license by a competitor claiming economic injury from the grant.[49] The reason for permitting standing in *Sanders Bros.* had not been the protection of the economic interest, but the airing of more general public challenges that the competitor, pursuing its private interests, would raise.[50] We can defer to the next chapter the details of standing doctrine; it is more directly pertinent to judicial review than to participation in agency proceedings. Although the legal standards for standing in the two contexts are said to be the same, in fact, access to courts and access to agencies raise quite different policy issues.[51] For instance, concerns about liberal public access to courts typically stem from the perception that it leads to judicial encroachment on executive (and in constitutional cases, on legislative) prerogatives, a separation-of-powers concern that has no relevance to public participation in agency proceedings.[52] Absent any interbranch encroachment, the only objection against standing to appear before the agency is the practical objection to expanding somewhat the scope of the agency proceeding and possibly adding to the agency's administrative burdens.[53] This essentially reduces to a comparison of costs and benefits.

The costs are fairly obvious: the greater the scope and degree of participation, the higher the administrative costs to the agency. The benefit side is a bit more complicated, for it involves an assessment of various purposes and values that are not merely incommensurable but almost indefinable. *Church of Christ* is illustrative. Involvement of the public groups in this case seems to rest on quite a different footing than that of the licensee; both were contestants, but contestants in quite a different sense than, say, two competing license applicants, or two litigants in a civil lawsuit. Just how those participants differ is not easy to explain, however. The conventional explanation would proceed to distinguish the two parties on the ground that one had a protected legal right at stake and one did not. But this is question begging, for the public groups were, in effect, claiming the equivalent of a legal right to participate with respect to those matters that affect the *collective* interests of the public. In any case, reference to legal rights in this context is hardly dispositive of the more basic question of whether public participation is useful and appropriate. For this we need to look more directly at the purposes and values of participation generally.

At the outset it must be conceded that the variety of administrative processes, as well as differences in the kind of interests affected, makes generalization about the purpose and value of participation somewhat suspect. This is precisely the difficulty encountered in attempting to prescribe constitutional requirements, as I suggested earlier in discussing *Matthews v. Eldridge.* Nevertheless, it is quite commonly assumed that participation involves values and instrumental purposes that are basically unaffected by the manifest differences in agency activities, functions, and interests at stake. Just what are those values and purposes is seldom given close reflective study, though I think one can capture their essence with two concepts.

The core liberal value of participation is generally taken to be individual autonomy and self-determination. The standard modern argument of liberal democracy is that individuals should have the opportunity to register their preferences on matters affecting their interests. This argument runs somewhat contrary to an older, more communitarian, theory of democracy that insists that participation is not simply a registration of individual preferences but a means of defining the public good. In the older view, participation serves an educative function, socializing the individual to civic responsibility—a more public-regarding consciousness. Although these two conceptions of participation have different philosophical thrusts, it is possible to embrace both, as did John Stuart Mill, in a general argument for political participation.[54] Hereafter I shall refer to the argument, in both its preference registration and civic socialization forms, as the argument from "political legitimacy."

Distinct from its legitimating value, participation serves a purely instrumental, utilitarian purpose of providing information and perspective to decision makers who are conceived as independent agents, that is, as Burkean representatives as distinct from mere surrogates of the public.[55] Ever receptive to simple phrases, I call this the "informing" model of participation. There is an overlap between the informing model and the legitimacy models, insofar as the latter models presuppose the furnishing of information about individual preferences and ideas of the public welfare. However, it is a distinctive feature of the information model that it assumes participants have information that political agents do not have, information that is objectively valuable, which is to say that it does not matter how or by whom this information is conveyed to the agent.

It is obvious that both the legitimacy and informing models have important roles in explaining and rationalizing participation. Just as obvious, both have their limitations, conceptual and practical. We can begin with the informing model, for it is the simpler conception and, at least as applied to broad *public* participation in rule making and in policy-relevant adjudications, it is the more conventional model of what participation is thought to be about.

The informing model fairly describes the central assumption of *Sanders Bros.* and its progeny involving expanded standing of individuals or citizen groups to participate in and appeal from agency proceedings. The idea is that such intervenors/appellants come to the agency or the court armed with particular information or views that will not be supplied by those parties who have directly affected rights or interests in the proceeding. As it later took hold in cases like *Church of Christ*, this concept became associated with participation by general, public-interest groups claiming to represent a broad segment of the public. This is not a necessary assumption of the model, as *Sanders Bros.* illustrates. The competitor granted standing in that case made no claims on behalf of the general public, nor did the Court assume any such representative motive. Standing was granted simply because it was assumed that the party had useful information or argument to contribute that would aid both courts and agencies in reaching a decision that served the public interest. This idea might be taken as simply an extension of political pluralism, kin to the traditional interest-group theory we examined earlier, broad participation rights being a means of diversifying the interests to be represented in public forums.[56] I think, however, the original premise of *Sanders Bros.* differed from simple political pluralism in supposing that administrative and judicial forums were not political but rationalistic in character. In this essentially technocratic model, participant preferences are not of primary significance except where the policy choices clearly embrace distributional issues, in which event participants' preferences offer useful information about those distributional effects. Nevertheless, participants are seen not as registering their preferences or involving themselves in a collective political activity; they are merely conveying practical information instrumental to a technocratic choice. At least that is the way the technocratic decision makers are supposed to view it. Preferences are important to motivating participants and are a kind of guarantee that the parties will be effective advocates, but the purpose of their involvement is to contribute information that is useful to the agency's public interest responsibilities.

There cannot be much doubt that the information function is important. Agencies have huge appetites for information of all kinds, technical, social, legal, even philosophical. And no matter how expert the agency, no matter how lavishly endowed with internal resources, the information required for most agency functions to operate must be generated from outside sources. Some of the information can be obtained through investigative methods, such as subpoenas, inspections, or noncompulsory inquiries by the agency that do not involve participation in administrative proceedings. However, investigative methods are very limited in their usefulness for major policy choices by agencies. The EPA cannot gain information sufficient to develop regulations for implementing clean air or clean water standards by sending a questionnaire to a list of industry, civil, and environmental groups. The FCC could not hope to generate sufficient information to promulgate regulations governing the marketing of telecommunications equipment by mailing queries to "interested" parties. For one thing, the agency often does not even know what questions to ask, or who to ask, without obtaining preliminary information and comment. More important, the nature of the information required is seldom amenable to simple exposition in response to a subpoena or other request. What is needed are multiple layers of response to particular lines of inquiry: "if this, what about that," and "what do you think of A's answer to question X?"

In short the ideal is not simply supplying information in the way that one would deliver milk. The idea is an interactive dialogue in which information in the form of facts, arguments, interpretation, and stories—the whole array of communicative elements—is exchanged, subject to rebuttal, evaluation, and critique. In adjudicatory settings, we would think of this function as embracing the presenting of evidence and the opportunity to challenge the evidence of antagonistic parties. In the rule-making context, cross-examination is seldom allowed, save in unusual instances where the rule making is conducted "on the record" of a formal hearing. However, even here the ideal is to design processes that allow participants not merely to respond to an agency's preformulated inquiry but also to challenge the relevance of the questions formulated by the agency, to suggest others that have not been asked, to take issue with responses by other parties, and so on. Perhaps needless to say, such *intensive* participation is at the expense of *extensive* participation. It is obviously practical only in proceedings where there are few participants. Too, it makes sense only where the participants are capable of bearing the costs of such intensive participation and making a meaningful contribution.

The informing model of participation does not have the kind of resonant sound to it that appeals to the popular democratic imagination in the same way that the legitimating model does. Those who pronounce the virtues of democracy are wont to see public participation as more a matter of political rights than of instrumentalist convenience, at least in the context of general policy-making proceedings. This rights perspective is congruent with pluralist political theory insofar as it rejects the earlier assumptions about rationalistic, technocratic, public decision making and focuses instead on the political element. From this perspective, the main purpose of participation is to register personal preferences, which are then translated into public choice decisions by the usual means of aggregation (via coalitions and bargains). It is this view that I have labeled the legitimation function of participation. The use of the term and the idea behind it call for some further explanation. What precisely is the attribute of participation in administrative proceedings that legitimates agency decisions? In adjudications of distinctive rights or interests, some type of participation by the affected person is the essence of due process protection. Participation is virtually synonymous with the opportunity to present facts and argument in defense of the protected interest. Absent such opportunity, decisions would be deemed arbitrary.

Yet it is not easy to articulate the underlying basis for this view. One common articulation invokes dignitary theories: participation is a way of recognizing the dignity of the individual.[57] The dignitary claim is probably unanswerable. One might question whether it is, in fact, the value individuals actually seek to vindicate by their participation. Many years ago as a nominee to a seat on the FCC, I was advised by Senator Warren Magnuson, then chairman of the Senate Commerce Committee (which oversees FCC activities), to be attentive but fair to all who came before the agency. All they want, he said without a smile, is to be given a "fair advantage." I suppose he might have said they also wanted to be treated with dignity, but I came to believe that mostly they just wanted a fair advantage.

Of course, it may be that it is not the immediately affected individuals we should consult on the point, since the value of participation can be considered a collective norm. Be that as it may, legitimacy as dignity takes us only so far in understanding participation in administrative proceedings. For one thing, the dignity argument has appeal only in cases involving real persons, for instance, an individual pressing a social security benefit claim. Important as these cases are, they are not the whole of bureaucratic justice. If the FTC institutes an unfair trade proceeding against General Motors, we would not ordinarily think to worry about GM's dignitary interests. Setting aside cases involving corporations, dignity theory is typically invoked only in particularized adjudications that target individual rights; it has only faint appeal in the case of proceedings in which the individual is affected only as a member of the general public, or some special segment of the public. Yet participation by interested individuals and groups in such proceedings is now generally allowed. Consumer groups, environmentalists, or competitors are frequent participants in adjudicatory cases involving matters affecting such interests, such as the *Church of Christ* case. And in rule-making cases, opportunity for some degree of participation on the part of the public (notice to and comment by) is prescribed by the federal Administrative Procedure Act. One would hardly rationalize such participation in dignitary terms, but it is not radical to think of such participation as somehow related to the legitimacy of the proceeding, in much the same way that public participation in the political process, inter alia by voting, legitimates political choice. In fact, I believe that is the central premise underlying provision for general public participation in agency rule making.

The analogy to voting, of course, only pushes the inquiry back a notch. How does voting "legitimate"? It is a question not often asked, either because the answer seems obvious or because there is no answer. Ask the ordinary democratic citizen why voting in elections legitimates political choice, and the response is likely to be a stare of curiosity that anyone would ask such a question. No doubt, sophisticates will no doubt try to answer by appealing to principles of individual self-determination and consent. Unfortunately, this explanation will not get us very far. It is trite to observe that modern social organization does not permit a fully consensual model of individualism. Such a model presupposes virtual consensus on every issue of public choice. Consensus or unanimous choice rules might be possible in some organizational settings—small clubs and the like—but they are manifestly unworkable in social organizations of the scale relevant to the present discussion.

The closest one comes to fully consensual public choice is in highly localized settings where individuals can move to another locale if their preferences are not satisfied. However, this "exit" option, as Albert Hirschman calls it,[58] or "shopping" option, as it has been sometimes described following Charles Tiebout's celebrated market model,[59] is more a theoretical than a real option for most matters of the public choice. Notwithstanding the exhortation of bumper stickers to "love your country (or state) or leave it," for most people that choice is a Hobson's choice. Even assuming the requisite mobility, the effective array of choices is limited by the way in which political goods come packaged.[60]

In the absence of an effective exit veto, Hirschman's voice option becomes the only alternative means by which the individual's preferences are registered. Unfortunately for those preferences, the individual's voice in the public marketplace is lost in the babble of the crowd: it is either ineffectual or redundant. Where voice does not entail a veto power—where decisions follow majority preferences—participation, through voting or through some other form of expressive activity, cannot be taken as an act of individual consent in the strict sense. "Consent" to majority preferences that are not one's own is simply an awkward way of describing a social decision-rule. Nor does one get very far supposing that prior consent has been "tacitly" given to majority rule; such prior consent is purely imaginary in political settings. The idea of a social contract may be a useful heuristic for thinking about the basis of political obligation,[61] but we should recall Hume's demonstration of the weakness of classical contract arguments to the extent that they are grounded in an assumption of actual consent.[62] The simple reality is that those who are bound by the social contract are not given a meaningful opportunity *not* to be bound.

Moreover, the idea of consent via the social contract, a prior consent to be bound by majority rule, rests (in any case) on the assumption that the individual has an opportunity to influence public choices. In most political contexts this would imply, at best, a very attenuated kind of consent. Consider voting as a form of participation. It is a notorious fact that the probability that any given vote will be determinative in a major election is so vanishingly small as to prompt some theorists to question the rationality of voting from the perspective of a narrowly specified utilitarian perspective.[63] Since we regularly observe people voting (albeit not as often in the United States as elsewhere),[64] it is necessary to formulate a richer model of purposive behavior.[65] As with voting in particular, so with political activity: in general, efforts to explain participation by reference to narrowly defined individual interest protection are embarrassed by everyday observation.[66]

But this is something of a tangent. The important point to make here is that, whatever the explanation for it, political participation is not very clearly related to actual consent. The most that can be said is that voting, or participation in general, is a kind of symbolic consent, a requirement that the decision maker at least consider the collective voice of participants. Inasmuch as the collective voice has strength and clarity in proportion to the degree of individual participation, individual votes thus have importance as a necessary, if very small, component of the larger "voice."[67] Notice that at this point the focus of the legitimacy model shifts away from the preference registration idea to a notion of public involvement as an independent political good. Economists are sometimes wont to describe independently desired activity as "consumption goods" and that term is sometimes applied loosely to political voting behavior. It is a somewhat misleading term in this context, however, for the social value of participation does not depend on the immediate pleasures of consumption by the individual, but on the long-term fulfillment to the individual and to the political well-being of the community. Think of it this way: political participation is not like actual shopping, but it is not like window shopping either. The value lies neither in the purchases one actually makes or in those one fantasizes making. Participation is more like being in a play or, perhaps to push an analogy too far, like going to church. In both instances, the self-realization is critically interdependent with how others act, and how they regard the activity.

This is a somewhat romantic view of political activity and one not well attuned to the modern liberal temperament, which likes to characterize participation merely from an individualistic, near-term instrumentalist perspective. The immediate payoff is what counts according to most such characterizations. Such a view is, however, socially mischievous. I am far from disparaging thee individual as an ultimate reference point in considering political legitimacy, but to focus on the individual in isolation and to attend only to his or her near-term expectations does not give us a full appreciation of what is valued in political participation. From such a perspective, it would certainly be hard to credit the much heard expression that voting—the most common and readily available form of participation—is not only a right but a social obligation. (In some countries it is even a legal obligation.) Such a notion cannot make sense if participation is purely an act of individual utility (utility understood either as expressing individual demand for public choices or as an act of purely individual consumption).

It is true, of course, that participating in administrative proceedings is not customarily conceived as voting in the sense applied to political votes. Not only are bureaucrats not elected, but their decisions are not usually thought to be *bound* by the preferences of those who participate in their proceedings in the same sense that elected officials are supposed to be bound by the wishes of their electorate. However, this reflects a misleading view of participation in both the political and administrative environments. Of course, bureaucrats, not being elected, do not have an electoral incentive but they share with elected officials other incentives to respond to public constituencies for various reasons. Among them are personal gain (setting aside immediate gain, there is the prospect of future gain if and when the bureaucrat pursues a career in the private sector), social congeniality (*routine* participants in agency proceedings often comprise the social milieu of the bureaucrat), and, not least, a sense of public accountability (participants' preferences are an important component of the "public interest"). This being the case, participation in administrative forums can be seen to serve much the same legitimating function as participation in the general political process. Moreover, as we have seen, to the extent that the legitimating force of participation comes from the collective political activity itself as much as from the individual registration of preferences, we should not regard it as essential that the representative is strictly bound by the particular aggregation of preferences. Indeed, even in the context of elected officials, the idea that representatives are strictly bound by constituent preferences in the sense of precisely replicating them (the "mirror" theory of representation) is, I think, neither very attractive nor realistic.[68]

One might still wonder whether the legitimating model of participation can be applied to the administrative arena insofar as the model presupposes a degree of public involvement that is not possible or, at least, not realized in practice. In this view, the fact that the administrative process ostensibly is open to general public participation conveys a false legitimacy, given the reality that effective participation is essentially confined to well-organized groups. Much as we might seek to open up the administrative process to all (everyone can at least send the agency a postcard with their views on pertinent policies), an inspection of who takes advantage of it suggests that effective participation is largely confined to a small number of repeat players who have recurring interests in the outcome. To the extent the legitimating model presumes otherwise, it misleads. Such is the argument.

But supposing this to be the correct view of the matter, what does it say about the *administrative* process that is different from the more general political process? For most citizens, political involvement consists of pulling levers in an election booth at most. It is a fairly perfunctory act, uninformed by more than cursory attention to vacuous political advertisements, prototypically in the form of thirty-second television "sound bites." Moreover, at best such votes are merely choices for elected officials, not for particular public choices.

Except in the unusual local referendum, people do not vote for particular laws or policies. A vote for a candidate is, at most, a vote for a mixed bag of programs and policies, some of which voters would choose separately and some they would not. Participation in the lawmaking process itself rarely involves mass public involvement. Effective political participation in legislative activity is essentially confined to small groups, just as it is for administrative activity. I speculated earlier that the requirements for effective participation in administrative proceedings might favor permanently organized interest groups to a greater degree than the requirements for legislative action. But neither forum provides much opportunity for unorganized public influence, and there is no basis for radically different expectations for public participation in the legislative and administrative forums.

What this suggests, then, is that the legitimacy model can claim at least as much respect in the administrative process as in the political process; further, it suggests that, where issues of significant public policy are involved, participation in administrative proceedings should not be limited to persons with particular interests. As a matter of general principle, which is to say setting aside practical limits on the scope and character of participation, an interest-based limitation is no more appropriate for participation in administrative proceedings involving public issues than would be a comparable limitation on the right to vote in political elections. While there are some types of elections where an interest limitation is appropriate, interest limitations on voting are generally considered so inappropriate as to be at least presumptively unconstitutional.[69]

Not to be misunderstood on the scope of the parallel, I should reemphasize the assumption I have been making all along that the proceeding is one in which issues of *public* policy are being considered. In rule-making cases, we can assume this to be the case for it is virtually inherent in the concept of rule making. The more controversial cases are those, like *Church of Christ*, where the agency is both adjudicating individual rights—the station licensee's statutory rights, or expectations—and matters of general public interest—the licensee's performance of obligations to the community. No doubt there are some such cases where the general public simply has no business being a regular participant, where its preferences are appropriately ignored. Routine sanction cases comparable to criminal trials are illustrative. But *Church of Christ* was not such a case. While the station licensee certainly was subject to a sanction in the form of nonrenewal of its license, that sanction was simply the flip side of its performance obligations to the community, about which the preferences of the community are relevant even if they are not dispositive. The case is, in this respect, no different than a general rule-making proceeding.

How far these abstractions about models can be made to yield practical lessons, useful in designing processes for administrative agencies, depends on how single-minded one wants to be in promoting abstract principles at the expense of practical program objectives.[70] It is not necessary to choose categorically between the two models of participation, however. It is only necessary to have some sense of how the purposes of participation diverge and what that implies for the design of process in the context of particular administrative programs.

Plainly the most fundamental practical difference between the two models is the degree to which they entail extensive or intensive involvement by the public. The legitimacy model is dominated by extensive involvement. Whether one characterizes this purpose as a function of simple preference registration or one of involvement in political activity for its own sake, it obviously is important to involve as many people as possible. The involvement need not be deep (particularly if the point is merely to register "votes"), though one would ideally choose a form of participation that gives the individual a sense of purposeful political engagement.

In the informative model, by contrast, intensive involvement is more likely to dominate. In most policy-making contexts, we have no reason to think that important technocratic information (as distinct from information about individual preferences) is widely dispersed. Where it is not, broad participation is unlikely to be cost effective, measuring the benefits of increased information against the cost of participation. Ideally, the informative model calls for a pure efficiency calculus equating the marginal cost and benefit of each incremental increase in the scope of participation. On the assumption made here, the marginal benefits of adding parties falls very sharply.

Given the conflict between the two models of participation, it is important for agencies, and reviewing courts, to decide what purpose dominates. I do not mean to suggest that one purpose always precludes the other or that an agency might not try to accommodate both. For instance, in *Church of Christ* one might seek to promote extensive participation by selecting a limited representative of different elements of the community and to promote intensive participation by allowing them limited participation as parties (with the right to submit briefs, oral argument, etc.). This would be a judicious (i.e., cautious) way to proceed. Odds are, however, it will just confuse matters. As it happens, the *Church of Christ* case was not one in which the agency needed much factual information from the community or from any other public group such as the Church of Christ. Virtually all pertinent facts were matters of record at the agency itself; the FCC certainly did not need information as to what the licensee, in fact, broadcast. Although local public groups can provide an important monitoring function that helps to initiate agency action, once action has been initiated, that function has been discharged. The most the agency might hope to obtain from the public representatives is information about local conditions that might shed some additional light on the licensee's performance. Sometimes this will be helpful, but in most such instances, including *Church of Christ*, I am inclined to think the local condition that is most important is the attitudes or preferences of local citizens.

In this latter respect the legitimating argument takes over. *Church of Christ* was an exceptionally appropriate case for the political legitimacy model of participation. If there is any argument for extended public participation in administrative proceedings as a means of registering preferences and of promoting civic consciousness, this is the case to which the argument naturally applies. The core issue in the case was the licensee's alleged racism in its programming in general, and its noncompliance with FCC policies governing balanced treatment of controversial issues in particular. The subject is obviously appropriate for allowing, and promoting, widespread public expression. One might imagine such a case to be the occasion for the agency to convene hearings in the community itself to maximize local participation, or at least to permit its staff to convene local meetings. I realize, of course, that the legal (statutory and constitutional) requirements for formal adjudications place limits on the extent to which the agency may conduct its hearings in an open forum without restriction on the type of communications made to the decision maker (I will come to this problem in a moment). But I am not suggesting a town meeting. That too easily causes public hearings to degenerate into riot— also a form of public participation, but not one that commends itself to the administrative process. Nevertheless, it should be possible to solicit an airing of local expression in a case such as this without unfair prejudice to the licensee. It is not, after all, the local citizens who will make the ultimate decision, so the unreflective prejudices of local citizens will be screened.

In *Church of Christ*, the FCC was acutely aware that the decision-making prerogative belonged exclusively to the FCC itself. What it neglected was the opportunity to use the occasion to share a sense of responsibility with the community. The commission's perception of the public role brought it before the same court a second time in the case, the court this time rebuking the agency for treating the public intervenor as a kind of hostile interloper, with a special burden of proof, rather than as a "friend of the agency."[71] Of course, the FCC is in the business of regulating communications, and I am not saying that it should subordinate its mandate to pursue an extraneous public policy of enhancing civic consciousness in the local body politic. Plainly its primary task in *Church of Christ* was to adjudicate aspects of the licensee's performance, not to conduct a public seminar in broadcasting responsibility. Still, if one accepts the premises of public participation as a form of political legitimation, some affirmative effort to encourage the public voice in these cases seems not too much to expect. For segments of the public that have strong interests or intense preferences, an affirmative effort by the agency is not required: people with such interests or preferences require no encouragement to come forth. It is the wider community that needs encouragement.

Formalized Decision Making

Designing administrative processes to promote the purposes of public participation is related to another question, how far should decision makers be confined to matters raised and explored in public proceedings? The question can be broken down into two problems: one deals with the extent to which participants or nonparticipants can communicate relevant information to the decision maker outside the formal proceedings; the second deals with the extent to which decision makers must bring to the proceedings an open mind, free of bias about the issues or the parties.

These issues are generally regarded as distinct. The first is an "ex parte communications problem," the second, a "bias problem." For expositional convenience, I shall treat them separately, but it is important to note, at the outset, that they both involve common problems of efficiency and fairness. Both implicate practical problems of managing and evaluating information. In the case of ex parte communications, a central concern is with the fact that the information is not subject to critical examination by the opposing party, nor, if it is never made part of the record, is it subject to review by appellate courts or the interested public. So too with bias; information or opinion that is locked away in the mind of the decision maker is beyond examination or scrutiny except to the extent it is publicly revealed. In both instances, the possibility that such unexamined information may be incorrect or incomplete obviously raises serious problems of social efficiency. Equally, in both instances, the efficiency concern is matched, if not overwhelmed, by a sense that this is simply unfair to the disadvantaged parties. It is the dignity point again, though it is deepened perhaps by the perception that the disadvantaged person is not merely ignored or being given insufficient attention but is being actively discriminated against. That is, she is the subject of focused hostility.

It is small wonder, then, that both the common law and the constitutional law of due process have long set such a store by the principle that in all adjudications, whether by judicial or by administrative tribunals, decisions must be made upon a record and must not be influenced by extracurricular communications or considerations.[72] Yet, despite ancient acceptance of the core principle, there are unanswered questions about the scope of its application in administrative proceedings. These questions have been raised in the context of some fitful attempts to extend the restrictions on bias and ex parte communications to informal rule-making proceedings as well as formal adjudications. The attempts have generally met with poor reception by courts and commentators, who have generally accepted the traditional distinction between formal and informal cases.[73] This traditional distinction may be the correct one to make, but on close examination it turns out to be a great deal less compelling or clear than has been thought, and this is the central point I want to explore.

We can begin with the problem of bias. Over 350 years ago, Lord Coke announced it as a settled principle of the common law and of natural justice that a person should not be a judge of his own cause.[74] Until fairly modern times, this principle was interpreted rather narrowly as merely a prohibition against adjudicatory decisions being made by persons having a pecuniary interest in the outcome. However, this narrow conflict of interest rule has been expanded to embrace a broader principle of impartiality that is everywhere accepted as the very essence of due process applicable to all adjudications, criminal, civil, judicial, or administrative.[75] It has not found comparable acceptance in agency rule-making proceedings. Indeed, the notion of disqualifying an agency rule maker or impeaching an agency rule on grounds of mere bias or prejudgment—apart from conflict of interest—was virtually unheard of until the recent *Association of National Advertisers* case.[76] A federal district court disqualified the chairman of the Federal Trade Commission from participating in a rule-making proceeding to consider rules restricting television advertising directed at children. The basis for the disqualification was a series of public statements and correspondence evincing prejudgment of the key issues. The test applied was that accepted for adjudicatory cases, whether a disinterested observer could conclude that the decision maker has prejudged the particular case in advance of hearing it.[77] The court of appeals reversed the finding of disqualification, holding that rule makers were subject to a different, less demanding standard of impartiality than adjudicators. The pertinent test for the former, said the court, was whether the rule maker evinces an "unalterably closed mind on matters critical to the disposition of the proceeding."[78] This test ostensibly retains a minimal standard of impartiality but, as a practical matter, the evidentiary burden imposed on parties seeking to challenge rule makers is not sustainable.

One can criticize the force of the distinction between judicial and legislative processes on the simple ground that agency rule making is not the same as legislation, as I emphasized earlier. Agency rule making is bound by statutory standards of rationality and fairness far more exacting than those to which legislation is subject by the Constitution. Similarly, rule making is constrained to follow statutorily mandated processes, while legislation is subject only to the very minimal constitutional criteria for enacting laws. (If, indeed, rule making were fully comparable to legislation, then the court's "unalterably closed mind" standard would be unwarranted, for no such standard of impartiality is enforced against legislators.) This implies that the legislative model is not wholly apt for administrative rule making in terms of the criteria by which ultimate choices are judged. It is certainly not unthinkable to apply a standard of impartiality for rule making similar to that applied in adjudication. Whether applying such a standard would fairly match our expectations for agency decision makers in the exercise of policy-making judgments is another matter. To revert to the *National Advertisers* case, what do we expect of an agency member in such a situation? The chairman had been long known for his strong general advocacy of consumer interests and his critical views on television advertising. Such views were, in fact, a major political reason for his appointment to the position. Politically, the chairman behaved as expected.

Of course, one might make pretty much the same argument with respect to adjudicatory cases. Suppose *National Advertisers* had involved an individual adjudication instead of a general rule making? Imagine the legal issues to be the same. (There is no reason to suppose they would be any different, since the statutory criteria for "unfair or deceptive" trade practices are the same regardless of the procedural form the agency chooses to enforce its mandate.) Applying accepted impartiality standards for adjudications, there is not much doubt the chairman would have been disqualified by reason of his public pronouncements. Yet if political expectations are the key, why the difference in outcomes? Again, we could analyze this in terms of the judicial-legislative distinction: courts often make law on particular matters in ways not materially different from legislatures, but we hold judges to different standards of impartiality than legislators. The appropriateness of these models, in turn, leads us once again to question public expectations about the respective roles of agency officials, judges, and legislators.

There is no point to pursuing this line about general expectations further, for if it has any clear resolution, I do not know what it is. Instead, I want to suggest a different kind of response, one that starts from the premise that there is no relevant distinction between agency officials acting as adjudicators and as rule makers, but then asks whether and to what extent they can be held to enforceable standards of impartiality in *either* role. At the outset, set aside questions of conflict of interest where there are clearly definable and objectively determinable interests or relationships (e.g., pecuniary or familial) that can and should be the basis for disqualifying any decision maker, whether adjudication or rule making (or I would argue, even legislation). When we set these aside, the central problem of bias is one of proof of state of mind. It is on just this point that the impartiality rule runs headlong into another principle of administrative law, one not quite as venerable, but firmly anchored in common wisdom all the same. It was long ago established that, in the exercise of their ordinary review power, courts could not "probe the mind" of decision makers, but must evaluate agency actions on the basis of officially proffered factual findings and legal reasons.[79] This rule is sensible; essentially it is designed to protect the institutional process of decision making and to avoid costly and ultimately feckless challenges to agency decisions based on what individual decision makers knew (or did not know) as opposed to whether the decision itself has a rational basis. But this "anti-mind-probe rule," known among legal cognoscenti as the "*Morgan IV* rule" after the name of the Supreme Court case establishing it,[80] makes it exceedingly difficult to question the impartiality of the decision maker. Disqualification for bias has thus been essentially confined to cases where there is some objective indication of bias—typically outside the record of the case—for example, public speeches or private communications by decision makers concerning the cases before them.[81] Such cases do arise from time to time, but with such infrequency that one could reasonably ask whether the impartiality principle has any practical bite.

Indeed, one must go further to wonder whether we really should care about impartiality. If this latter statement seems unduly provocative, it must be set in the context of the anti-mind-probe rule. Insofar as that rule rests on the principle of accepting *institutional* accountability and objective criteria in judging agency decisions, it undermines the whole basis for insisting on the subjective impartiality of individual decision makers. In effect, we judge the fairness and reasonableness of decisions on the basis of the record, the findings and the reasons given, and not on the basis of what individual decision makers knew or thought in the secret recesses of their minds.

In other words, if a decision is fair and reasonable on the basis of the record, why are we concerned with how it was derived? One answer might be that we are concerned to maintain the *appearance* of fairness. Although this is, in fact, often said in cases involving challenges for bias,[82] it seems to me a bit puzzling. Apart from actual fairness, judged on the basis of record, why should we be concerned with appearance? Public confidence in the system? But why should we encourage the public to place confidence in appearances; why should they not be asked to evaluate decisions simply on the basis of objectively determinable criteria? If there is an answer, it must proceed from the assumption that "objectively determinable criteria"—the record, the official findings and reasons—are insufficient guarantees for the integrity of agency decision making. They are insufficient because there is some discretion allowed to the decision maker in any one case, some range of choice over alternative outcomes, any of which can be justified by the facts and legal criteria being applied. The purpose of an impartiality rule is to ensure that, among the objectively acceptable choices, the decision maker's actual choice is a fair and honest one.

Still, the fact remains that since we do not permit decision makers to be cross-examined about their motives or the state of their mind, the occasions when the rule can be invoked are so few as to create doubt whether, aside from clear conflict-of-interest cases, the impartiality principle has any utility or credibility. I do not mean to say that the principle is not an attractive ideal, and on that ground alone, perhaps, it should be retained, not to promote appearances but to declare our ideal of fairness, a symbol of our commitment. I could not object to that. But if it is symbols we are after, why not a similar symbol for rule-making cases as well? Again, the question of expectations for rule makers: is impartiality even an ideal? If it is not, how do we explain all of the legal process constraints and rationality standards that are imposed on agency rule makers? We may gain some yards on this play if we shift our attention to the ex parte problem.

As with the bias problem, the problem of ex parte communications has traditionally involved a sharp dichotomy between adjudication and rule making. The basic principle is fairly straightforward and universally accepted. In formal adjudications heard on a record, all ex parte communications relevant to the merits of the case are unlawful; by contrast, in informal rule making, ex parte contacts traditionally have been allowed, even in a sense encouraged as a means of "informing" agency rule makers.[83] In 1959 in an obscure case involving a contest over a change in geographic television allocations, an exception was created for proceedings involving "conflicting private claims to a valuable privilege."[84] However, this exception went virtually unnoticed until *Home Box Office v. FCC* in 1977, where the Court of Appeals for the District of Columbia Circuit relied on it, in part, in banning ex parte contacts in *all* informal rulemakings.[85]

The case involved revision of FCC rules restricting pay exhibition of programs on cable systems and broadcast stations. The rule-making proceeding followed the general form prescribed by the Administrative Procedure Act, with public notice and opportunity to file written comments. During the proceeding, the FCC imposed no restrictions on informal, ex parte contacts between commissioners, staff, regulated parties, and other public groups. Such contacts occurred throughout the proceeding, including extensive lobbying—primarily by cable and broadcast representatives—after formal oral argument had taken place and the record for public discussion had been closed. On appeal from the commission's order adopting the revised rules, a public-interest group argued that the ex parte communications were improper, at least insofar as they occurred after the period for public comment supposedly had expired. The court agreed, but was not content simply to rule that the agency was required to adhere to the spirit of the "public comment" period. Instead, it seized the occasion as an opportunity to fashion a radical departure from prior understanding. The court announced a general rule, applicable to all informal agency rule making, and invalidated not only ex parte communications occurring after oral argument, but also all such communications after issuance of the public notice of proposed rule making.

Home Box Office seemed nothing short of revolutionary to many observers and practitioners. The revolution, however, was soon aborted. A different panel of the same court shortly thereafter criticized the rule;[86] more recently, a panel of the District of Columbia Circuit appears to have repudiated it altogether by treating it as merely an application of the "conflicting-claims-to-a-valuable-privilege" situation.[87] This is a disingenuous description of *Home Box Office*, but we can set that aside. What is important is the court's obvious intent not to restrict ex parte communications save in unusual cases.

I confess to some ambivalence on the whole question, though not so much as formerly. I should also admit to being a member of the FCC when it decided *Home Box Office*. I was not personally involved in the ex parte contacts, not because I regarded them as improper or unlawful (they were not then unlawful and almost no one then regarded them as improper), but because my vote on the rules was too unimportant to the parties involved to warrant the extra lobbying effort.[88] In support of allowing ex parte contacts is the argument from participation: ex parte contacts promote such participation by lessening the burdens thereof. This rationale seems particularly appealing from the perspective of the informative model of participation. Burdening information flows with the formality of notice to other parties and incorporation of information into an official record may not be an unusual burden to place on someone seeking to communicate with the agency, but, in some instances, such a burden may be enough to discourage valuable communications with interested persons.

Moreover, informal communications can facilitate a real dialogue on policy issues. The greater the formality surrounding communications and information gathering, the more difficult it is to engage in an active discussion among participants and between participants and agency officials. Confronted with often prodigious quantities of information in the form of briefs and written comments, the decision makers find themselves searching for some way to get to the heart of the matter. Of course, the agency always has its staff to help reduce elephantine records to manageable proportions, to sharpen the issues, and so on. But such staff assistance presents a problem of its own. Particularly where it must be processed through several layers of institutional staff, the reliability of the information becomes a serious problem for officials.[89] Ex parte communications between officials and outside parties is a way of checking staff-provided information and interpretation. It is a means of avoiding the problem of "staff capture," which is one of the most frustrating problems confronting higher echelon agency officials.

However, if the foregoing considerations argue against restrictions on ex parte contacts, they do so equivocally. The goal of promoting informal information flows to the decision maker is, by the same token, an excuse for casual investigation and deliberation. When interested persons are able to present their facts and arguments to individual agency members and staff off the record, there is no check on the reliability of information presented to the decision makers. This raises obvious concerns of fairness, as well as substantial problems of effectiveness and efficiency, given the problems inherent in evaluating such information. Allowing unfettered ex parte communications also undermines the incentive for interested persons to submit reliable, carefully prepared documents, because such documentation is so easily lost in the shuffle of off-the-record encounters. Regulatory policymakers are often forced to place great reliance on oral briefing and discussion because of the massive quantities of paper confronting them. However, this produces a situation where even the most carefully produced commentary of one party can be negated by the offhand comments of another. Informal exchanges reinforce the natural disposition of busy agency officials to define data as the plural of anecdote. The inability or unwillingness to work through a complex record leads to an often desperate search for salient features and simplification. Personal exchanges with interested parties can provide both, reducing elephantine dockets to a few memorable stories or slogans suitably slanted to their interests.

This may be acceptable at the level of high politics. Certainly it was widely accepted of President Reagan, for whom complex social issues were apparently meaningful only as they were embodied in simple stories (many of which were fictional). But at the level where vague public philosophy is translated into operational policies, that is, at the level of the working bureaucracy, we expect more. It is one thing for President Reagan to give moral instruction to the country by invoking some movie fantasy; it is quite another for an agency to make concrete policies on the basis of anecdotal (and often concocted) reports about Aunt Minnie's problems with product label warnings. Democratic principle may require that we indulge the former; it does not require us to tolerate the latter.

As to the point that ex parte communications help to promote a real dialogue among the parties, which, inter alia, facilitates compromise and negotiated settlement, it must be asked whether this is the proper aim of agency rule making. Even where rule making is a zero-sum game among different interests, agencies should be sensitive to minimizing the losses to any particular group as a consequence of the rule being adopted. Bargaining may or may not be the appropriate means for resolving disputes (it depends on the nature of the interests at stake), but in no circumstance is it appropriate without rules that prevent public policy decisions turning on who was able to contact whom, when, and so forth. This is the whole point of having a structured rule-making process with public notice and comment, and in some cases (*Home Box Office*, for instance) even oral argument. Unless this structured process is to be just a warm-up for private negotiations, there must be some restrictions on private, off-the-record discussions.

The problems are neatly illustrated by the *Home Box Office* case. Although the basic policy issues before the commission there were not especially complex, they had generated an extraordinarily complex set of proposed rules, devised in the main by two separate, antagonistic staff bureaus that represented the cable and broadcast industry clientele, for the most part. (The third major industry interested in the rules, the film industry, was essentially aligned with the broadcasters.)

My view, then and now, was that the rules were difficult to justify, particularly in the almost baroque detail in which they were drafted; but the first task was to understand the problems they were supposed to address. (Broadly speaking, the problems reduced to a fear that unrestrained pay television via cable would siphon programs away from advertiser-supported television, to the detriment of those who did not have access to cable or could not afford it.) From the material in the rule-making record—all of the formal comments and staff analyses, together with three days worth of oral argument— one could gain such an understanding, but only at the cost of nonnegligible effort. Too, it was not easy to glean from the record the intensity of the parties on particular matters: how did they *really* feel about, say, restrictions on subscription carriage of old movies? In these circumstances it was natural, it was convenient, to confer with the major participants off the record.

However, such informal, unannounced consultations, while lawful, were potentially unfair to those not having easy access to agency members. Equally bad, these consultations undermined the integrity of the decision-making deliberations, as the underlying factual premises of the proposed rules took a back seat to the commissioners' assessment of the intensity of the leading protagonists' preferences. This was a voting model of participation run amuck; it was not even a matter of trying to follow the median voter's preference. Effectively, the ex parte votes were given special weight. Now, this sort of interest assessment is a normal and, up to a point I suppose, legitimate element of the legislative process. But the notion that agencies are constrained by legal standards and formal processes, if it means anything, must mean that the administrative process is constrained by tighter standards of regularity and objectivity. If we wanted to turn the political process loose on the problem of pay television, the respective interest groups should have been relegated to Congress.

Again, translating abstract principles into practical rules turns out to be a vexing task. This is a matter of no small difficulty here, for there is a terrible enforcement problem. The enforcement problem is admittedly somewhat easier in the case of ex parte contacts than in the case of bias. A ban on ex parte contacts admits of reasonably objective enforcement, or at least an objective determination of what constitutes a violation. It is not necessary to probe minds to ascertain whether information has been impermissibly communicated or received. The problem is rather one of defining the scope of the ex parte proscription in ways that effectively regulate communications relevant to particular proceedings without insulating the agency from all informal contacts with the outside world. This is easy to accomplish in adjudicatory proceedings because of their (generally) limited duration and issue focus. However, for major rule-making cases, which may remain in open docket for many years and may involve a host of broad policy issues, a ban on all ex parte communications is another matter. Particularly where, as will be often the case, the agency has numerous such proceedings open at any given time, an ex parte ban would be more than a minor nuisance for agency and interested public alike. It is not difficult to imagine that agencies, chafing under such restrictions, would seek to evade the ban by the simple expedient of deferring the beginning of rule-making proceedings until after it had its surfeit of unrestricted communications. For better and for worse, agency officials do not live in a well-controlled environment, hermetically sealed against the influences from industry and other interested groups. Trying to prohibit EPA officials from informally talking with representatives of the coal industry or representatives of public utilities about acid rain would not be much easier than preventing them from reading an article on the subject in the *New York Times* (or worse, a drug store tabloid).

We may be left with symbols only. As with impartiality, there is something to be said for articulating even an unenforceable rule as a kind of aspirational command. One could even formulate the rule, as in *Home Box Office*, to ban all ex parte contacts after the formal beginning of a proceeding. That would permit easy avoidance as I said, but it would give at least symbolic force to the idea that agency processes are not completely free-form and that the formalities prescribed for such procedures are not mere conveniences to be followed or dispensed with as the agency and the parties choose for each occasion.

Participation, Formalism, and Special Interest

I said at the outset that there is an apparent conflict between open participation and formalized decision making insofar as the effect of the latter is precisely to foreclose certain types of influence and communication that the former might naturally pursue. The conflict exists, however, only if we assume that administrative discretion is comparable to that of the legislature, an assumption that is quite incorrect, as I have stressed throughout. No doubt restricting the kinds of influence that are permissible requires some sacrifice in the full realization of the purposes of participation; still, the restrictions are not so confining as to rob participation of its essential purposes. In fact, for the run-of-the-mill participant, the restrictions will not be felt at all. Those most likely to feel the pinch from restraints on ex parte influence, and from the more general requirement that decision makers justify their decision by formal record evidence, are the highly organized special-interest groups that have easy, continuous access to the decision makers. In this respect, broadened participation with restrictions on informal communications and influence work together in dampening the effect of special-interest political influence.

Home Box Office is again instructive. In terms of public participation, the agency's proceeding was faultless, up to the final stages. Not only industry groups with immediate economic interest, but representatives of a broad array of public groups participated, both through the submission of formal written comments and in oral argument. To be sure, many of the groups were mere stage props for the industry groups. Both the broadcast and cable industry parties recruited representatives from minority groups, commerce, labor, and agricultural organizations to support the respective industry positions, both in written comments and oral argument. The film-producing industry even delivered a clutch of Hollywood stars to deliver oral pleas to the agency, a gambit that at least ensured a packed hearing room and media coverage. But this is a time-honored form of political influence and is not necessarily to be despised where everyone knows what the game is and everyone can play. It would be hard to fault the agency's efforts to allow and encourage as wide and diverse a participation as could be practicable.

Unfortunately, much of the value of open participation, at least to participants, was effectively defeated by the subsequent backdoor lobbying by a handful of special players, representatives of the major industry protagonists. No one supposes that these subsequent informal influences canceled out all of the information and arguments made on the record. Nevertheless, as the court of appeals later observed, there was no way of sorting out the respective influences. (Of course, the *Morgan IV* anti-mind-probe rule effectively ruled out any examination of the commissioners to determine this.) And in terms of the value of participation to the participants themselves, the effect of permitting these later influences could hardly contribute to any sense of legitimation; one could even understand a cynic thinking that the formal process had been simply a setup, a Potemkin village.

One could perhaps correct part of the problem by simply announcing to everyone at the outset what the nature of the game was. But I doubt this would matter much for the reason mentioned earlier; only the well-organized, well-funded groups are likely, in most cases, to be able to sustain the kind of effort required to play at this game. Anyway, it misses the central point to say that everyone can do it if the "it" is not what we want. If what we are looking for is some set of constraints on the process that will help to ensure reasonably principled judgments by administrative decision makers, then it is necessary to set some formal boundaries on the kind of influences that are appropriate. The rule of law demands no less.

CHAPTER 5

Judicial Review of Administrative Decisions

In 1928, Ernst Freund, a pioneer in the field of administrative law, wrote, — "administrative law continues to be treated as law controlling the administra- — tion, and not as law produced by the administration."[1] By law controlling the — administration, Freund had in mind the law of judicial review. This is still — what it means for the most part. While administrative lawyers today treat — many different facets of administration and its control, the point of reference for the *law* is the law of judicial review of agency action.[2] Important as administrative due process is as an internal embodiment of the rule of law, it is the external enforcement of law by the courts that lawyers habitually regard as the wellspring of legal principle. In part, the emphasis on the judicial role reflects a strain of American legal positivism that defines law in terms of what courts will enforce. Representative is Justice Holmes's famous (and in my view incorrect) statement: "The prophecies of what the courts will do in fact, and nothing more pretentious, are what I mean by law."[3] Behind that perspective is a normative conception of law, embedded in Anglo-American tradition, that views courts as the quintessential instrument of legitimacy to which government power must answer under a rule of law.

Enforcing the Rule of Law

The rule of law was historically defined almost entirely in terms of the judicial enforcement of legal rights and duties. It is not, therefore, surprising that the explosion of administrative agencies in the 1930s should have been greeted with some degree of alarm by the legal establishment, who proposed federal legislation that would have given courts an unusually large role in overseeing agency policies.[4] The bill was vetoed by President Roosevelt; the furor passed, aided by the intervention of World War II. By the late 1940s when the Federal Administrative Procedure Act was enacted, the "felt necessities of the time" (Holmes again) had forced a recognition of administrative agencies as independent instruments in the creation of legal rights and duties. However, that recognition came in the form of an accommodation, not a surrender, to administrative authority. The concept of a judicially oriented rule of law was not abolished, merely transformed. While no longer the sole or even dominant instrument of law, the judiciary retained a critical supervisory function that has made it, with rare exception, the final interpreter of legal rules. The most important contribution of the Administrative Procedure Act was not in prescribing basic agency procedures—"due process"—but in securing and broadening judicial review.

This rule-of-law principle of judicial review has been selectively applied. As we saw earlier, judicial enforcement of this principle has had almost no important content when applied directly to conventional legislative action. Legitimacy can be circumvented by wholesale transfers of legislative power to bureaucracies and, even, to purely private groups. Rationality is drained of any content by presuming that whatever the legislature does, there must be a "reason" which it is not the business of courts to gainsay, except where "personal" liberties are threatened or the legislature discriminates among persons on the basis of suspect criteria.

On the other hand, administrative action, even when it is in scope and substance the same as legislation, is subject to more exacting standards of reasonable (public) purpose and a reasonable relationship between that purpose and the means chosen to effect it. An agency rule that does not pass muster under the conventional "rational basis" (is not "arbitrary" or "capricious")[5] standard for review of agency action would typically be approved pro forma under the minimal rationality standard used to test the same rule enacted as a statute by the legislature.[6]

This distinction between review of legislation and comparable administrative action is so well established that hardly anyone pauses to consider whether the disparity in standards is warranted. Most observers would justify the disparity by pointing to the obvious fact that, in the case of administrative agencies, review is prescribed by the legislature itself, so none of the problems associated with judicial interference with popular sovereignty arise. In short, the "countermajoritarian difficulty" that so troubles strict constructionists is absent where the courts are acting simply as agents of the legislature to superintend the actions of another legislative agent. This is a neat justification, but also a bit strained in its assumption that the legislature effectively defines the terms of judicial review in all instances. In fact, the review power, while chiefly legislative in origin, is largely self-defined by the courts with rather little direction from the legislature. About the most one could say for the legislative responsibility is that the legislature has delegated to the courts a kind of common law power to define the relevant standards of review.

In identifying the system of judicial review as largely the creation of the courts themselves I imply no criticism on that score. On the contrary, whether or not the courts are responding to specific legislative directions in formulating standards of reviewability and review, they are reflecting a sense quite deeply rooted in our legal culture that the use of government power, to be legitimate, must at some point be reviewed by courts. The need for active judicial review of *agency* action is enhanced, not diminished, by the fact that the courts have largely declined to supervise *legislative* purposes. At least some of what we have lost in the way of constitutional principle as a consequence of the Supreme Court's refusal to enforce exogenous standards of public good and rationality by legislatures may be retrievable through the review of administrative decisions. If Congress, for example, enacts legislation that transparently is for the purpose of transferring wealth to a favored group at the expense of the general public and that has no *credible* public purpose other than benefit to the favored group, it is unlikely to be stopped by the Supreme Court's constitutional precedents as they now stand.[7] It presumably would not matter whether such a transfer is effected directly by the legislation or is part of a program administered by an administrative agency, so long as the agency was given no discretion in implementing Congress's preferences. In the more common situation where the preferences are administered by an agency exercising some discretion, however, a court reviewing the exercise of that discretion can demand a standard of rational public purpose beyond the preferences that appear to be reflected in Congress's design. The fact that Congress can directly order its preferences to be implemented without inviting significant judicial scrutiny is not a convincing reason to permit it to do so by indirection, shifting responsibility to the agencies, and to the courts insofar as they are expected to cooperate by deferring to vaguely defined legislative purposes.

This is not a new idea. Numerous public law scholars have argued for a form of creative judicial interpretation of statutes along these lines.[8] Even Judge Richard Posner, the quintessential realist, has suggested that courts may take seriously expressions of public ideals that are often found in statutes, even when the ideals are contradicted by the political reality of the legislative design.[9] While Posner's suggestion is offered as an alternative to Gerald Gunther's proposal for a similar constitutional requirement of legislative candor that I discussed in chapter 2, I do not think one must choose between the two. Indeed, in a sense constitutional evaluation and nonconstitutional interpretation are interrelated. The power to scrutinize legislative and executive/administrative power for constitutional legitimacy implies some lesser power to use constitutional criteria as a base norm for ordinary adjudication. I do not mean simply that a court can use interpretation to save the constitutionality of legislative or administrative choices, though that is part of the point.[10] I mean to suggest that the courts' whole approach to nonconstitutional review is properly informed by conceptions of legitimate public purpose that underlie substantive constitutional scrutiny. If some rational public purpose is a legitimate constitutional expectation, courts are justified in reaching out to find such purposes, where they can do so without turning the statute on its head. This idea is roughly similar to Ronald Dworkin's idea of interpretation, making a text "the best it can be."[11]

The argument for a little "creative idealism" in statutory interpretation applies easily and naturally to cases involving review of agency action, that is, review of agency interpretation and implementation of legislative directives. Indeed, the case for judicial creativity here is even stronger, for the court can claim prerogatives of legislative authorization similar to those of the agency itself. If the reviewing court liberally construes its power to correct agency choices, it does no more than the agency itself typically does with its grant of legislative power. And, of course, it is always open to the legislature to correct errant courts no less than errant agencies by enacting pertinent legislation. This is often ignored by conservatives who oppose active judicial review of agency action. Against active judicial review of legislation one may make the reasonable claim that legislatures are the repositories of popular sovereignty. The argument from democracy ignores the central and democratic premise of constitutionalism, as I pointed out earlier, but it does have at least the veneer appeal of democratic principle. The same claim cannot be credibly made on behalf of administrative agencies. Their democratic legitimacy is entirely derived from whatever powers and discretion have been transferred to them by the legislature. Against the agencies' claims to delegated power and discretion, courts can counter with the same claim. Without a close look at exactly what powers and discretion have been transferred to whom there is no a priori *political* basis for presumptively favoring one agent over another.

This notion that courts have a liberal warrant for creative interpretation is obviously controversial. Those who believe in the virtue of judicial restraint in constitutional matters make similar arguments for restraint in the administrative context as well. In their view, there is no role for a common law of judicial review except to the extent the legislature itself has clearly provided for it: the courts no less than administrative agencies are instruments of—agents for—the legislature, and whatever discretion they have been given must be exercised in the spirit of promoting those political choices made by the legislature and not some external purposes claimed by the court to be in the public interest.[12] If the point of insisting that courts act merely as agents of the legislature in regard to judicial review is to admonish courts not to substitute their personal policy preferences for those of agencies, it is unexceptionable. It is also inconsequential. Even those apologists for judicial activism like myself, who argue for a broad common law of judicial review, suppose that the court must invoke *some* legislative or constitutional source of jurisdiction and authority. The question is, what is the scope of that jurisdiction and authority—what is the range of choices the court may make on the basis of its own evaluation of public principle and policy.

We can quickly dispose of cases where a statute itself contains text bearing directly on the issue, and the task of the reviewing court is to select among a member of alternative meanings. Such cases may present a host of difficult problems of statutory interpretation: what are the appropriate canons of construction (on which too much has been written), the appropriate use of legislative history (which has not been adequately explored), and the like.[13] A court's choice of interpretive techniques obviously will profoundly affect the kind of role it plays, and thus be influenced by how it conceives its role, vis-à-vis the agency and the legislature. However, it is not specific (if ambiguous) legislative texts that expose the most vexing problem of judicial review in administrative law. The real problem arises where legislative intent is not merely ambiguous but indeterminate because no legislative choice has been made with respect to the issue in controversy. Instead, the power to make the choice has been delegated to the agency, subject to judicial review on such general terms as those of the Administrative Procedure Act (agency action generally must not be "arbitrary or capricious," formal agency adjudications must be supported by "substantial evidence," etc.). It is in the case of broadly delegated legislative power that courts have the broadest freedom to determine the rationality and legitimacy of agency action.

On first acquaintance, it may seem counterintuitive that the court's discretion should be most uninhibited precisely in those cases where the agency's own powers are most expansive. One might suppose that agency and courts could not simultaneously possess delegated power; to the extent power to make a particular choice between action A and B has been given to the agency, there would seem to be no basis for a reviewing court to make a different choice—or to invalidate the agency's choice. However, the transfer of legislative power is seldom exclusive. The legitimacy of the court's intervention is given by the fact that the legislature has transferred power to it, as well as to the agency. The mere fact that delegation of power to the courts is vague, and more implicit than explicit, is irrelevant, for the same is true of delegations of power to agencies. The agency is given a general power to make choices, but almost invariably those choices are subject to some legal constraints, however vague they may be. At the very least, the agency's choice must be nonarbitrary, which is usually translated into an affirmative requirement that the action have a rational basis. To the degree that rationality is not clearly defined by the pertinent statute, the court is free to define for itself the pertinent standards of reasonableness. In doing so, the court should not regard itself bound by what it, qua political investigator, believes were the particular political alignments in the legislature. As an independent agent of the law it is free, within the capacious boundaries of rational interpretation and subject to legislative correction, to imagine an ideal purpose, whether or not that purpose is politically realistic.

Not to be misunderstood, let me underscore that I do not argue judges should aspire to be public philosophers, detached from the political reality that shapes the laws and the controversies before them. Confronted with the problem of interpreting a particular statute and fitting it to a particular agency program and decision, one does not expect judges to seek solutions in Aristotle's *Politics*. By the same token, one does not expect them to seek them in the latest issue of *Public Choice* either.

No doubt judges will, as they should, bring to the task of review such general learning and experience as they have at their disposal, and this will certainly include a sense of political practice. Indeed, in the nature of things, the latter is likely to be the largest part of their intellectual portfolio, for most judges come from a background of involvement in political affairs. That is how they came to be appointed to the bench. However, for just this reason they need no special prompting in the ways and means of political action or special tutelage in political behavior; what they need is more reflection about the distinctive role of courts in the process of making and implementing public choices. That role is distinctive precisely insofar as courts do not serve simply as agents of the political process. That is what we have administrative agencies and executive officers for. What is not needed, and not wanted, is merely another set of bureaucratic agents adding their political and technical judgments on top of that of the initial decision makers. In other words, judges should not see themselves as simply another (more or less final) tier in the hierarchy of political qua bureaucratic decision makers; they should see themselves as involved in a separate enterprise, one of ensuring that, whatever the political objectives being sought, the minimal formal requirements of the rule of law have been met.

The last point deserves emphasis in light of a modern tendency to portray the courts as purely agents of the legislature, as students of modern public choice theory in particular are wont to do.[14] I noted that courts, like agencies, claim coordinate authority from the legislature and thus can make claims to legislative powers that are broadly similar to those on behalf of agencies. One should not on that account think of courts as simply alter egos of executive agencies, however; they may act in the same play but they do not, or at least should not, perform the same role. In this respect, Judge Harold Leventhal's now popular characterization of the court-agency relationship as a "partnership in furtherance of the public interest," and the reviewing court as "in a real sense part of the total administrative process, and not a hostile stranger to the office of first instance," is misleading.[15] While one must be cautious not to read too much into rhetorical phrases, this particular phrase is potentially mischievous insofar as it connotes an alliance in purpose and outlook that undermines the court's independent and distinctive role. The pertinent appeal is to a partnership in the same sense that an auditor can be said to be in partnership with a firm whose books are audited. The auditor and audited are partners only in the very loose sense that, ideally, both stand ultimately to gain by a successful relationship.

Whatever the correct simile, it is obviously necessary to define the terms of the relationship. It is not my purpose to attempt to draft such terms. I doubt it is possible to do so in meaningful detail, generalizable across the entire spectrum of agency programs. Instead, I want to consider two broad aspects of judicial review that I think capture most of the elements of important controversy about the role of courts in monitoring the "administrative state." The first of these aspects is the question of access or standing, who can seek judicial review of agency action. The second is the question of the level of scrutiny to be given by the courts in review, commonly labeled the scope of review issue. These are the two most important and most troublesome questions encountered in defining the court-agency relationship.

There is an anterior question of reviewability, whether agency decisions are subject to *any* review. However, as a matter of general principle, reviewability is not often an important issue in contemporary administrative law. There is a strong presumption of reviewability; only rarely is the presumption rebutted by showing specific legislative intent to withhold review or by showing administrative discretion so broad as to be virtually unreviewable.[16] For most agency decisions, the question of reviewability reduces to questions of who can seek review and what degree of scrutiny is to be given by the courts to agency findings and judgments.

Access to Courts

Criteria and Confusion

Determining who has access to the courts—who has standing to seek review of agency decisions—is in one sense a preliminary jurisdictional determination. So it has been viewed by the courts at least. This view is misleading. The question of standing cannot be practically separated from an assessment of the merits of the claim being presented for review, and this necessarily takes the court beyond jurisdictional preliminaries. For this reason, an inquiry into standing rules entails a debate about the basic character of the agency-court partnership. It is not surprising, then, that debate over standing, over who should be given access to courts to review agency action, aligns with the liberal-conservative positions on judicial review generally.

Interestingly, neither side of the debate over principle seems to be very satisfied with the present state of legal doctrine. This dissatisfaction is not new. The law of standing has vexed generations of administrative lawyers. One searches the legal literature in vain for favorable commentary on the pattern of federal precedents laid down by the Supreme Court over the past half-century.[17] It is not that the Court has failed to articulate either purposes or a set of criteria for standing. The purposes are tolerably clear—at least they are fairly easy to recite: restrictions on who has standing to seek review are supposed to limit judicial review to concrete, particularistic claims involving distinctive injury that can be effectively resolved by judicial action, as opposed to presenting ideological or abstract claims that are not suitable for judicial resolution. For federal courts this concept has a constitutional dimension in the "case or controversy" requirement of Article III, a requirement that rests ultimately on a separation-of-powers principle of preventing "undue" interference with executive and legislative political prerogatives.[18] As to criteria, these have been a bit less clear over the course of the last fifty years, but the Supreme Court at least nominally now adheres to a threefold requirement: a person seeking review must show (a) an "injury in fact" (b) linked to agency action and redressable by the judicial relief sought, which is (c) arguably within the zone of interests that is protected by the statute or constitutional provision that the litigant seeks to enforce.[19]

If these criteria and the purposes that supposedly underlie them are tolerably plain, they are not sensible. One problem is they are not logically or in fact connected one with the other. The supposed link between injury in fact and concrete adversariness, for instance, is adventitious at best; and as injury in fact has been actually defined by the Supreme Court, one would have to say that it serves virtually no purpose in guiding courts along the correct and appropriate path, deciding only appropriate "judicial" matters and avoiding trespass on executive and legislative prerogatives. In fact, it is difficult to see how such a purpose can be served by focusing on the *identity* of the party as distinct from the merits of her claim. The most the injury-in-fact criterion tells us is something about this particular litigant's stake in the controversy. In itself that does not inform us whether the claim presented is a serious, justiciable issue of law. Much the same point can be made about the redressability criterion, which is really an extension of the individual injury notion. As to the zone-of-interests criterion, this is little more than an awkward way of asking whether the claim has merit, a question quite distinct from the party's identity. But I run ahead of myself. It is necessary to retreat just a bit to take note of some of the development of standing law and a few of the leading precedents. This will be a spare summary, mindful of the fact that there is a rich literature on standing law.[20]

When administrative law was in its infancy, standing was coincident with a claim of legal right; a party seeking judicial review of administrative action was required to show not merely an interest in or an injury from the agency's action, it was necessary to show that the agency invaded a legally recognized interest, a right conferred by common law, statute, or constitutional provision. Of course, in such cases where a legal right is involved, standing has no independent significance; it is merely an awkward way of describing the fact that a person's interest is judicially protected. The legal interest test had the virtue of simplicity; its vice was that it clashed with the emerging notion that the task of judicial review was not simply the vindication of private rights, but was the enforcement of the rule of law as a constraint on bureaucratic decision making.

The Supreme Court first breached the traditional legal interest test in the 1940s in cases that involved statutory provisions granting a right of appeal to "persons aggrieved" or "adversely affected" by an agency order. Essentially what the Court did was to interpret these provisions to allow standing to interested (affected) parties even though they had no legally protected interest. The leading case, *FCC v. Sanders Bros.*, was briefly noted in the previous chapter.[21] The case involved a protest by a broadcast licensee to the grant of a license to another in the same market. The petitioner's claim here was that it would suffer the ill effects of new, unwarranted competition, the alleged effect of which would be to injure petitioner's ability to provide "public service" to its community. By reason of the economic injury, the petitioner could, the Court said, claim to be a "party aggrieved" by the FCC's order. The Communications Act does not protect broadcast licensees against competition; petitioner had no statutory or other "right" to be free of competition. However, allowing petitioner standing would make it possible to hear legal objections that might implicate general public-interest concerns.

Sanders Bros. and its progeny can be explained in terms of either of the participation models of chapter 4. Here, as before the agency, a party can argue for liberal standing as a matter of legitimacy or as a matter of informing. The Court itself, in *Sanders Bros.* and subsequent decisions, explained the standing principle in terms that suggest the latter more than the former: interested parties could function as "private attorneys general" who would promote the public interest by exposing administrative error.[22] The Court suffered no illusions that "aggrieved" parties were really motivated by public concerns. It simply assumed that, in seeking to vindicate their private interests, they would necessarily expose *any* failings in the administrative action, and that this exposure would redound to the general public good. The assumption ought to be familiar; it is essentially a version of the process theory of politics, an anticipation, if you will, of David Truman, John Hart Ely, and kindred spirits, though the particular application is not one that most interest-group partisans would approve, since it has the effect of expanding the reach of the judiciary into the political realm of public choice.[23] This expanded standing concept was confined to appeals taken pursuant to specific statutory charter until 1970, when the Court essentially eliminated any distinction between statutory and nonstatutory forms of appeal.[24] In doing so it articulated a twofold criteria of injury in fact and zone of interests. Since 1970, most of the controversy has arisen over the "injury-in-fact" requirement and a third criterion, subsequently added, that the injury and relief sought must be causally related, that is, the requested relief must redress or remove the injury on which standing is claimed. The zone-of-interest test was virtually ignored by the Supreme Court for the better part of twenty years, causing some observers to speculate that it had been abandoned. The recent revival of the zone test in 1987 ended that speculation, but it is still uncertain how much weight will be placed on it.[25]

The variousness of outcomes reached by the Supreme Court in applying these tests reveals not only elements of vagueness in the standing criteria, but a deep ambivalence about the wisdom of liberal standing. A sample of leading cases will illustrate. We can begin with a celebrated environmental case from the 1970s, *Sierra Club v. Morton*.[26] The Sierra Club challenged actions of the Forest Service and Department of Interior permitting private development of a ski resort on public lands in Mineral King Valley. On the merits, the Sierra Club claimed the proposed development contravened various laws governing preservation of national parks, forests, and game refuges, all of which would be affected by the development. As a basis for standing, the Sierra Club asserted a "special interest in the conservation and sound maintenance" of such parks, forests, and refuges. The Court acknowledged that an interest in "aesthetic, conservational or recreational values" could meet the injury-in-fact test of standing. However, it held that the allegations here were insufficient to show that petitioners would be among those suffering such injury inasmuch as they did not claim that club members used Mineral King for any purpose, let alone use it in any way that would be significantly affected by the proposed actions.

The Court's insistence on alleging "individualized" injury, for instance alleging that individual club members hiked in Mineral King Valley, is rather perverse in terms of the instrumentalist premises of *Sanders Bros*. If one wants reliable and effective "private attorneys general" to police the administrative process, the Sierra Club (as an organization) is a more effective advocate than an individual backpacker on several counts: one, the organization has more resources to devote to the legal task; two, because it can capture more of the benefits of its "public action," it has a greater incentive to undertake litigation where the benefits are diffuse—precisely where the legal stakes are most likely to be a matter of general public interest; three, the Club will, by the Court's own implied assumption, represent a broader (more "public") range of concerns than the individual.[27] The last point is what most bothered the Court. It worried that recognition of the Sierra Club, *pro se*, would imply acceptance of purely ideological litigants seeking to embroil the courts in abstract or political disputes,[28] and it would be impossible to control demands on the courts' time and energy. Of course, this assumes that limiting access to litigants who profess individual interest effectively screens out such ideological litigants. The assumption is quite unfounded.[29] One has only to imagine the scenario that the Court invites to demonstrate the ultimate artificiality of this distinction between ideological and nonideological interests in this context. When an individual backpacker comes forward to claim, as his interest, the interference with his personal enjoyment of Mineral King Valley (a cognizable interest under the Court's own criteria), is he less ideological than the Sierra Club?

In any event, the Court has not faithfully followed this distinction between ideological and nonideological litigants cum abstract and concrete issues. A year after *Sierra Club*, the Court upheld a grant of standing to a group of law students in Washington, D.C., to challenge the ICC's refusal to suspend railway freight rate increases for the transport of recyclable goods.[30] The students alleged that the increased rates would lead to reduced substitution of recyclable for nonrecyclable goods, which in turn would require increased use of natural resources, which might be taken from national parks in the Washington, D.C., area, and which might result in more refuse being discarded in such parks. Since the students enjoyed the use of such parklands, they were "injured." In holding the students had standing on the strength of this wondrously contrived scenario, the Court stressed that, in judging the sufficiency of the *complaint*, it had to accept factual pleadings as true. This embrace of formalism over common sense could be ascribed to a reflexive adaptation of a lesson learned in a first-year civil procedure course. However, it also suggested a broader substantive principle of standing doctrine, a principle that any allegation of injury would suffice if some state of affairs could be imagined that would make it true. This use of judicial imagination is not, of course, confined to standing doctrine, as will be recalled from my earlier discussion of judicial review of legislation under the "rational basis" test.

The suggestion of a policy of judicial imagination to support the requisite inquiry for standing was made all the stronger a few years later in applying the causal nexus test in a case challenging the constitutionality of the Price-Anderson Act, which limits civil liability of nuclear power plant operators for nuclear accidents. An environmentalist/citizens group claimed injury from the siting of a nuclear power plant; the alleged nexus between that injury and its complaint was that, but for the limitation on liability, the power plant would not have been built and the group would not have suffered the anxieties of suffering a nuclear accident. Drawing on its singular facility for imagination, the Court accepted this allegation as sufficient.[31]

At this juncture one might infer that the Court's concern about ideological litigants has disappeared. Alas, no. The Supreme Court's indulgence for environmentalists has not been extended to other citizen groups. For example, the Court's tolerance for speculative allegations of causation in the nuclear power case was a marked departure from a decision, two years earlier, where it denied standing to a group representing indigents who sought to challenge an IRS ruling that allowed favorable tax treatment to hospitals that limited indigent care to emergency services.[32] Similarly, the Court would not speculate that tax policies that supported racially segregated schools "caused" injury to minorities who claimed to be thereby deprived of educational opportunities.[33] Other decisions show a similar pattern of unexplained variation.[34]

The confusing pattern of decisions on what constitutes a cognizable interest and injury is made even more so by the fitful invocation of the zone-of-interests test, which was introduced in 1970, only to be forgotten for more than a dozen years (the test was occasionally applied by lower courts that also occasionally wondered aloud about the status of the criterion). There was good reason for thinking that the Court's disregard of the criterion was a purposeful recognition of its essential irrelevance. The irrelevance follows from the simple fact that, if a particular class of person is clearly identified by statute as an intended beneficiary, standing is coincidental with a legally recognized interest and thus has no independent function to perform in directing access to the courts and to judicial relief. However, given the thrust of modern standing doctrine to identify a wider class of persons who are deemed appropriate litigants, useful statutory guidelines are hard to find. Indeed, in most instances, the search for legislative purpose is bound to be little more than a stylistic gloss on the courts' common law inventions. Had the Court said as much or, by its silence, at least allowed us to think this was its view of the matter, the law would be the better for it. Unfortunately, it turned out otherwise. The Court has not only revived the test, but done so in a way that maximizes confusion.

The zone test was revived, in fact but not in name, in *Block v. Community Nutrition Institute*.[35] The case involved a suit challenging a milk marketing order issued by the Secretary of Agriculture pursuant to the Agricultural Adjustment Act of 1937. That act established a scheme of milk marketing orders setting minimum prices that dairy product "handlers" (processors) must pay "producers" (farmers) for dairy products. Orders are promulgated by means of an administrative rule-making proceeding in which members of the public (consumers included) may participate. The rulemaking process here is not conclusive, however. Approval of handlers representing at least half of the milk covered by the order and at least two-thirds of the producers is required before the order can become effective; the secretary can override the refusal of the handlers to approve it as the "only practical means of advancing the interests of the producers." The expressed purpose of this official cartel scheme is to curb "destabilizing competition" among dairy farmers, to raise producer prices, and "to insure that the benefits and burdens of the milk market are fairly and proportionately shared by all dairy farmers."

The particular order in the case involved regulations governing the pricing of reconstituted milk, which were challenged on the grounds that they made reconstituted milk uneconomical for handlers. Plaintiffs included three individual milk consumers, a nonprofit organization representing consumers, and a handler. Although the act did not speak to the question, the Court found congressional intent to preclude judicial review by consumers. The evidence of such intent was derived largely from an interpretation of the statute as an attempt to benefit producers and handlers, not consumers. The Court believed that consumer participation, via standing to challenge the action in court, "would undermine the congressional preference for administrative remedies" and disrupt administration of the congressional scheme.

It is odd that the Court treated the issue as one of preclusion and did not even advert to standing under the zone-of-interest test; on the facts, the two are indistinguishable. Perhaps the Court, at that time, was uncertain whether to revive the long-ignored zone test. In any case, three years later when the Court explicitly revived the zone test in *Clarke v. Securities Industry Association*,[36] it recognized *Community Nutrition Institute* as directly relevant to its application. In contrast to the earlier case, the Court in *Clarke* was able to discern a general legislative intent to protect the interests of persons in the same general class as petitioners; *Community Nutrition Institute* was distinguished as involving a clear legislative intent to preclude. The respective findings of legislative intent in the two cases are due more to the Court's inventiveness than any reliable evidence of congressional purpose. In *Clarke*, the Court acknowledged that the standards of proof in support of finding plaintiffs to be within the zone were not meant to be "especially demanding" and that there need not be any "congressional purpose to benefit the would-be plaintiff."[37] This liberal view of standing is quite at odds with the spirit of *Community Nutrition Institute*, but, given the inconsistency of the cases noted earlier dealing with injury and interest, the orthogonal relationship between these two zone-of-interest cases is, in and of itself, of marginal importance.

Consistency aside, the attitude of the two cases is noteworthy. They imply quite different views concerning the degree of liberality with which one should interpret congressional intent, which in turn suggests continued ambivalence about access to the courts generally. As to congressional intent, it is hard to find any useful general rule that can explain both cases. Commenting only on *Community Nutrition Institute*, Frank Easterbrook applauded the Court's political realism, from the vantage point of public choice/interest-group political theory.[38] The statute in that case, he argues, was the product of an interest-group "bargain" in which Congress sought to advance the interests of agricultural groups by increasing the prices of agricultural products. Inasmuch as this was necessarily at the expense of the consuming public, the "bargain" plainly did not contemplate protecting consumer interests by allowing them to participate, according to Easterbrook. Therefore, Congress's failure to provide for consumer participation is sufficient indication of an intent to foreclose challenges by such groups in court.

Easterbrook's interpretation overlays a bargain model on Earl Latham's Hobbesian account of the legislative struggle that I noted in chapter 1. Realistic or not, his interpretive model is not a helpful way to approach this issue, even if we assume that the reviewing courts are obliged to make political realism one of their canons of statutory interpretation. To begin with, both the Court's decision and Easterbrook's gloss of it pretermit a disputed question: was the Department of Agriculture's action authorized by the "bargain." By necessary implication, the consumer group's claim on the merits was an argument that the order in question was not, in fact, authorized by the legislative bargain. To reject the challenge on the ground that it is made by someone not protected by the bargain assumes we know what the terms and conditions of the bargain were. In effect, the rejection is a decision on the merits of the claim, though it is one informed only by the identity of the claimant. No matter how the legislative action is characterized, a reviewing court must engage in interpretation, of course, and it is not obvious that the bargain model aids materially in this endeavor. Whether one calls legislation a bargain, a sovereign decree, or an epiphany, it is still necessary to have credible interpretive criteria for determining what it means: what is the bargain, decree, or revelation?[39]

Why should we suppose (without clear evidence of legislative intent) that, because this legislation was not for the benefit of consumers, Congress intended to deny them standing? Easterbrook apparently thinks it inherently implausible that a legislature would authorize such challenges by persons who are not intended beneficiaries of the statutory scheme. A similar assumption is at least suggested by the Court's opinion. It is not beyond imagination, however, that even legislators predisposed to favor dairy farmers' interests might think it imprudent to legislate on their behalf without making some bow to the consumers, providing some opportunity for consumers to challenge certain price-fixing schemes. The Court conceded that "the general purpose sections of the Act allude to general consumer interests." Such references are, of course, the routine stuff of legislative preambles, whatever the real political motive force of the legislation, and the realist will dismiss such references as atmospheric—blowing smoke, as they say. Still, the fact that the legislature finds it necessary or convenient to blow such smoke is not altogether unimportant. If it helped legislative draftsmen gain public acceptance for what otherwise would be seen as pure rent seeking, should not a court consider that fact? Why is this smoke-blowing bow to consumer interests not an operative term of the bargain? How much a court should read into such vague references is a hard question to answer in the abstract, but, as I suggested at the outset, it does not strain the court's role to give life to references that allude to a public purpose, if only to enforce legislative honesty.

It is important here to emphasize that even a politically "realistic" theory of legislative intent must take into account relevant background laws of legislative or common law origin. In bargain argot, we might say that every legislative bargain must be construed against the background of prior meta-bargains. I do not refer here specifically to the Constitution though it is, of course, a relevant metabargain. In this particular case, the relevant background consisted of a fairly well-established tradition, developed mostly by the courts, of general reviewability and of liberal standing. If the cases are not consistent, they nevertheless ought to be consulted as relevant background, part of the metabargain, if you will. The Court in *Clarke* was mindful of this; the Court in *Community Nutrition* was not. In both cases, specific legislative intent was a phantom; the Court in *Clarke* implied as much in falling back on general principles, specifically the "not especially demanding" zone of interests standard. Given the amorphousness of that standard, one has to ask whether this interpretive enterprise is a profitable one. As with the interest/injury criterion of standing, the question is, what is the point of asking this question? Why should we care whether litigants can locate themselves in some "not especially demanding" zone of interests? It cannot be a matter of implementing actual legislative purpose. As the Court acknowledged in *Clarke,* the zone test only entails inquiring whether standing would be *incompatible* with the legislative design, broadly conceived. This is no more than a rule of judicial prudence, subject to a legislative negative. As for the concern about being swamped by ideological plaintiffs, this has not been a real factor in most cases where the zone-of-interests test has been raised. I suppose one might regard *Community Nutrition Institute* as raising the danger of ideological plaintiffs. But surely it does not raise it any more pointedly than myriad other cases brought by general consumer groups, cases that are a staple feature of administrative appeals. The inability of the Court to provide clear and consistent rulings on who should have access would not be so troubling if one could be certain that the ultimate object were worthwhile. In fact, however, the erratic and confusing jurisprudence only underscores a deep confusion about the purposes and principles being advanced by restricting access.

Purpose and Principle

One supposed purpose of standing doctrine is to ensure that courts are confronted only with concrete claims. If, however, the point is to limit courts to concrete claims, it is hard to see how that can be done without at least peeking at the claims themselves to see if they present justiciable legal issues. By assumption, the function of standing rules is to foreclose a look at the claims themselves; instead a generalization is made about the claims on the basis of who makes them. The distaste for "ideological" plaintiffs makes sense only on the assumption that their claims are not appropriate for judicial resolution, that is, they are truly too abstract or political to warrant legal examination. Why should we make such an assumption? We may take as a given that the Sierra Club is, in the usual sense of the word, an ideological plaintiff. Why should we assume from that fact alone that its claims in *Sierra Club v. Morton* were nonjusticiable? It is on just this ground that the whole injury-in-fact criterion has been attacked as a confusing irrelevancy. Numerous critics of standing law have insisted that the pertinent question is not a jurisdictional or threshold question, but one going to the merits of the claim, whether appellant has a cognizable claim under the substantive law relied on.[40] Perhaps justiciability is not the true concern. On closer inspection, the standing concern appears not to be about the appropriateness of the case to be heard in court as much as it a more general concern about law enforcement. There are two arguments, related but distinct. The first argument is directed primarily at the conservation of judicial resources, the second directed at a separation of powers. Neither argument is convincing.

In popular expressions, the first argument takes the form of the familiar fear of the flood and the notion that some form of restricted access is necessary to prevent courts from being inundated by hoards of citizen-dissidents. Less colorfully, but to the same practical point, the argument is that restrictions on standing are appropriate in order to conserve judicial resources, a rationing function made necessary by the fact that the costs of using those resources are only partly borne by litigants.[41] The interest in resource management is legitimate, but the argument linking it to standing rules is misguided. It assumes that those legal claims denied judicial consideration under standing rules are not meritorious. There is no basis for that assumption. The absence of effective cost constraints on access to the courts generally might be a legitimate concern, but standing rules are not an appropriate way to address it. We now subsidize adjudication on the theory that it produces a kind of public good in the form of legal rules, which public good ought not to be wholly dependent on a pricing mechanism.[42] The very nature of that choice, the essence of the public goods character of the resource, presupposes a desire to promote judicial resolution of meritorious claims. Of course, ideally we would like some mechanism to avoid wasting the judicial resource on non-meritorious claims. But standing rules do not reliably differentiate between claims on the basis of merit. Moreover, any economic screening of claims would rightly start not with public actions of the kind we are concerned with, but with private cases, for it is the latter that presumptively are least in need of public subsidy and support. In other words, if the object is to promote some kind of economic conservation of resources, it is the ideological plaintiffs who seek some broad vindication of a public interest, as they perceive it, that have the best claim to public support.

The second argument for restricting legal enforcement is also animated by a fear of the hordes, but the thrust of the concern is more political than economic. The tenor of recent conservative challenges to liberal standing rules seems less concerned with preserving the judicial resource than with protecting executive prerogative.[43] One part of the argument sees liberal standing as an interference with the president's power and prerogative "to take care that the laws are faithfully executed." Insofar as liberalized standing allows citizens, in effect, to seek enforcement of broad public interests not firmly anchored to private grievances, it interferes with the executive's prerogative to enforce the public law. The *Sanders Bros.* "private attorneys general" theory is, on this view, a constitutional oxymoron.[44] Another part of the argument is not targeted specifically on law enforcement prerogative, but on a more general objection to the overjudicialization that is perceived to result from an expansion of the types of claims courts are asked to adjudicate. Neither part of the argument provides support for current standing limitations.

The argument from executive enforcement prerogative is fatally overambitious; given that private standing cases involve statutory or constitutional challenges to executive authority, to assert that private parties cannot challenge such action may be, in effect, to immunize the executive (administrative agencies thereof) from the rule of law. The Supreme Court, in affirming the constitutionality of the independent prosecutor statute in *Morrison v. Olson*,[45] quite appropriately rejected the notion of such an immunity in the guise of executive enforcement prerogative. Notice too that the argument from executive enforcement prerogative necessarily presupposes a fixed, a priori conception of the distinction between claims of right and "mere" claims of standing, for it is only the latter that raise any conflict with executive prerogative. No one would seriously argue that a person who seeks to "enforce the law" in defense of a personal claim of right usurps an official law enforcement prerogative. There are literally numberless private rights of action, grounded either in common law or statute, that replicate public law claims. It would not be silly to say that private enforcement of these rights of action interferes with public enforcement discretion,[46] but it would be quite dotty to say that the creation of such private rights is a constitutional encroachment on executive law enforcement prerogative. That would precisely reverse the liberal premises of the Constitution.

Consider, for instance, a common law products liability suit, a staple of private tort law. Such a suit against GM for making a defectively designed Buick may very well interfere with regulatory policies of the National Highway Traffic Safety Administration (within the Department of Transportation), an agency charged with prescribing standards for automobile safety design. While such interference might support an argument for interpreting the statute to preempt the common law,[47] it cannot make sense to say that congressional tolerance of the common law is an unconstitutional limitation on executive powers. Only where a private individual or group is given standing for *purely* instrumentalist reasons as a private attorney general would it make sense to say that the executive prerogative is implicated. Even here the long accepted practice of authorizing law enforcement by private bounty hunters suggests that we ought not to be greatly concerned about instrumentalist standing to appeal agency actions. In most instances, such private law enforcement actions, known as *qui tam* suits, displace executive control of enforcement and, to that extent, arguably violate separation of powers. However, given their long history and given the Supreme Court's recent decision in *Morrison*, such private enforcement actions do not appear vulnerable to constitutional challenge.[48] Acceptance of such suits would seem to silence any objection to instrumentalist standing to appeal, which is far less intrusive on executive prerogative than the right to initiate an enforcement action.

Quite aside from the precedent of private law enforcement, the distinction between instrumentalist standing and claims of right is a vague one. It is exaggerated to say, as does Cass Sunstein, that the line is wholly anachronistic, based on nineteenth-century conceptions of legal rights,[49] but it is almost unarguable that in the modern state the distinction has become too vague to be constitutionally enforced. The point can be underscored here by reference to *Sanders Bros.* again. The Court's view of standing there was frankly instrumental; the competitor granted standing did not have (on the Court's interpretation of the statute) a personal "right" to be free from competition, yet it was given (again on the Court's interpretation of the statute) a "right" to challenge the agency's authorization of a competitor, claiming agency violation of the statute. What is the difference between the two rights? Ultimately, the argument from executive prerogative fails because there is no definable limit on Congress's power to create "rights," even if those rights are essentially process rights.

The other political argument against liberal standing, the argument of overjudicialization, can be disposed of quickly. This argument simply returns us to the question of justiciability and to the assumption that claims brought by persons who do not make claims of right are ipso facto not suitable for judicial review. That assumption is not justified as a general rule, and even if it were justified in some cases, the present standing rules are hopelessly misleading in identifying nonjusticiable claims.

In the end, the separation of powers arguments for restricting standing take us back to the argument against judicial review in general—whether and how far the political process (including the administrative process) should be constrained by legal formalities enforced in court. Those who argue against liberal private standing do not do so in terms of defending lawlessness, of course. The argument is cast more reasonably in terms of political, qua administrative, discretion. I concede this is not tantamount to an approval of lawlessness. Yet, if discretion is unbounded by any *enforceable* rule of law (unenforceable for want of any litigant having standing to seek enforcement), it may easily come to the same thing. I am not talking about lawlessness in the sense of criminal conduct, but simply lawlessness in the sense that administrative agents are able to satisfy their personal preferences, and those of their clientele interests, without significant legal restraint. In other words, the agents are able to follow convenient political preferences without consulting less convenient principles of public law or public interest. It is not necessary to believe that providing liberal access to the courts will guarantee enforcement of those principles in order to recognize that a foreclosure of access to all litigants except those who can point to formally protected legal rights effectively removes from judicial monitoring a whole range of cases where official action may be unlawful, that is, without statutory or constitutional authority, but is so diffuse in impact that it does not invade a legally protected interest. In refusing to review a case because a party lacks standing, the court impliedly concedes the party's claim on the merits—the claim of unlawfulness. It does so, that is, unless the standing disposition is simply taken as an awkward way of expressing summary judgment on the merits.

I do not say it is never appropriate to generalize about the justiciability of certain types of claims, and to establish appropriate general rules for dealing with them wholesale. How such limits are to be characterized is perhaps a detail. Most critics of standing doctrine continue to believe in limitations on the justiciability of certain kinds of claims, and they continue to use "standing" as the appropriate label.[50] However, the use of the standing concept only seems to perpetuate the confusion of the claimant's identity and the character of the claim, a confusion that these same critics deplore. To avoid that confusion, it would be better simply to eliminate the concept of standing and to have the courts declare certain types of claims to be nonjusticiable, or at least to establish certain pleading requirements that would distinguish general political grievances from concrete, clearly defined legal claims.[51] No doubt it would be very difficult to craft such rules, which may be why the Supreme Court so often retreats to doctrines of avoidance like standing. However, it is doubtful the courts would do any worse job of fashioning generic rules about justiciability and pleading than they have done in articulating coherent standing principles. The important thing in all events is to be clear about the public purpose to be served. Standing rules, as they have been crafted and implemented by the Supreme Court at least, have obscured more than clarified this purpose.

Scope of Review

One might characterize judicial review as a dialogue between agency and court in which the former sets the terms of the discourse. The agency explains what it did and why and offers relevant factual and legal support for its rationality. The court responds with a critique of the adequacy of the explanation and of the supporting documentation. If the court finds the agency action sufficiently explained and supported, the dialogue is ended. If either explanation or support is found deficient, the case is usually not terminated, but remanded to the agency for further agency consideration, which may produce a change in the agency's decision or may simply produce a better explanation or justification. The dialogue label has become quite fashionable as an idealized characterization of the process of constitutional review of legislative choices. In a sense, it has more apt application to the nonconstitutional review of agency decisions, however, insofar as it is more likely to involve not a one-shot debate in court but a recurring review, possibly over many years and several agency decisions. This is because a reversal of agency decisions almost invariably involves a subsequent opportunity for the agency to correct its decision; on occasion this will involve a return to the same court for a new round of debates.

More important, perhaps, is the fact that the court-agency dialogue is, as a practical matter, more a matter of mutual persuasion than that of the court and legislature, at least as review is now structured. If the Supreme Court overturns a congressional choice on constitutional grounds, no doubt it would like to convince Congress of the reasonableness of its action, since a decision perceived to be to be arbitrary is likely to generate political dissatisfaction that will ultimately undermine its effectiveness. Still, in the nature of things, even arbitrary judicial declarations of unconstitutionality are usually accepted as final (in the near term, at least) for want of any effective political response. In the case of agency decisions, a reversal of an agency decision typically is not the end of the project or policy of which it is part. An agency determined to persist in its program can often maneuver around a single judicial decision. In some cases, they can do so by formally refusing to acquiesce, inviting further decisions, by a different court or a different panel of the same court.[52] More typically, an administrative agency seeking to resist a judicial precedent will narrowly interpret the court's decision or will shift its own rationales and press on with its previous policy in the expectation of outlasting efforts by litigants and courts to change the policy.[53] The agency's ability to remobilize its resources and energies in this way is, of course, one of the characteristics that distinguishes it from the legislature. Some count this ability a virtue; it is at least an advantage, and one that bears importantly on its relationship with the reviewing court.

The standards by which the court judges the adequacy of the agency's part of the dialogue are described generally by administrative lawyers as a scope of review question; with equal appropriateness they could be called a burden of proof question (the challenger, not the agency, bears the formal burden of proof, but this does not change the practical accuracy of the characterization). No matter how the inquiry is described, it has proved to be all but impossible to capture in useful formulas. The federal Administrative Procedure Act contains a bewildering array of criteria. Reviewing courts are enjoined to "decide all relevant questions of law, interpret constitutional and statutory provisions and determine the applicability of the terms of an agency action." They are further directed to set aside agency action that is (*a*) "arbitrary, capricious, an abuse of discretion, or otherwise not in accordance with law," (*b*) "contrary to constitutional right, power, privilege or immunity," (*c*) "in excess of statutory jurisdiction," (*d*) "without observance of procedure required by law," or (*e*) in certain cases for which an on-the-record hearing is required, "unsupported by substantial evidence."

Locating a clear and useful set of directives in this army of adjectives is not an easy task. Some of the words cannot be given their literal meaning, and others have none. For example, "arbitrary and capricious" does not mean to an administrative lawyer what it means in *Webster's*. To say that agency action can be reversed if it is "whimsical or capricious" (*Webster's*) is to imply no more than a test of seriousness or sobriety. It is difficult to imagine administrative decisions so aberrant as to flunk that test. Bureaucrats may not always be sweetly reasonable, but they are not idiots or children. In fact, conventional judicial usage has made the phrase synonymous with "unreasonable"; this is a fairly open-ended concept but is, at least, more demanding than a standard that only corrected "capricious" decisions. "Substantial evidence" on the other hand has no obvious literal meaning. The term "substantial" conveys a sense of what is wanted, but it is a somewhat misleading sense in that the term is intended to denote a relative but not absolute measure of the weight of the evidence. It is, in other words, a way of describing the persuasive power of evidence for and against a particular proposition.

Linguistic translation of the APA's directives has not been the main problem, however. In fact, the APA review provisions have been more ignored than interpreted. At most they have provided a kind of loose vocabulary for a set of rules and practices that bear no very close relationship to the APA. In some instances, the courts have not even followed the APA vocabulary, but have invented their own. For example, the courts have formulated a so-called hard look test that requires agencies to take a hard look at the issues and arguments before them; whatever the usefulness of this test, it has no obvious relationship to anything found in the Administrative Procedure Act or any other statutory instrument.[54]

It is not my intent to belittle the courts for their creativity, however. In contrast to the area of standing, where I argued the Supreme Court has made a muddle of legal doctrine for no very good purpose, scope of review questions are inherently less well defined. At bottom, the question is how much deference a reviewing court should give to an agency's findings and its judgment. Traditional formulas for judicial review distinguish between factual and legal questions to mark the opposite poles of deference. Courts are supposed to defer very substantially to factual findings and not at all to "pure" legal questions such as matters of statutory interpretation; somewhere between these poles is the realm of judgment involving, so the formula goes, "mixed questions of law and fact," as to which courts must respect "reasonable" agency judgments.[55] These traditional formulations have never been very useful for the simple reason that almost all interesting questions fall into the latter category, where the guidelines are the most indeterminate. At the fact end of the spectrum, agencies do, of course, often make adjudicatory or rule-making findings about the existence or nonexistence of relatively simple facts, facts in the sense of journalistic reportage. But agencies, unlike newspapers, are not in the business of mere reportage. When an agency finds certain facts, it does so with a purpose of rendering a judgment on them. The judgment entails an evaluation of the interrelationship of facts and significance for legal policy judgments. Except in very simple adjudicatory contexts, the line that separates evidentiary facts and judgmental gloss is extremely fuzzy at best.[56]

The same can be said of the other end of the deference spectrum, legal interpretation. The number of important instances where the task of interpreting a statute is simply a search for authorial intent in the abstract is too small to care about. My point here is not some deep hermeneutic lesson about the contingent, agent-relative nature of meaning, though on a deep level of interpretation that point could also be made.[57] What I mean to emphasize here is merely the homely observation that, in the workaday world of administrative activity, legal interpretations, like factual findings, are usually made for some policy objective from which the activity of pure interpretation cannot be separated.

It should come as no surprise, therefore, that modern courts have not rigidly adhered to the classic conception of deciding issues of statutory interpretation (issues of "law") for themselves in favor of a standard similar to that traditionally used for "mixed" questions of law and fact, involving the interpretation of a statutory directive in a context where judgment is unavoidable. The Supreme Court's much celebrated decision in *Chevron, U.S.A. v. Natural*

Resources Defense Council Inc.,[58] involving review of agency interpretation of statutes, will illustrate my point.

Chevron was the culmination of a long-running controversy over the EPA's implementation of a so-called bubble concept in implementing provisions of the Clean Air Act requiring EPA to implement emission standards governing permits required for "new or modified major stationary sources" of air pollution. The bubble concept essentially involves enforcing emission standards on the basis of an entire industrial plant, as opposed to applying the standards separately for each emission source within the plant. Prior to *Chevron*, the EPA had implemented the bubble policy only in so-called attainment areas where the air quality standards had been met and the aim of regulation was to prevent significant deterioration of existing air quality. In nonattainment areas where the EPA sought to improve the level of air quality, the EPA imposed its stationary source standards on either the plant or any of its components. The effect of doing so was to force a firm either to forego construction for new facilities (for example, a furnace and smokestack) or meet the high, and costly, air quality standards imposed for "new or modified sources," even though the pollutant emissions of the new facility could be offset by reduced emissions elsewhere. The discrimination between attainment and nonattainment areas had been mandated by the court of appeals in two prior decisions that discerned such a policy from the basic purposes of Congress in enacting the Clean Air Act. In 1981, shortly after the "Reagan revolution" began, the EPA revolted against the court of appeals' mandate and promulgated new regulations permitting the bubble policy to be applied to plants within nonattainment, as well as attainment, areas. EPA asserted that Congress had not defined *stationary source* to exclude a plantwide definition, and the narrower definition (applied to nonattainment areas) made no sense insofar as it discouraged new investment and modernization and encouraged the displacement of older pollution sources that were dirtier than the new ones. On appeal, the court of appeals followed its earlier decisions mandating the dual definition of stationary source and reversed the EPA. The Supreme Court, in turn, reversed the lower court. The Court did not purport to review the reasonableness of the EPA's bubble policy as such; the question it addressed was whether the statutory phrase "stationary source" permitted that policy. That question, in turn, was reduced to whether the EPA's interpretation of the phrase was entitled to deference. The Court set to one side cases where the statute is clear; obviously, no deference is due in such cases—the statute is to be enforced according to its assumedly clear terms. Where the statute was ambiguous, however, the Court treated this as an implied delegation of power to the agency, similar to an express delegation, to which courts must accord deference.

Though the issue was addressed as a question of statutory interpretation—ostensibly a question of law—it plainly was not a matter of textual exegesis. The naked language of the statute contains no relevant instruction. As it happens, neither does the legislative history, as the Court found. Even the lower court, in reversing the EPA, conceded the legislative history was at best contradictory. It justified its interpretation by reference to the basic purpose of the Clean Air Act, and specifically its view of Congress's purpose to force nonattainment areas into compliance with prescribed quality standards by imposing drastic penalties on new construction. Anyway, whatever it is called, the pertinent issues to be decided were plainly not questions of law except in the sense that the law on this subject is the set of reasonable policy choices that are made within the broad purpose of clean air enforcement. *Chevron* has become the most controversial opinion on the subject of judicial review of agency action in recent years. Some saw it as a new landmark in the definition of the agency-court relationship.[59] This assessment is itself the subject of debate, however, much of which is tied to a debate over what the Court meant by "statutory interpretation" and what it meant by "deference."

Unfortunately, the Court's opinion obscures both questions by framing the question as one of statutory interpretation. Putting it as a question of interpretation and thereby suggesting that it was a matter of narrow textual exegesis, the Court's ruling invited justifiable criticism that its deference requirement amounted to judicial abnegation.[60]

Subsequently, the Court indicated it did not intend deference in matters of simple textual exegesis, holding that in cases of "pure statutory interpretation" no deference is due.[61] This "clarification" has not settled the on-going controversy sparked by *Chevron*; nor has it settled all confusion among courts and commentators on this issue.

The Court's conflation of statutory ambiguity and delegation was unfortunate. Ambiguity need not, and often does not, imply a purposeful delegation. However, in this case, one might sensibly say that the ambiguity produces the same result as an implied delegation in that it permits the agency to proceed to exercise its *general* regulatory authority to regulate stationary source emissions subject only to *general* standards of reasonableness (under the APA and Clean Air Act), thus incorporating a requirement of judicial deference to agency policy judgments. In other words, in the context of an admitted delegation of general authority to regulate, the choice of a particular regulatory strategy is within the reasonable discretion of the agency, unless something in the statute clearly precludes such a choice. It would be otherwise, of course, if there were uncertainty as to the agency's general authority to regulate in the field or to deal with a particular subject; such was not the case in *Chevron*. The EPA's authority to make some policy choices concerning stationary source emissions was not in doubt; it was only its use of the bubble concept that was in dispute. Once it was ascertained that nothing in the statute dealt with this concept, the agency should be allowed to use reasonable judgment in exercising its general authority. It is in this highly context-specific sense that one could equate ambiguity with delegation. In *Chevron*, "stationary source" had no intrinsic meaning (at least none that can be discovered) apart from a choice between two types of emissions regulations. To define the term is thus to make a judgment about which of those choices is most sensible.

On this view of *Chevron*, the Court should have taken note of its decision a year earlier in *Motor Vehicle Mfr's. Ass'n v. State Farm.*[62] As in *Chevron*, the review issue involved the validity of agency rules (in this case revocation thereof), but the question was not framed as one of statutory interpretation. Rather, the question was framed in terms of the reasonableness of the agency's action in revoking certain rules. More specifically, the issue was whether the agency had provided an adequate (rational) basis for its action, applying the "arbitrary-capricious" test that the Administrative Procedure Act prescribes for all agency action. The underlying controversy in *State Farm*, again like that in *Chevron*, was long running and involved several twists and turns. The action reviewed here was a revocation of rules requiring the installation of automotive passive restraint systems (automatic seat belts or airbags). The rules have had a checkered political history, going back to 1969, when passive restraint rules were first proposed by the Department of Transportation. From that time forward, rules in some form were adopted, modified, suspended, reinstated, and finally revoked, the last action being the occasion for the Court's review in *State Farm*. Although it somewhat oversimplifies the story, it is fair to say that the ebb and flow of the rules corresponded to changes in political administrations; the final revocation was one of the early objectives of the Reagan administration. The revocation was preceded by the requisite rule-making formalities; there was no complaint about the process. The claim (by State Farm) was that the revocation was arbitrary inasmuch as the agency (NHTSA, the bureau within the Department of Transportation responsible for highway safety rules) had not given reasonable grounds for its action. Essentially, NHTSA's explanation came down to the following syllogism. First, the major premise: the original judgment in support of mandatory passive restraints was based on a calculation of significant safety benefits, which calculation assumed that auto manufacturers would install airbags in 60 percent of the cars and automatic seatbelts in the rest (the latter option being given them by the rules). Then the minor premise: it became apparent (conveniently, just after a new administration took office) that manufacturers planned to install automatic seatbelts in 99 percent of the cars, which seatbelts could be and would be readily detached by owners. Second minor premise: detached seatbelts will not produce significant safety benefits. Conclusion: the rules are no longer reasonable.

The court of appeals and the Supreme Court both found NHTSA's explanation insufficient, though on somewhat different grounds. The lower court thought the agency's action called for specially intensive scrutiny because of Congress' demonstrated support for mandatory passive restraints, which support did not result in actual legislation, however. The Supreme Court rejected the notion that the pertinent standard of review could be modified based on congressional opinion that was not part of the governing statute itself. Nevertheless, it agreed that NHTSA's action was arbitrary under the usual standard of review because its explanation was flawed. One flaw lay in the agency's dubious assumption that installation of detachable passive seatbelts would not increase usage above the level of manual belts. A more obvious flaw, however, lay in NHTSA's basic syllogism. The agency reasoned that because it had provided a choice of passive restraint systems and the manufacturers had picked one that turned out to be unsatisfactory (because of detachability), *therefore* the passive restraint requirement was ineffective. The "therefore" is incorrect. It does not follow that the system requirement is ineffectual; the most that follows is that manufacturers (hence consumers) should not be given the option of detachable belts.

In dissent, Justice Rehnquist defended NHTSA's explanation on the seatbelt usage point but ignored the logical fallacy point. The main thrust of his defense, however, did not rest on rational justification but on political prerogative. In a masterpiece of understatement, he observed that the agency's "changed view of the standard seems to be related to the election of a new President of a different political party." Anticipating a dictum to come in Justice Stevens's opinion in *Chevron*, Justice Rehnquist thought deference should be given to such political determinations, "as long as the agency remains within the bounds established by Congress."

If the Court missed the relevance of *State Farm* to *Chevron* on the question of review standards, it was not alone. The standard treatment by legal glossarists puts the cases in different boxes: *Chevron* involves a question of law, cum statutory interpretation; *State Farm*, a question of mixed law and fact, that is, judgment. The distinction between the two boxes is important, of course, only if an important element of judicial review turns on it. Some think it does. For instance, on the basis of the traditional law-fact formula it has been suggested that the Court got *Chevron* and *State Farm* backward: the Court should not have deferred to the EPA in the former but should have given greater deference to NHTSA in the latter.[63] This is empty law-fact formalism. The question in *Chevron* reduced simply to a question of the general reasonableness of the bubble policy in light of the general objectives of the Clean Air

Act and the fact the Congress itself had not determined this particular issue. Perhaps the Court might have considered the EPA's justification for the bubble more closely, but that approach would only bear out my point that the question was one of reasonable judgment, which puts it in the same box as *State Farm.* As to the flip side of the foregoing criticism, the Court's failure in *State Farm* to give adequate deference to NHTSA's judgment, this too misses the mark. What would greater deference mean in such a case? NHTSA's explanation of its policy choice was clearly flawed; its syllogism contained a gap. What was the Court to do when it saw such a gap, disregard it as inconsequential on the assumption that the agency probably could supply some other good reason for its action? In fact, this last point is close to what NHTSA argued by insisting that the rationality standard for agency rule making was no more exacting than the minimum imagined rationality standard applied to legislatures under the due process clause.[64] As I remarked earlier, this interpretation of the review standard for rule making has long been rejected, and for good reason. It is bad enough to have no principled standards for legislation; it would be worse to have none for agencies either.

This is not to say that political choices are not to be accorded respect. There is some force to the argument that deference should be given to the fact that the rules in question were the product of a new presidential administration. However, if the rule of law means anything, it means that the laws survive changes in political administrations. The Administrative Procedure Act, and the corpus of related administrative law concerning reasoned justification for administrative action, is not suspended each time a new occupant enters the White House.

It is still necessary to ask, of course, how much weight should be accorded to political factors, such as a new face in the White House or in the agency itself, within the realm of discretion that the law accords agencies. It is a question that has not been answered, and probably cannot be answered in the abstract, for it will vary with the nature of the administrative program and legislative instructions. The relevance of politics is not separate from the generic issue we have been pursuing, what is the appropriate level of judicial deference to the agency's standards of rational justification? In other words, there is not any separate dollop of deference for "political" decisions over and above that accorded "technical" decisions. For purposes of determining the scope of review, it should not matter whether the issue is technical or political. It simply makes no sense to try to make that kind of distinction as a preliminary to examining the proffered reasons for the agency's decisions.

Is it possible to say anything useful about deference in general, or are we compelled to conclude that every generalization must be qualified by "it all depends on . . . "? To judge from the amount of print devoted to the subject in legal journals, it would seem that everything that can be said has been. As

Peter Schuck and Donald Elliott wryly note in a recent empirical study of judicial review, legal scholars analyze the subject with "Talmudic intensity," searching for rules or criteria or general principles.[65] Without much success. Most of the analysis is ex post and particularistic, focusing on critiques of individual decisions (as I have done above) but with no formulations that have useful generality.

Of those who have sought to formulate a general perspective, perhaps Colin Diver has come as close as any to offering practical criteria, although, as I shall show, his analysis breaks down at critical points. Diver seeks to define the respective roles of court and agency in terms of their comparative competence as lawfinders and lawmakers.[66] He begins his analysis by distinguishing between two distinct perspectives on the judicial task: interpretation seen as *lawfinding* and interpretation seen as *lawmaking*. The distinction, as he concedes, is somewhat artificial; it is primarily a heuristic tool for analyzing the judicial role.

Viewing the interpretive task first as an exercise in lawfinding (as opposed to lawmaking), several factors are relevant: access to sources of legislative meaning (other than the statute itself, to which court and agency have equal access), appreciation of public expectations and understanding of legislative meaning, understanding of consequences of alternative interpretations, institutional processes by which alternative meanings and consequences can be explored, and political neutrality and objectivity. Unfortunately, application of these criteria is far from unambiguous.

Consider, for example, the first two criteria. Diver suggests these favor the agency insofar as it has better resources to devote to the search for relevant legislative history and might have a better sense of the political intent of the legislation because they have participated in legislative formulations or are in closer contact with the legislators than the courts. In fact, on neither criterion does the agency have an edge over courts. Since the agency must put its arguments and its research before the court, the latter effectively captures the use of the agency's superior research capabilities in the same way that a judge uses the research capabilities of the lawyers who brief it. As to the agency's political sense, no doubt agency decision makers have closer ties than courts to the legislature and to the political process. But these ties are typically to the current legislature and the contemporary political scene, which are in most instances quite different from the legislative/political environment that produced the statute in question. Contemporary FCC commissioners are no closer to the politics that produced the Communications Act of 1934 than is a reviewing court. The politics that produced the FTC and the ICC are not even a memory for anyone in those agencies (or, one hopes, anyone sitting on any court). That agency decision makers may be closely tied to contemporary legislative and political thinking is, of course, no reason to prefer their choice of original meaning. Indeed, the very opposite is noted by Diver when he considers the factor of objectivity ("motive" in his parlance): the independence of the courts insulates them from political pressure and, hence, ensures unbiased enforcement of legislative programs according to the intent of their authors. By contrast, administrative agencies are not independent and are free to accommodate subsequent political efforts to alter earlier arrangements.[67]

Of course, the argument from objectivity depends critically on the assumption that the administrative program is both well defined and stable. As we saw in chapter 3, it is a common feature of many administrative programs that they are in fact, and are assumed to be in purpose, constantly "changing with the times" as they say. Presumably, for such programs the political sensitivity criterion trumps objectivity. At this point Diver's framework directs us to a different paradigm of agency decision making, the agency as *lawmaker*. The criteria we look at under the lawmaking model changes our perspective but does not yield much more certainty to the definition of roles.

Viewing the interpretive question as one of lawmaking, Diver identifies two major criteria that are central to the allocation of responsibility here, "intrinsic soundness" and "internal coherence."[68] The intrinsic soundness criterion involves a Dworkinian distinction between decisions based on principle and those based on policy, the former heavily weighted with "deontological reasoning" while the latter is oriented to "utilitarian instrumentalist justifications."[69] For Dworkin, adjudication from principle is the essence of the judicial function. Courts appeal to principle, not to social policy, in deciding "hard cases" (those not clearly governed by precedent or other clear rules). Legislatures and agencies, on the other hand, enjoy a comparative advantage in making utilitarian choices insofar as those choices partake of technocratic arguments about relevant tradeoffs rather than adherence to enduring principle. It follows from Diver's analysis that courts should give least deference on matters of principle and greatest deference on matters of policy. The central difficulty here is, obviously, to identify which is which. We might revert to the *State Farm* case for a moment to see if we can sort these out. At first glance, the issue here seems to be a quintessential policy issue in which both technocratic and political factors are preeminent. Whether to require a passive restraint system is surely not a matter of "deontological reasoning," but of "utilitarian, instrumentalist justification." But notice the question for the Court is not whether restraints should be mandated, but whether the agency has rationally justified its latest decision (of several, recall) on the matter. Now, rationality of discourse is not necessarily a matter of deontology, but it is the very essence of legal principle all the same, in Dworkin's system as in any other.

The "internal coherence" criterion involves several aspects of coherence: geographical uniformity, temporal continuity, harmony among different decisions and policies, integration of policy making and enforcement, expedition. From the first two considerations one might infer a rule favoring relatively greater judicial lawmaking responsibility; appellate courts are especially situated to review the effect of agency actions as they affect on different regions and, as agents of "principle," they are arguably more attuned to consistency over time. Unfortunately, as Diver points out, the former assumes a single venue for appeals when, in fact, many agencies are subject to multiple venues, the frequent result of which is inconsistency *among courts*. As for temporal continuity, the argument draws us back to the earlier choice between principle and policy, the former stressing adherence to settled decisions, the latter a flexible accommodation to changing social, economic, and political variables. As Diver puts it, "the choice . . . depends on one's diagnosis of administrative behavior. Which is the greater problem: bureaucratic inertia or capriciousness?"[70]

We could go further in this vein, but without much profit. In the end, Diver's criteria, though useful to some degree, turn out to be so ambiguous in application that they fail to provide us with much more than the vaguest of guidelines: courts are to admonish agencies to be consistent (but flexible), objectively rational (but politically responsive), and so on.

The Missouri Compromise

We are left with no criteria that permit us to formulate reliable general rules defining the respective responsibilities of courts and agencies. The absence of such general rules is unfortunate; it is not fatal. In chapter 2, I suggested a more activist judicial review of legislative choices. As I have emphasized at several points in this chapter, the rules are and should be more demanding for review of administrative choices. But common to both tasks is the unapologetic acceptance of the fact that there is an important role for the courts not as alternative decision makers, but as skeptical critics. The *State Farm* case that I examined earlier is illustrative. I do not say the Court's decision was correct on the merits (though I think it was), but it was the correct stance to take toward the agency's decision. On its face, NHTSA's new rule was not, by any reckoning, silly or arbitrary. But, as a change in the status quo, the rule came burdened with a requirement that it be justified by a story of how it would better serve the purposes of the agency's safety mandate than the rule it replaced. The Court properly saw its task not as one of laying down rulings but throwing down challenges: "I'm from Missouri, show me." The Missourian version of judicial review does not imply that the courts place themselves in an authoritarian posture vis-à-vis agency decision making; being stubbornly skeptical is not the same as being hostile. The important thing is that, while the court should try to understand what the agency is about, it is not part of its responsibility to share the agency's purpose or outlook. The court is not, in this sense, a partner, but an adversary—at least a devil's advocate.

I am mindful that this discussion of the ambition of judicial review is all quite atmospheric, a matter of attitudes more than hard criteria, but the main point of my treatment of Colin Diver's thoughtful attempt to develop criteria was to show how ambiguous his basic criteria were when it came to establish-ing concrete general rules and to suggest, in turn, that attempting to formulate very specific guidelines for review is unlikely to prove successful. Schuck and Elliott's quip about the Talmudic intensity with which administrative lawyers (judges too) study the decisions was preface to a study of whether and how judicial review affects agency decisions. Of particular interest is their finding that the way in which the scope of review test is formulated (in the terms of the degree of judicial deference required toward agency choices or interpreta-tions) does affect the Courts' review of those decisions.[71] It may be so. Still, one may doubt whether this justifies the Talmudic intensity that lawyers have devoted to the subject. If it is possible to devise criteria that can make a difference, it does not follow that they will be the right criteria. Some very general guidelines allocating decision-making responsibility and burdens of proof are appropriate, but the quest for some kind of algorithm of review seems to me a waste of time. Our "language games," to borrow Wittgenstein's famous phrase, do not have the necessary precision to make this game worth the candle.

More important is to establish some agreement about the basic roles of agency and courts, about the basic premise of judicial review. I suggested earlier, in the context of arguing for liberal access to the courts, that judicial review was a check on lawlessness, a check on administrative agents making choices based on convenient personal or political preferences without substan-tial concern for matters of inconvenient principle. I follow here the Kantian notion that it is the nature of a principle to be inconvenient; that sets me apart from the liberal pluralists who are wont to make principles out of practice, which is to say principles of convenience. I do not include in this category all the political realists, merely those who fail to observe the distinction between positive descriptions and normative evaluations of the political process. Un-fortunately, as I pointed out earlier, it is very easy to cut political ideals to fit what one observes to be political reality. In this regard, the trend in political science over the past half-century toward a more realist appreciation of the private interests that drive the political process have combined with econo-mists' models of the rationality of market interactions to create not only a powerful, positive theory of politics and public law but a powerful theory as well. Thus, bargain-theory metaphors that are now widely used by public choice theorists to explain political behavior have become a justification as well, by appeal to the private marketplace where such bargains are welfare enhancing ("Pareto superior") to alternative mechanisms.

In the melding of political and economic models some old and valuable learning somehow got lost. The appeal of bargains in private markets is that they are generally nonbinding on other parties. In the public sector, political bargains are invariably coercive of others who are not privy to the bargain. It is no answer to say that everyone has a chance to form a coalition and to strike a bargain of their own. In the private sector, if two persons, A and B, bargain with one another and a third, C, is excluded, we do not say C is bound because she might have struck a bargain with A or B. We do not even say she is bound because a reasonable person would want to be a party to the bargain; at least we do not bind C on the ground that she consented. Fictitious consent to a decision or an action does not become actual consent simply because the action or decision is reasonable. Recalling the Wisconsin consumers excluded from the milk marketing bargain between producers and handlers in *Community Nutrition*, why were they bound by the bargain? Because they were parties? According to Easterbrook's explanation, the Court's refusal to give consumers standing was that they were *not* part of the bargain, that is, not part of the winning coalition. If so, it is passing strange to say they are bound *because* there was a bargain. Whatever the political reality of the situation, it is simply nonsense to invoke bargain theory, with its appeal to voluntary self-ordering, to justify binding nonconsenting parties. That stands contract theory on its head. The only credible claim that can be made for binding the consumers is that they are ultimate ("in the long run" as they say) beneficiaries of political choices that sometimes, at least in the short term, cause them hurt. Of course, put in these terms, the appeal is to a discernable if diffuse benefit; the promise is of a *public* good, and it is precisely on that score that we wish some degree of neutral monitoring by the courts, to prevent private bargains from making phony claims to public purpose.

There is an irony in the appeal by Easterbrook and others to modern public choice theory in order to support a normative principle of judicial restraint in reviewing agency action. As I suggested in chapter 3, modern public choice theory has given us a new appreciation of the political dynamics that drive the bureaucratic, as well as the legislative, process. Building on the somewhat unfocused insights of political realists such as David Truman, the public choice theorists have been successful in undermining the Wilsonian idealism that has been the foundation of bureaucratic discretion for over a half-century. The legal principles in which reviewing courts were admonished to defer to agencies were founded on this Wilsonian notion of agency expertise. To this day, conventional debate over judicial review is framed in terms of the appropriate deference owed to experts. Public choice theory reveals the false premise in this debate by showing that agency policy choices are not, in reality, driven by expert judgments so much as by ordinary preferences and political interests that are not different in character from those that animate legislative action.

Like Toto in *The Wizard of Oz*, who runs behind the curtain and shows us an ordinary old man manipulating levers that make the great Oz roar, public choice theorists have exposed the bureaucratic wizardry that once held us in thrall as mostly just whistles and bells manipulated by ordinary folks like old Frank Morgan (who played the role of Oz in the original movie version). Having thus exposed the shaky premise of judicial deference, public choice theorists might well have left it to others to draw their own normative conclusions. After all, it is the foremost pretention of public choice theory to be positive, not normative. However, the distinction between positive and normative theory is often ignored, as I have suggested. Easterbrook's account of the bargain theory is illustrative of the switch from positive to normative.

Of course, by virtue of their exposure of the reality underlying public choices, deference can no longer rest on traditional grounds of agency expertise; it must now shift grounds; it must now be deference to political choice. Oz the Wizard is gone. In his place is someone who looks, for all the world, like someone off the street. How does he command our respect? Presumably by being just like us, that is, by being part of the everyday business-as-usual process his choices become legitimized to the same extent that political choices generally are supposed to be respected in a democracy. The flaw in this perspective is the assumption that, because courts defer to political judgments made by legislatures, they should defer to agencies when, as often happens, the agencies make "legislative" judgments. No principle of democratic choice requires this. No respectable notion of the rule of law should tolerate it. Even if majoritarian principles require us to pretend that the preferences of elected legislators represent preferences of the median voter, they do not require us to suffer the same illusions about the preferences of unelected bureaucrats.

It is important to recognize precisely what is at issue in any event. It is not who gets the final say about what public policy choices will be made. No conception of judicial review yet advanced by even the most ardent exponent of active judicial review imagines that courts will have the final say on all (or even most) public choices. It would be a practical impossibility not only because of the number of decisions the courts would have to oversee, but because it would require sustained attention to each decision reviewed, often sustained over a period of years as decisions were remanded, redecided, re-reviewed, etc. This is not to deny that courts can have an effect on policy choices. If they did not, there would be scarcely any point to judicial review (and also, incidentally, very little point to debate about it one way or another). Nor could one reasonably deny that the effects of review are sometimes not benign. We have very little reliable information on the long-term effects of review. Some recent studies have produced evidence of a negative character, showing dysfunctional results on agency policies.[72] Of course, it is the nature of the subject that dysfunctional results produce more highly visible trails and are, therefore, more readily discovered, while the benign effects of review are masked by other elements of agency decision making. Indeed, the nature of the judicial role makes it impossible for courts to claim any significant credit for those policies that are successful, however much their intervention (or threat of intervening) may have contributed to that success.

We proceed largely on faith and some intuition born of experience. If that seems frail support for such a large enterprise, it might be recalled that it is the same support that underlies our continued commitment to liberal democracy.

Conclusion

In 1938, James Landis, a scholar and practitioner of government, echoed
another scholar cum practitioner, Woodrow Wilson, in praising the new administrative state.

> The most superficial criticism which can be directed toward the develop-
> ment of the administrative process is that which bases its objections
> merely upon numerical growth. A consequence of an expanding interest
> of government in various phases of the industrial scene must be the
> creation of more administrative agencies, if the demand for expertness is
> to be met. . . . Efficiency in the processes of governmental regulation
> is best served by the creation of more rather than less agencies. And it is
> efficiency that is the desperate need.[1]

If Landis's enthusiasm for administrative agencies and expertise in government did not go unchallenged in 1938, it was very much more in fashion then
than it would be today. Landis's belief in government by experts, and his
assumption that creating more administrative agencies is the way to secure it,
would invite smiles among modern observers of the political scene. We know
better today.

Or do we? While most modern sophisticates will smile at Landis's naive
faith in government by experts, there are still some who do not. And quite
apart from what "sophisticated" people think, our political actions conform to
Landis's prescription, albeit for political reasons he never appreciated. If we
have learned something about bureaucracies in the half-century since Landis's
era, if we have learned about the political uses of agencies to produce something other than a common good and about the errant ways of "expertise," we
quite evidently have not learned what we should do about it. Indeed, the
conventional wisdom among modern political scientists, as we saw in chapter 1,
is that there is nothing to be done, nothing, that is, so long as we are
committed to liberal democratic choice with its emphasis on honoring individual preferences. Given such a commitment, it is simply unrealistic ("impossible" according to the strict mathematical logic of individual choice) to derive
an objective public good; there is only a process for registering the prefer-

ences of individuals. What that process produces *is* the public good. That is the political reality. So we are told.

It is exceedingly difficult to argue against "reality." Those who do so are called romantic or crazy, depending on the intensity of their argument. Of course, it helps to know what the alternatives are, and here the realists are powerfully supported by the difficulty of finding plausible alternatives to interest-group pluralism as a model for democratic society.

The communitarian model has received attention as a competitor to individualistic liberalism in recent years. Some of its proponents are associated with "critical" political theory, loosely, and variously, derived from Marxist theory. Marxist, or more precisely post-Marxist, theory has never taken a very firm root in American intellectual soil. For good reason; as recent events in eastern Europe have brought to light, the performance of those regimes has been dismal in virtually all social dimensions—economic efficiency, individual freedom, and social justice. The record of such regimes prompts a positive distaste for the associated political theory, however far removed the latter may be from socialist practice. A model of communitarian political theory more congenial to the American temperament, and now enjoying a revival of sorts among theorists at least, is that of civic republicanism. The republican ideal of politics has had a strong appeal in American political thought, notably in the colonial and constitutional eras. The communitarian orientation of civic republicanism, with its emphasis on disinterested political participation and civic virtue, now appears as a stark contrast to the individualistic, self-interested orientation of liberalism. In the vagaries of early American political thought the contrast was obscured. Persons as individuals could have natural, inviolable rights anterior to the state, but as citizens they could be imagined willing to suspend their individual interests in disinterested pursuit of social welfare. Today, that reconciliation seems more difficult somehow. At least it has been quite widely doubted by modern liberals that such a reconciliation can be produced by legal means, least of all by *constitutional* law.

It is often explained that this follows democratic principle. Officials will be held to political account for their actions, principled or not. In truth this explanation is a bit disingenuous; the system of political accountability does not work that finely. Therein lies one of the conventional arguments for judicial review. But constitutionalism does not depend on any lack of political accountability. Quite the contrary, constitutionalism has the ultimate purpose of bounding the domain of political choices, whether or not they are made by accountable agents acting on instruction from the people. Where *conventional* personal rights are involved, no one questions this obvious proposition. Unfortunately, we have gulled ourselves into thinking that an individual has no personal right to be free of coercive wealth transfers in the form of unprincipled legislation.

There remains the problem of criteria and standards. I do not profess to have any simple solution to this problem. The burden of my argument in chapter 2 was the unoriginal thesis that courts should search for fundamental values despite the problem of locating them in any particular time frame that surrounds the occasion for implementing them. It was not my assumption that these values are forever fixed in time, though historical continuity is certainly an important element in separating enduring principles from evanescent convenience. On the assumption that values, even fundamental values, change, I concede that some accommodations to public choices are constitutionally legitimate today that might not have been legitimate in, say, the *Lochner* era. The reverse is also true (as the history of constitutional adjudication of so-called personal rights such as free speech attests). To say this is not to confirm the notion, widely held by defenders of the Court's post-*Lochner* jurisprudence, that there is today a fundamental difference between personal and economic liberties. As Robert McCloskey said of this distinction, it is redolent of the tastes of academic dons more than ordinary (working) folks.[2] Modern political experience, here and elsewhere around the world, should have demonstrated for us the symbiotic relationship between all individual rights.

But in the end the Supreme Court's retreat from *Lochner* says more about its ambitions for constitutional rights. Looking back on *Lochner*, the Court somehow came to believe that it could not sustain a meaningful substantive review of social legislation without unduly interfering into the heart of democratic processes. The key word here is *unduly*. Why it should be more undue to interfere with the democratic process in the case of regulatory legislation than in the case of, say, legislation prohibiting flag burning is something of a mystery.[3] Indeed, in terms of interfering with broad public preference, as distinct from those of coalitions of organized interest-groups, the flag burning case is a far more notable interference with democratic choice.[4] This is not to challenge the Court's decision on flag burning—it seems to me correct—but merely to dispel the illusion that judicial review in one type of case, where it is generally accepted (personal rights), is less an interference with popular sovereignty than it is in the other (economic rights).

If a return to Lochnerian judicial review of public choices would not put an end to liberal democracy, it would also not make a large dent in the welfare cum administrative state. The reaffirmation of general substantive principles of limitation on public choice would be salutary in my view, but quite modest in its effects.

Likewise, the constitutional demands of procedural due process must be seen as having a salutary but limited effect on the everyday workings of the administrative bureaucracy. Constitutional procedural due process, like substantive due process, is a way of fixing "first principles." This is not unimportant but it hardly exhausts the rule-of-law requirements for public choices. On the more routine level, the rule of law is a composite of "internal" law—a law governing procedural formality and fairness—and "external" review of agency action.

As to the internal law, I argued in chapter 4 for greater openness and greater formalism for administrative action. While there is some tension between these two objectives, they ultimately advance, in my conception, the same purpose of limiting bureaucratic discretion. On the one hand, open participation levels the playing field on which different public constituencies seek their "fair advantage," to recall Senator Magnuson's wry phrase. On the other, the demands of formalism keep the pressures and the agency's own deliberations within the bounds of a structure that can be evaluated after the fact.

The after-the-fact evaluation introduces the external law. To generations of American administrative lawyers, practitioners and academics alike, the role of the courts has been seen as virtually indispensable to the rule of law. While this may, in part, be related to the reductionism of legal realism reflected in Holmes's famous dictum that the law is what courts say it is, at a deeper level it is the product of a belief that only the courts have the requisite disinterest to provide the objective rationality that is supposed to inhere in the rule of law. The idea of a bureaucracy controlled only by legislators or executive officers is troubling on precisely this score. Recent speculations by political theorists about the interdependence of bureaucrats and legislative and executive officers only reinforces the disquiet. As we saw in chapter 5, ordinary judicial review of administrative action does not pose the "countermajoritarian difficulty," as Alexander Bickel called it, that arises in the context of constitutional review of legislation. The assumption of the former is that it implements legislative design (hence, by further assumption, majoritarian choice). Critics of judicial review have sometimes implied the contrary, on the quite mistaken premise that legislative delegations to courts are inherently suspect and should be interpreted restrictively. But this is tantamount to a preference not for democratic political choice over judicial choice, but for bureaucratic choice over all others. On no credible theory of democracy or political supremacy can this latter preference be sustained.

The critical issues of judicial review depend less on general presumptions of reviewability than on two more focused questions: who has access to the courts to challenge administrative action, and what is the scope of review? As to the access question, much of the hostility to liberal access to the courts rests on an assumption that standing restrictions serve to screen out claims that are inappropriate for judicial resolution. If inappropriate means that the claims have no legal merits, there is no foundation for that assumption. If inappropriate means that public actions by "ideological" groups are an interference with executive prerogative, the objection simply begs the question of how far we should allow that prerogative to go unchecked in cases where it works a public injury too diffuse to invade discrete, legally protected interests. As to scope of review the controversy over greater or less deference to agency action has become mired in a too-refined debate over highly artful, if not artificial, distinctions that have obscured more than clarified what is really at stake. Ultimately, most arguments about particulars depend on an unarticulated judgment about the relationship (or lack thereof) between political choices and legal principles. Here is where the debate over judicial review should be focused. As with the issue of constitutional review, it comes down to a question of just how far we want to insist that political choice be subject to a rule of law.

It would be fatuous to claim that the argument for principled restraint on political choice is self-evidently true. Jefferson notwithstanding, there are no self-evident truths about social or political organization, at least not if "self-evident" is a reference to some argument of natural law. Still, there are some truths that fit better than others with the values that we (as in "we the people") have generally embraced in our more reflective moments. One of these truths is that there must be effective, enforceable legal restraints on the power of government, whether it is acting in its legislative, executive, or judicial capacity. Another is that this legal restraint is meaningless unless it is tied to some articulation of principles that transcend vagrant sentiments or particular interests. I do not suggest anything here that quite approaches deontological principle, merely something that claims respect because it represents a judgment about enduring social values. There is a popular school of thought that sees all this emphasis on the rule of law as simply a disguise for the rule of lawyers. James Harrington, to whom we owe the thought that government is "the empire of laws and not of men," did not imagine that an empire of laws meant an empire of lawyers. In fact, he thought the judgment of lawyers, like that of "divines," was entitled to no more respect than that of "so many tradesmen."[5]

Harrington lived in a simpler age. Today, sad to say, we have not learned, in America at least, to have an enforceable rule of law without lawyers—lots of them. Also sad to say, we have not learned to have politics without politicians or bureaucracy without bureaucrats. This professionalization, if you will, of all three of these elements of modern social life may be regrettable, but it seems unavoidable. What is needed, then, is to define the balance of power in the triumvirate of law, politics, and bureaucracy that runs the modern administrative state.

Notes

Chapter 1

1. For general histories of federal administrative government see, e.g., Peter Woll, *American Bureaucracy*, 2d ed. (New York: Norton, 1977); Lawrence C. Dodd and Richard L. Schott, *Congress and the Administrative State* (New York: Wiley, 1979); Leonard D. White, *The Federalists: A Study in Administrative History* (New York: Macmillan, 1948); White, *The Jeffersonians: A Study in Administrative History, 1801–1829* (New York: Macmillan, 1956); White, *The Jacksonians: A Study in Administrative History, 1829–1861* (New York: Free Press, 1954); White, *The Republican Era, 1869–1901* (New York: Macmillan, 1963). A short history by James Q. Wilson, "The Rise of the Bureaucratic State," *Public Interest* 41 (1975): 77, is very useful.

2. The dispute first came to a head in 1789 in debate over a bill to create a Department of Foreign Affairs that specifically provided for removal of the secretary by the president without the advice and consent of the Senate. Congress approved this removal power. However, the question was reopened by the Tenure of Office Act of 1867, which required Senate approval for removal of officers whose initial appointment was subject to advice and consent. After an amendment that minimized its practical importance, the act was repealed in 1887. The issue arose again in 1926 in a constitutional challenge to an 1876 statute that provided for removal of certain postmasters only with the advice and consent of the Senate. In Myers v. United States, 272 U.S. 52 (1926), the Supreme Court held the restriction on removal was unconstitutional, but, eight years later in Humphrey's Executor v. United States, 295 U.S. 602 (1935), it ruled that *Myers* had no application to "independent" regulatory agencies (in this instance the FTC). The *Myers/Humphrey's Executor* distinction has been much criticized in recent years by legal scholars, but was reconfirmed by the Court's decision in Morrison v. Olson, 108 S. Ct. 2597 (1988), upholding the constitutionality of the independent counsel statute.

3. See Buckley v. Valeo, 424 U.S. 1 (1976) (legislative appointment of officers of the United States unconstitutional); INS v. Chadha, 462 U.S. 919 (1983) (legislative veto of executive rules or orders unconstitutional); Bowsher v. Synar, 478 U.S. 714 (1986) (delegation of executive functions to congressional agent unconstitutional).

4. White, *The Jeffersonians*, supra note 1 at 71. See also Noble E. Cunningham, Jr., *The Process of Government under Jefferson* (Princeton: Princeton University Press, 1978).

5. The figures are taken directly or estimated from data reported in U.S. Department of Commerce, *Historical Statistics of the United States, Colonial Times to 1970*

(Washington, D.C.: GPO, 1976), 8, 224, 1103, 1114, 1115. The GNP is a crude estimate because there are no reported GNP figures for this period. The earliest period for which historical figures are given in the Department of Commerce statistics is the decade 1869–78, when GNP was estimated at an average of $7.4 billion. Taking this average, and discounting by an estimated average annual productivity growth of 4 percent (Cf. Moses Abramovitz and Paul David, "Reinterpreting Economic Growth: Parables and Realities," *American Economic Review* 63 [1973]: 428, 430), I derived a figure of $406 million for 1800 GNP. This is much smaller than the estimate of Robert F. Martin, *National Income in the United States, 1799–1938* (York: National Industrial Conference Board, 1939), 10, who reports a personal income figure of $674 million in 1799. His estimate implies a lower growth rate (about 3 percent). I have opted for a 4 percent growth rate based on Abramovitz and David.

6. *Economic Report of the President, February 1990* (Washington, D.C.: GPO, 1990), 329, 383. The GNP is estimated.

7. See *Historical Statistics*, supra note 5, for GNP and spending up to 1970. The 1990 ratio is calculated from figures in *Economic Report of the President*, supra note 6.

8. See U.S. Department of Commerce, *Statistical Abstract of the United States, 1989* (Washington, D.C.: GPO, 1989), 321.

9. See, e.g., the provocative and interesting history by Stephen Skrowronek, *Building a New American State: The Expansion of National Capacities, 1877–1920* (Cambridge: Cambridge University Press, 1982), chaps. 5 and 8, which uses the Interstate Commerce Act as one of three models to describe the "building" of the modern bureaucratic state (the other models are the development of the civil service system and of the modern army).

10. Solon Buck, *The Granger Movement: A Study of Agricultural Organization and Its Political, Economic, and Social Manifestations, 1870–1880* (Cambridge, Mass.: Harvard University Press, 1913).

11. The Pennsylvania oil interests are emphasized by Gerald D. Nash, "Origins of the Interstate Commerce Act of 1887," *Pennsylvania History* 24 (1957): 181. The New York merchants are identified by Lee Benson, *Merchants, Farmers, and Railroads: Railroad Regulation and New York Politics, 1850–1887* (Cambridge, Mass.: Harvard University Press, 1955).

12. Gabriel Kolko, *Railroads and Regulation, 1877–1916* (New York: Norton, 1965).

13. Edward Purcell, Jr., "Ideas and Interests: Business and the Interstate Commerce Act," *Journal of American History* 54 (1967): 561.

14. This requires qualification. As Wilson, supra note 1 at 88, points out, there was a precedent. The Pension Office, established in the Department of Interior in 1833 to administer veterans' pensions, had a similar clientele mission. However, the more open commitment to the farmers, purely by reason of their political status, makes the Department of Agriculture the better exemplar of clientele government.

15. On the history and functions of the Department of Agriculture, see John M. Gaus and Leon O. Wolcott, *Public Administration and the United States Department of Agriculture* (Chicago: Public Service Administration, 1940).

16. E. Pendleton Herring, *Public Administration and the Public Interest* (New York: McGraw-Hill, 1936), 258–59.

17. Until 1903, the principal federal agency interested in commercial and industrial activity was the Department of Treasury. Following the Civil War, commercial interests and labor interests alike agitated repeatedly for separate institutional recognition in the form of departments devoted to their respective interests. Labor interests had partial success as early as 1884, when Congress created a Bureau of Labor, nominally within the Department of Interior but semiautonomous. A Department of Commerce and Labor was created in 1903 and the Bureau of Labor was transferred to the new department. In response to arguments by labor interests that the combined commerce and labor responsibilities created a conflict of interest, Congress transferred the labor functions to a separate Department of Labor in 1913, the commerce functions residing unconflicted in a renamed Department of Commerce. See George C. Thorpe, *Federal Departmental Organization and Practice: The Executive Departments, Bureaus, and Independent Establishments of the United States Government* (Kansas City: Vernon Law Book Co., 1925), 383–86, 495.

18. Advocates for departmental status were particularly concerned about budget constraints on veterans' benefits, enforced by OMB oversight. Departmental status for veterans affairs, it was argued, would allow veterans' benefits to avoid OMB review and go directly to the president. See, e.g., *Department of Veterans Affairs Act: Hearings Before a Subcommittee of the House Committee on Government Operations*, 100th Cong., 1st sess., 1987, 43–45 (statements of Congressmen Montgomery and Solomon; hereinafter *Hearings*).

19. *Hearings*, supra note 18 at 95 (testimony of Thomas Miller, spokesman for Blind Veterans of America).

20. Michael Weisskopf, "Raising EPA to Cabinet Status: Bush, in Policy Shift, Endorses Idea," *Washington Post*, January 25, 1990, A25. As this is written the latest report is that the proposal for EPA cabinet status has been stalled by disagreement between Congress and the White House on peripheral issues. Michael Weisskopf, "Drive to Elevate EPA to Cabinet Status is Stalled," *Washington Post*, October 12, 1990, A19.

21. See William Letwin, *Law and Economic Policy in America: The Evolution of the Sherman Act* (New York: Random House, 1965).

22. Not all the agencies mentioned are independent in the same sense as the ICC. Some, like the FDA, NHTSA, and OSHA, are mere bureaus within a department; others, like the EPA, are independent of any department, but still subject to direct presidential control.

23. Bruce Ackerman and William Hassler, *Clean Air/Dirty Coal* (New Haven: Yale University Press, 1981), 79. Just how faithful their phrase is to the New Deal ideal may be seen by reading James Landis, *The Administrative Process* (New Haven: Yale University Press, 1938). Landis was a leading academic proponent of, and participant in, New Deal programs.

24. On the origins of social security, see Charles McKinley and Robert W. Frase, *Launching Social Security, 1935–1937* (Madison: University of Wisconsin Press, 1970).

25. Federal outlays for all social welfare programs (including: social security, public aid, health care, veterans benefits, education, housing, and miscellaneous welfare and aid programs) for 1986 was $472.4 billion (*Statistical Abstract of the United*

States, supra note 8 at 347). Civilian employment for the Departments of Health and Human Services, Education, the Social Security Administration, and the Veterans Administration in 1987 was 452,729 (ibid. at 321).

26. Herbert Kaufman, *Are Government Organizations Immortal?* (Washington, D.C.: Brookings, 1976), 78.

27. See his "Inaugural Address," January 20, 1981, *Public Papers of the Presidents of the United States: Ronald Reagan, 1981* (Washington, D.C.: GPO, 1982), 2 (hereinafter *Public Papers of the Presidents*). I think most people came to interpret Reagan's program as seeking an absolute reduction, however, and he did little to dispel this popular understanding.

28. See Jonathan Rauch, "The Fiscal Ice Age," *National Journal*, January 10, 1987, 58.

29. Ibid. at 60.

30. Ibid. at 63.

31. See Robert W. Crandall, "Whatever Happened to Deregulation," in *Assessing the Reagan Years*, ed. David Boaz (Washington, D.C.: Cato Institute, 1988), 271, 286 (expenditures for EPA, OSHA, and NHTSA programs).

32. William Niskanen, *Reaganomics* (New York: Oxford University Press, 1988), 325.

33. "Inaugural Address," January 20, 1981, *Public Papers of the Presidents*, supra note 27 at 1.

34. Quoted in John A. Vieg, "The Growth of Public Administration," in *Elements of Public Administration*, ed. Fritz Morstein Marx, 2d ed. (Englewood Cliffs, N.J.: Prentice Hall, 1959), 13.

35. Charles A. Reich, "The New Property," *Yale Law Journal* 73 (1964): 733.

36. See Kaufman, supra note 26 at 48–49.

37. See Hugh Heclo, "Reaganism and the Search for a Public Philosophy," in *Perspectives on the Reagan Years*, ed. John L. Palmer (Washington, D.C.: Urban Institute Press, 1986). Heclo fits Reaganism into this amalgam of individual liberalism and communitarianism, noting that it neatly appealed to both strains. Its free market, antigovernment program appealed to liberal individualism while at the same time appealing to communal values on moral issues such as abortion, school prayer, etc. Even welfare reform (curtailment) could be married both to individualism and communitarianism, Heclo notes, by saying that institutionalizing welfare measures both suffocates the true communitarian moral impulse of private (individual) initiatives (charity) while also suppressing individualism among those dependent on welfare.

38. Walter Lippmann, *The Public Philosophy* (Boston: Little, Brown, 1955), 114–15. The difficulty of determining a true public interest in a liberal democratic society was an old theme in Lippmann's writings. See Ronald Steel, *Walter Lippmann and the American Century* (Boston: Little, Brown, 1980). Similar sentiments were expressed by John Dewey, who acknowledged his debt to Lippmann's earlier writings on this point. See John Dewey, *The Public and Its Problems* (New York: Henry Holt, 1927).

39. Earl Latham, *The Group Basis of Politics* (Ithaca: Cornell University Press, 1952), 38. Compare the imagery in the title of a contemporaneous textbook: Bertram

M. Gross, *The Legislative Struggle: A Study in Social Combat* (New York: McGraw-Hill, 1953).

40. David Truman, *The Governmental Process: Political Interests and Public Opinion* (New York: Knopf, 1951), 159, 348, 512–24 and passim. Truman never quite specifies the nature of these rules. They appear to be primarily procedural and constitutional protections of individual rights and guarantees of political participation. But he also hints that the rules include "norms, values, expectations about the legitimate use of political power," an idea that sounds vaguely like a public interest criterion.

41. The field is sufficiently ill defined to confound the bibliographer. Probably the best introduction to the main themes (and general bibliography) is Dennis C. Mueller, *Public Choice* (Cambridge: Cambridge University Press, 1979). Somewhat more daunting is a text by two of the leading political scientists in the field, William H. Riker and Peter C. Ordeshook, *An Introduction to Positive Political Theory* (Englewood Cliffs, N.J.: Prentice Hall, 1973). Peter H. Aranson, *American Government: Strategy and Choice* (Cambridge, Mass.: Winthrop, 1981) is an excellent interweaving of public choice theory into an introductory text on American government. Public choice has begun to find its way into legal scholarship. See generally Daniel A. Farber and Philip P. Frickey, "The Jurisprudence of Public Choice," *Texas Law Review* 65 (1987): 873; "Symposium on the Theory of Public Choice," *Virginia Law Review* 74 (1988): 167; Herbert Hovenkamp, "Legislation, Well-Being, and Public Choice," *University of Chicago Law Review* 57 (1990): 63. Opinions are sharply divided concerning both the analytical usefulness and the normative implications of public choice applications to public law. For a sample of perspectives pro and con see, e.g., Cass R. Sunstein, "Interest Groups in American Public Law," *Stanford Law Review* 38 (1985): 29 (criticizing the public choice perspective of legislation on normative and descriptive grounds); Mark Kelman, "On Democracy Bashing: A Skeptical Look at the Theoretical and Empirical Practice of the Public Choice Movement," in "Symposium," supra (general critique of public choice theory); Frank H. Easterbrook, "Statutes' Domain," *University of Chicago Law Review* 50 (1983): 533 (applying public choice theory to statutory interpretation); William Landes and Richard A. Posner, "The Independent Judiciary in an Interest Group Perspective," *Journal of Law and Economics* 18 (1975): 875 (use of public choice theory to explain the judicial role). My own view of public choice theory is ambivalent. Analytically I think it can be a very useful perspective in many contexts, but there is a regrettable tendency among adherents to apply it uncritically. Normatively, I think public choice theory, as conventionally interpreted, does not provide an appropriate model for political governance, though I am quick to add that the premise of liberal individualism that underlies public choice is an appropriate point of departure.

42. The diversity is illustrated by comparing the work of three economists, Kenneth Arrow, George Stigler, and James Buchanan, each of whom earned the Nobel Prize for work associated with the field. See, e.g., Kenneth J. Arrow, *Social Choice and Individual Values*, 2d ed. (New York: Wiley, 1963); James M. Buchanan and Gordon Tullock, *The Calculus of Consent* (Ann Arbor: University of Michigan Press, 1962); George J. Stigler, "The Theory of Economic Regulation," *Bell Journal of Economics and Management Science* 2 (1971): 3.

43. The assertion that Arrow's work provided the "foundation" of public choice is common. See, e.g., Frank H. Easterbrook, "Ways of Criticizing the Court," *Harvard Law Review* 95 (1982): 802, 813. However, if one regards the central perspective of public choice as concerned more with modes of strategic behavior than with the mathematics of formulating collective-decision rules from individual preferences, it would seem sensible to give that distinction to the work of Anthony Downs (e.g., *An Economic Theory of Bureaucracy* [New York: Harper and Row, 1957]) or that of Buchanan and Tullock (e.g., *The Calculus of Consent*, supra note 42) or that of William Riker (e.g., *A Theory of Political Coalitions* [New Haven: Yale University Press, 1962]).

44. In addition to Stigler, supra note 42, see, e.g., Sam Peltzman, "Toward a More General Theory of Regulation," *Journal of Law and Economics* 19 (1976): 211; Richard A. Posner, "Theories of Economic Regulation," *Bell Journal of Economics and Management Science* 5 (1974): 335.

45. Posner, supra note 44, is one of the few discussions of Stigler's contribution that calls attention to the similar work of political interest-group writers, including but not limited to "industry-capture" arguments of political scientists. Probably the most notable of the latter school is Marver H. Bernstein, *Regulating Business by Independent Commission* (Princeton: Princeton University Press, 1955).

46. The difficulty of forming coherent and effective groups on a broad basis is preeminently a problem of free riding. Essentially, the benefits of broad-based, group action are a kind of public good that cannot be withheld from those who do not pay to produce it. This obviously undermines individual incentives to join or support such groups. See Mancur Olson, *The Logic of Collective Action: Public Goods and the Theory of Groups* (Cambridge, Mass.: Harvard University Press, 1965).

47. William Riker and Steven Brams, "The Paradox of Vote Trading," *American Political Science Review* 67 (1973): 1235.

48. See, e.g., David R. Mayhew, *Congress: The Electoral Connection* (New Haven: Yale University Press, 1974); Morris P. Fiorina, *Congress: Keystone of the Washington Establishment* (New Haven: Yale University Press, 1977); Anthony Downs, *Inside Bureaucracy* (Boston: Little, Brown, 1967).

49. See, e.g., Joseph P. Kalt and Mark A. Zupan, "Capture and Ideology in the Economic Theory of Politics," *American Political Science Review* 74 (1984): 279.

50. See, e.g., William A. Niskanen, *Bureaucracy and Representative Government* (Chicago: Aldine-Atherton, 1971).

51. John K. Galbraith, *The New Industrial State* (Boston: Houghton Mifflin, 1967), 212–15.

52. For a general political analysis of recent deregulatory measures (focusing on airline, trucking, and telecommunications deregulation), see Martha Derthick and Paul J. Quirk, *The Politics of Deregulation* (Washington, D.C.: Brookings, 1985).

53. The airline deregulation story is narrated in Derthick and Quirk, supra note 52, and in Michael E. Levine, "Revisionism Revised? Airline Deregulation and the Public Interest," *Law and Contemporary Problems* 44 (1981): 179.

54. The basic deregulatory moves in telecommunications are summarized in Glen O. Robinson, "The Titanic Remembered: AT&T and the Changing World of Telecommunications," *Yale Journal on Regulation* (1988): 517. For mass communica-

tions there is no single source. The main initiatives, in cable television, are reported in Stanley M. Besen and Robert W. Crandall, "The Deregulation of Cable Television," *Law and Contemporary Problems* 44 (1981): 77.

55. See Derthick and Quirk, supra note 52; Thomas G. Moore, "Rail and Truck Reform—The Record So Far," *Regulation* (November/December, 1983): 33.

56. See Ronald R. Braeutigam, "The Deregulation of Natural Gas," and W. David Montgomery, "Decontrol of Crude Oil Prices," both in *Case Studies in Regulation: Revolution and Reform*, ed. Leonard W. Weiss and Michael W. Klass (Boston: Little, Brown, 1981), 142, 187.

57. Cutbacks in antitrust enforcement have reflected a major shift in legal and economic thinking about antitrust policies and priorities, particularly a turning away from the populist, small-business orientation of antitrust policy of the 1950s and 1960s. See, generally, Herbert Hovenkamp, "Antitrust Policy after Chicago," *Michigan Law Review* 84 (1985): 213. In part it also reflects changes in economic circumstances: the economic internationalization of markets and, hence, of competition has diminished the importance of domestic trade activities, such as mergers, that once were a major occupation of antitrust laws.

58. The FTC's near shutdown in 1980 was a product of congressional dissatisfaction with its performance (most importantly, some of its recent ventures into regulating "unfair" practices) and the Reagan administration's dissatisfaction with its existence. In the end Congress, responding particularly to small business interests, rescued it. See Stanley E. Cohen and Richard L. Gordon, "How FTC Escaped Stockman Ax," *Advertising Age*, March 9, 1981, 1, 74. The CPSC was also on the Reagan administration's list for elimination in 1981, but the agency survived, albeit with a reduced budget. See Michael deCourey Hinds, "Consumer Product Agency: Small but Busy," *New York Times*, April 30, 1983, 17.

59. The obvious tension between deregulation on the one hand and modern positive political theories of regulation (along the lines summarized above) on the other is explored by Levine, supra note 53, in the context of airline deregulation and noted by Derthick and Quirk, supra note 52, in the context of airline, trucking, and telecommunications. In a sense, the tension is symbolized by Levine himself. As a top level staff member at the CAB he played a key role in deregulating airlines "in the public interest"; before that he was an academic student of regulation and of public choice theories that stress the private interest bases underlying regulation. I should, at this point, acknowledge having had a somewhat similar experience as an academic and a regulator (an FCC commissioner in the mid-1970s). Unlike Levine, I could not quite describe what I observed at the FCC as public interestedness, but I agree with him that the fact of deregulation is very difficult to reconcile with modern political theories of regulation.

60. 90 Stat. 1038 (1985). The act originally gave the Comptroller General, an agent of Congress, authority to determine whether deficit reduction targets were met. After this was declared unconstitutional as an invasion of executive prerogatives (Bowsher v. Synar, 478 U.S. 714 [1986]), Congress transferred the authority to OMB.

61. On the accounting manipulations, see Peter Milius, "Cooked Books," *Washington Post*, April 24, 1989, A11.

62. Omnibus Budget Reconciliation Act of 1990, 104 Stat. 1388 (1990).

63. See Anne Wexler, "Son of Gramm-Rudman," *Washington Post*, October 28, 1990, C7.

64. See Jon Elster, *Ulysses and the Sirens* (Cambridge: Cambridge University Press, 1979), 36–111; Thomas C. Schelling, "The Intimate Contest for Self-Command," *Public Interest* 60 (1980): 94.

65. On the classic republican tradition, see J. G. A. Pocock, *The Machiavellian Moment: Florentine Political Thought and the Atlantic Republican Tradition* (Princeton: Princeton University Press, 1975); the essential elements of civic republicanism are summarized in Gordon S. Wood, *The Creation of the American Republic, 1776–1787* (New York: Norton, 1972), 49–75.

66. See, e.g., Roberto Mangabeira Unger, *Knowledge and Politics* (New York: Free Press, 1975).

67. A classic defense of "market socialism" is Oscar Lange and Fred M. Taylor, *On the Economic Theory of Socialism* (Minneapolis: University of Minnesota Press, 1938).

68. The radical differences between Hobbes and Locke in regard to political organization often obscure their common ground in basic liberal premises. On this common ground and their divergent paths from it, see Leo Strauss, *Natural Right and History* (Chicago: University of Chicago Press, 1953), 165–251.

69. John Plamenatz, *The English Utilitarians* (Oxford: Basil Blackwell, 1949), explores the development of English utilitarian theory from Hume to Mill and also relates it to the work of Hobbes and Locke. For recent critical perspectives on utilitarianism, particularly as an ethical theory, see Amartya Sen and Bernard Williams, eds., *Utilitarianism and Beyond* (Cambridge: Cambridge University Press, 1982).

70. See, e.g., Charles Taylor, "What's Wrong With Negative Liberty," in *The Idea of Freedom: Essays in Honor of Isaiah Berlin*, ed. Alan Ryan (Oxford: Oxford University Press, 1979), 175–93. The classic liberal defense of negative liberty, challenged by Taylor, is Isaiah Berlin, *Four Essays on Liberty* (Oxford: Oxford University Press, 1969), 118–72. The binary distinction between negative and positive obscures a more elaborate set of different conceptions of freedom. See Richard E. Flathman, *The Philosophy and Politics of Freedom* (Chicago: University of Chicago Press, 1987).

71. It would also call for a rethinking of constitutional principles inasmuch as they are based on these liberal distinctions and priorities. For a lucid discussion, see Louis Michael Seidman, "Public Principle and Private Choice: The Uneasy Case for a Boundary Maintenance Theory of Constitutional Law," *Yale Law Journal* 96 (1987): 1006.

72. John Rawls, *A Theory of Justice* (Cambridge, Mass.: Harvard University Press, 1971).

73. Adam Smith, *The Wealth of Nations*, ed. James E. Rogers (Oxford: Clarendon Press, 1880), 2:272–73.

74. Lionel Robbins, *The Theory of Economic Policy in English Classical Political Economy*, 2d ed. (London: Macmillan, 1978), 37.

75. On Smith's eclecticism, see Jacob Viner, *The Long View and the Short:*

Studies in Economic Theory and Policy (Glencoe: Free Press, 1958), 244: "He saw a wide and elastic range of activity for government and he was prepared to extend it even farther if government, by improving its standards of competence, honesty, and public spirit, showed itself entitled to wider responsibilities."

76. For a good sample of the modern literature of welfare economics, see, e.g., Kenneth J. Arrow and Tibor Scitovsky, eds., *Readings in Welfare Economics* (Homewood, Ill.: Richard D. Irvin, 1969). William J. Baumol, *Welfare Economics and the Theory of the State*, 2d ed. (Cambridge, Mass.: Harvard University Press, 1967) is an important theoretical synthesis that also discusses some of the earlier works in political economy on the scope of the public sector. Among the more lucid and accessible summaries of economic theories of the public sector is Peter O. Steiner, "Public Expenditure Budgeting," in *The Economics of Public Finance*, ed. Alan S. Blinder and Robert M. Solow (Washington, D.C.: Brookings, 1974), 243–82.

77. See A. C. Pigou, *The Economics of Welfare* (London: Macmillan, 1920).

78. Paul A. Samuelson, "Diagrammatic Exposition of a Theory of Public Expenditure," *Review of Economics and Statistics* 37 (1955): 350, "The Pure Theory of Public Expenditures," *Review of Economics and Statistics* 36 (1954): 387. Earlier contributions to the theory are noted by Samuelson and by Steiner, supra note 76 at 264, who observes that the theory might be properly called "the Sax-Wicksell-Lindahl-Musgrave-Bowen-Samuelson . . . tradition, to recognize the apparently valid theorem that no one ever has an original idea."

79. See Steiner, supra note 76 at 250.

80. On this particular example, see the exchange between Jora R. Minasian, "Television Pricing and the Theory of Public Goods," *Journal of Law and Economics* 12 (1964): 11, and Paul A. Samuelson, "Public Goods and Subscription TV: Correction of the Record," ibid. at 81.

81. For a very good, concise discussion of this point using the broadcasting example, see Otto A. Davis and Andrew B. Whinston, "On the Distinction Between Public and Private Goods," *American Economic Review* 57 (1967): 360.

82. Modern discussions of externalities do not necessarily embrace Pigou's choice of corrective measures or even government intervention. See, e.g., James M. Buchanan and William Craig Stubblebine, "Externality," *Economica*, n.s. 29 (1962): 371; Ronald H. Coase, "The Problem of Social Cost," *Journal of Law and Economics* 3 (1960): 1.

83. Pigou reasoned that additional investment in the productive capacity of the poor would produce more social benefits than would equivalent investment in the rich (Pigou, supra note 77). A more sophisticated, modern argument is that wealth redistribution establishing a minimum level of wealth contributes to economic security which, in turn, is a benefit enjoyed by the society as a whole insofar as it contributes to both political and economic stability. An especially insightful treatment of income redistribution as a public good, which also examines other analyses, is William Breit, "Income Redistribution and Efficiency Norms," in *Redistribution Through Public Choice*, ed. Harold M. Hockman and George E. Peterson (New York: Columbia University Press, 1974), 3.

84. 467 U.S. 229 (1984).

85. This is the "minimal rationality" test applied in Williamson v. Lee Optical, 348 U.S. 483 (1955) and other cases.

86. Though the landowners were compensated, by necessary assumption the compensation was less than would have been demanded in an uncoerced market transaction. That, of course, is what eminent domain is all about.

87. See Richard A. Epstein, *Takings: Private Property and the Power of Eminent Domain* (Cambridge, Mass.: Harvard University Press, 1985), 161–62. Epstein complains that the Court's equating the public use requirement of the takings clause with the minimal rationality test applied to the general police power trivializes the former. However, the real problem lies in the minimal rationality test, not in making the public use test coterminous with it. In fact, it would be illogical to make the public use test *more* restrictive than the rationality test. To do so would imply that the power of the state to destroy property rights without compensation, under the police power, is greater than its power to take property with compensation under the eminent domain power.

88. See, e.g., Stigler, supra note 42, and Posner, supra note 44.

89. See George C. Wilson, "Navy Lobbies to Add 2 Carriers," *Washington Post*, March 29, 1987, A5. The strategy was not original with the Navy; the Air Force and the Lockheed Corp. used essentially the same tactic in a 1982 campaign to sell Congress more transport planes.

90. Arrow, supra note 42. Arrow's "impossibility theorem" derives from the well-known voting paradox in which voting cycles can defeat any attempt to aggregate individual preferences into a coherent majority choice. The paradox has been recognized since at least the eighteenth century and has survived recurrent attempts to solve it. For a history, see Duncan Black, *The Theory of Committees and Elections* (Cambridge: Cambridge University Press, 1958).

91. Ironically, Carroll (Charles Dodgson) devised a method that he thought solved the cyclical voting problem that is the heart of the "impossibility" of a democratic social welfare function. See Black, supra note 90 at 224–34.

92. See, e.g., Pocock supra note 65.

93. See Bernard Bailyn, *The Ideological Origins of the American Revolution* (Cambridge, Mass.: Harvard University Press, 1967), 24, 28; Wood, supra note 65 at 6–8.

94. See Wood, supra note 65 at 8.

95. For instance, in the classical version, liberty was seen principally in terms of the right of self-determination in the sense of political participation more than in the sense of individual autonomy outside political society. However, in the American political literature, the two senses of liberty are commonly intermixed in ways that reveal no obvious awareness of the conflict between the two types of liberty. On the two different meanings of liberty, and yet a third meaning associated with institutional balance of power, see Joyce Appleby, *Capitalism and the New Social Order: The Republican Vision of the 1790s* (New York: New York University Press, 1984), 16–22.

96. See Wood, supra note 65 at 606–19.

97. A skeptical view could be supported by the fact that the antifederalists' economic interests nicely reinforced their republican "principles." See Jackson Turner

Main, *The Antifederalists: Critics of the Constitution, 1781–1788* (New York: Norton, 1974), 1–20.

98. The Federalist No. 10, at 78 (J. Madison) (New American Library ed., 1961).

99. See The Federalist No. 51, at 322, 323 (J. Madison). See also The Federalist No. 73 at 441–47 (A. Hamilton). For an extended textual analysis of The Federalist, with particular emphasis to Madison's contributions, see David F. Epstein, *The Political Theory of The Federalist* (Chicago: University of Chicago Press, 1984). On The Federalist views generally, see Wood, supra note 65 at 471–564.

100. See, e.g., Douglas Adair, "The Tenth Federalist Revisited," *William and Mary Quarterly* 8 (1951): 48.

101. Sunstein, supra note 41 at 47. See also Epstein, supra note 99 at 5–9, who emphasizes the professed ambition of The Federalist to preserve the basic principles of republicanism.

102. See Wood, supra note 65 at 505. Wood notes Madison's belief that the new constitutional scheme would be conducive to bringing to power men of merit and broad vision, who would rise above "factious tempers," "local prejudices," or "sinister design." In this belief in aristocratic rule Madison, and the Federalists generally, kept faith with the elitist strain in classical republicanism. See, e.g., Wood, supra note 65 at 70–75; Appleby, supra note 95 at 8–9.

103. On Madison's views, see Wood, supra note 65 at 304.

104. Although the framers' views on this point (nowhere expressed in the Constitution) have been debated, it now is generally accepted that they contemplated some power of judicial review. See, e.g., Alexander M. Bickel, *The Least Dangerous Branch: The Supreme Court at the Bar of Politics* (Indianapolis: Bobbs Merrill, 1962), 14–15. For some of the evidence, see Wood, supra 65 at 453–63 (reviewing contemporary state court decisions and other statements including Hamilton's The Federalist No. 78).

105. See Cecilia M. Kenyon, "Men of Little Faith: The Anti-Federalists on the Nature of Representative Government," *William and Mary Quarterly*, 3d ser., 12 (1955): 3.

106. 5 U.S. (1 Cranch) 137 (1803).

107. See, e.g., Cass R. Sunstein, "Lochner's Legacy," *Columbia Law Review* 87 (1987): 873, criticizing the Supreme Court of the *Lochner* era for taking the common law standards and status quo as a baseline from which to determine constitutional principles.

Chapter 2

1. John Hart Ely, *Democracy and Distrust: A Theory of Judicial Review* (Cambridge, Mass.: Harvard University Press, 1980). For illustrative critiques see, e.g., Mark Tushnet, "Darkness at the Edge of Town: The Contributions of John Hart Ely to Constitutional Theory," *Yale Law Journal* 89 (1980): 1037; Laurence Tribe, "The Puzzling Persistence of Process-Based Constitutional Theories," *Yale Law Journal* 89 (1980): 1063.

2. See, e.g., Sanford Levinson, "The 'Constitution' in American Civil Religion," *Supreme Court Review* (1979): 123. For an incisive criticism of the metaphor and the ideas behind it, see Thomas C. Grey, "The Constitution as Scripture," *Stanford Law Review* 37 (1984): 1.

3. Standard references include Raoul Berger, *Government by Judiciary* (Cambridge, Mass.: Harvard University Press, 1977); Robert Bork, "Neutral Principles and Some First Amendment Problems," *Indiana Law Journal* 47 (1971): 1; Henry Monaghan, "Our Perfect Constitution," *New York University Law Review* 52 (1981): 353.

4. See, e.g., Michael J. Perry, *The Constitution, the Courts, and Human Rights* (New Haven: Yale University Press, 1982); Laurence H. Tribe, *American Constitutional Law*, 2d ed. (Mineola, N.Y.: Foundation Press, 1988), 1302–1435; Harry Wellington, "Common Law Rules and Constitutional Double Standards: Some Notes on Adjudication," *Yale Law Journal* 83 (1973): 221. Citing the foregoing under simple labels such as "fundamental moral principles" or "shared social values" obscures the considerable variation in this vein of constitutional scholarship. For a critical review of the fundamental rights/values perspective, and its critics, see Paul Brest, "The Fundamental Rights Controversy: The Essential Contradictions of Normative Constitutional Scholarship," *Yale Law Journal* 90 (1981): 1063.

5. The terms appear to have been first introduced by Thomas Grey, who has since regretted doing so (see Grey, supra note 2). Grey rightly notes the misleading character of the terms inasmuch as everyone is an interpreter; the differences lie in the degree to which interpretation is seen as an act of creative imagination and how much it is seen as a form of textual exegesis.

6. See Frederick Schauer, "Precedent," *Stanford Law Review* 39 (1987): 571.

7. See John Austin, *Province of Jurisprudence Determined*, 2d ed. (London: John Murray, 1861), 1:5.

8. H. L. A. Hart, *The Concept of Law* (Oxford: Oxford University Press, 1961), 20–25.

9. I do not argue that this legitimacy requires, as Lon Fuller insisted, congruence with some fixed ("natural") moral principles, or merely, in Hart's theory, a "rule of recognition." See Hart, supra note 8; Lon L. Fuller, "Positivism and Fidelity in Law— A Reply to Professor Hart," *Harvard Law Review* 71 (1958): 630. It is noteworthy, however, that Hart, a positivist in the Austinian tradition, and Fuller, an exponent of natural law, both rejected the simple command-compulsion theory of law.

10. For an excellent review of the Court's uses, and misuses, of history, see Charles A. Miller, *The Supreme Court and the Uses of History* (New York: Simon and Schuster, 1972).

11. A fascinating account of the deficiencies in the records of the Constitutional Convention concludes that it would be impossible to reliably derive the intent of the framers from those records. See James H. Hutson, "The Creation of the Constitution: The Integrity of the Documentary Record," *Texas Law Review* 65 (1986): 1.

12. James Madison, Letter to William Cogswell, *The Records of the Federal Convention of 1787*, ed. Max Farrand (New Haven: Yale University Press, 1937), 3: 533.

13. The differences between Federalists and antifederalists on the basic question of national versus state power is only illustrative of divergent interests and ideologies

(which, of course, existed within as well as between these two major groups). For an excellent discussion of these interests and ideologies, see Forrest McDonald, *Novus Ordo Seclorum: The Intellectual Origins of the Constitution* (Lawrence: Kansas University Press, 1985), 57–96, 185–224.

14. An important example is the range of interpretations among the framers about the scope of the contracts clause (art. I, sect. 10). See McDonald, supra note 13 at 270–75; Stephen R. Boyd, "The Contract Clause and the Evolution of American Federalism, 1789–1815," *William and Mary Quarterly*, 3d ser., 44 (1987): 529. See generally, H. Jefferson Powell, "Rules for Originalists," *Virginia Law Review* 73 (1987): 659, 684–87.

15. See H. Jefferson Powell, "The Original Understanding of Original Intent," *Harvard Law Review* 98 (1985): 885.

16. I say this mindful of the fact that, for forty years, the Court took the view that wiretaps and electronic surveillance were not a concern of the Fourth Amendment. See Katz v. United States, 389 U.S. 347 (1967), overruling Olmstead v. United States, 277 U.S. 438 (1928). However, the reason for withholding protection was never grounded on the notion that the framers could not have been familiar with modern surveillance technology.

17. See Monaghan, supra note 3.

18. The volume of the historical literature frustrates any attempt to capture it in a footnote. McDonald, supra note 13 at 57–96, gives an overview of republican and other theoretical influences. Other important references on republican influence include J. G. A. Pocock, *The Machiavellian Moment: Florentine Political Thought and the Atlantic Tradition* (Princeton: Princeton University Press, 1975); Gordon S. Wood, *The Creation of the American Republic, 1776–1787* (New York: Norton, 1972), 49–75; Bernard Bailyn, *The Ideological Origins of the American Revolution* (Cambridge, Mass.: Harvard University Press, 1967). The discovery of republican influence by constitutional law scholars is more recent. Good discussions include Cass Sunstein, "Interest Groups in American Public Law," *Stanford Law Review* 38 (1985): 29; Frank A. Michelman, "The Supreme Court, 1985 Term—Forward: Traces of Self-Government," *Harvard Law Review* 100 (1986): 4. See also "Symposium: The Republican Civic Tradition," *Yale Law Journal* 97 (1988): 1493, featuring lead articles by Michelman and Sunstein and a set of critical commentaries.

19. A recent symposium on Gordon Wood's seminal book, supra note 18, illustrates the character of the controversy. See "Forum," *William and Mary Quarterly*, 3d ser., 44 (1987): 549–640.

20. See Gerald Stourzh, *Alexander Hamilton and the Idea of Republican Government* (Stanford: Stanford University Press, 1970): 38–39. Stourzh notes that even those who opposed monarchial or aristocratic elements nevertheless foresaw an evolution toward them. The constitutional guarantee of a "republican government" was seen by them as more a "holding action" than a permanent barrier to nonrepublican government.

21. On the different political meanings, see Stourzh, supra note 20 at 38–75.

22. On the relationship between American republicanism and the "country" faction of eighteenth-century English Whigs, see Lance Banning, *The Jeffersonian Persuasion: Evolution of a Party Ideology* (Ithaca, N.Y.: Cornell University Press, 1978).

23. See Wood, supra note 18 at 421.

24. The tension between classical republican theory and the social, political, and, above all, economic conditions of America as it developed after the Revolution is explored in Drew R. McCoy, *The Elusive Republic: Political Economy in Jeffersonian America* (New York: Norton, 1980). As McCoy discusses, the conflict between theory and reality did not escape the notice of the leading figures of the time; Franklin, John Adams, Hamilton, and Madison all expressed skepticism, at least, on the possibility of a republic of virtue. Even Jefferson could set aside the classical republican model when political circumstances dictated, as the Louisiana Purchase dramatically shows. See ibid. at 204.

25. Among the most cogent of Jefferson Powell's "rules for originalists," supra note 14 at 672–74, is not to treat historical figures as our contemporaries merely because they use familiar, modern words and phrases. As Powell points out, the framers' discussions of constitutional politics "took place in a thought-world, and were conducted in a political language, distinct from our own" (ibid. at 673). A notorious example of the common disregard of this lesson is the frequent identification of Madison as a progenitor of modern interest-group theory. There is doubtless some kinship between Madison's analysis of factions (most notably in his essay in The Federalist No. 10) and contemporary analysis of interest groups. But the translation of Madison into contemporary terms has resulted in a significant loss of Madison's political conceptions, most notably his republican ideals. See Wood, supra note 18 at 505; Sunstein, supra note 18 at 42.

26. Ronald M. Dworkin, *Law's Empire* (Cambridge, Mass.: Harvard University Press, 1986), 56–59. I do not mean to suggest here that the legal and literary interpretations have the same purpose and effect. Manifestly they do not. See Richard A. Posner, *Law and Literature: A Misunderstood Relation* (Cambridge, Mass.: Harvard University Press, 1988), chap. 5. 1351. I do intend to suggest that, if one is willing to free legal interpretation (constitutional interpretation in particular) from a strict historical environment, Cavell's interpretive technique has strong appeal in the realm of law, no less than in the realm of literature.

27. See Richard Rorty, "The Historiography of Philosophy: Four Genres," in *Philosophy in History*, ed. Richard Rorty, J. B. Schneewind, and Quentin Skinner (Cambridge: Cambridge University Press, 1984), 49–75.

28. A total of fifty-five delegates attended the Constitutional Convention, most of them men of social distinction and privilege—the "ruling class" as Farrand reports (Max Farrand, *The Framing of the Constitution* [New Haven: Yale University Press, 1913], 39).

29. Madison himself, it should be noted, accepted the fact that the Constitution would receive interpretations different from those originally intended and thought that, once publicly accepted, they should not be disturbed. See Powell, supra note 15 at 939–41.

30. See Louis Michael Seidman, "Public Principle and Private Choice: The Uneasy Case for a Boundary Maintenance Theory of Constitutional Law," *Yale Law Journal* 96 (1987): 1006.

31. Alexander M. Bickel, *The Least Dangerous Branch* (Indianapolis: Bobbs-Merrill, 1962), 16.

32. See "Wapner v. Rehnquist: No Contest," *Washington Post*, June 23, 1989, A21. Some 53 percent of the sampled public said they approved of the job the Court was doing, 28 percent disapproved, the rest did not know enough to say. Interestingly, those who knew more about the Court, as shown by their ability to name one or more justice, were more likely to approve of what the Court was doing than the others. It is not reported whether they approved of Judge Wapner's work on "The People's Court."

33. See Richard A. Epstein, *Takings: Private Property and the Power of Eminent Domain* (Cambridge, Mass.: Harvard University Press, 1985).

34. See Hawaii Housing Authority v. Midkiff, 467 U.S. 229 (1984).

35. See, e.g., Epstein, supra note 33 at 161–62; Ellen Frankel Paul, "Public Use: A Vanishing Limitation on Governmental Takings," in *Economic Liberties and the Judiciary*, ed. James A. Dorn and Henry G. Manne (Fairfax, Va.: George Mason University Press, 1987), 357.

36. The verbal distinction is between a use of the general "police power" and a "taking." There are some bright-line rules that stake out the "easy cases" within the scope of one or the other. For instance, physical occupation of property by the government is a taking, Loretto v. Teleprompter Manhattan CATV Corp., 458 U.S. 419 (1982), while interference with property for the purpose of correcting a "nuisance" is not, Hadacheck v. Sebastian, 239 U.S. 394 (1915). However, the vast grey area of regulatory actions that diminish property values in order "to promote the general welfare" continue to be subject to vague criteria such as the degree of diminution in value. As an illustration of the confusion, compare, e.g., First English Evangelical Lutheran Church v. County of Los Angeles, 107 S. Ct. 2378 (1987) (taking) with Keystone Bituminous Coal Ass'n v. DeBenedictis, 107 U.S. 1232 (1987) (no taking). For critical commentary on the Court's recent decisions, from radically different perspectives, see, e.g., Frank Michelman, "Takings, 1987," *Columbia Law Review* 88 (1988): 1600; Richard A. Epstein, "Takings: Descent and Resurrection," *Supreme Court Review* (1987): 1.

37. Some constitutional scholars insist that, as a matter of literal textual exegesis or original intent, due process is purely a procedural concept. See, e.g., Ely, supra note 1 at 18. The textual exegesis seems to me hypertechnical given the latitude now accorded other constitutional provisions; the original intent argument seems similarly wanting for all the reasons discussed earlier. In any event the original intent is anything but clear. Accepted wisdom traces the phrase "due process" to Magna Carta's "law of the land" provision governing court adjudications of life, liberty, and property, and the accepted interpretation of these provisions is that they were not binding on Parliament (see, e.g., Robert P. Reeder, "The Due Process Clauses and 'The Substance of Individual Rights,'" *University of Pennsylvania Law Review* 58 (1910): 191, 214). However, the framers did not accept the basic premise of English constitutionalism, the supremacy of Parliament, which undercuts the assumption that they necessarily accepted the English content of the Magna Carta guarantee by accepting its form.

38. 348 U.S. 483 (1955).

39. On Lochner v. New York, 198 U.S. 45 (1905) and its "era," see Tribe, supra note 4 at 434–49. I place "era" in quotes advisedly. In truth, this activism—which effectively began in 1897 with Allgeyer v. Louisiana, 165 U.S. 578 (1897), and ended in 1937 with West Coast Hotel v. Parrish, 300 U.S. 379 (1937)—was not uniform in its treatment of economic legislation. Most economic legislation was sustained against challenge, and of that which was invalidated, less than half was invalidated under due process. See Tribe, supra note 4 at 435.

40. Corroborative evidence, if any is needed, is found in the fact that the statute also forbade advertising the sale of eyeglasses (and even frames). The Court rejected the due process challenge to this portion of the law, reasoning that regulation of advertising, even of frames, might be thought necessary to effective regulation of the general field of optometry. (This was before the Court discovered a First Amendment interest in commercial advertising in Virginia Pharmacy Board v. Virginia Consumer Council, 425 U.S. 748 [1976]).

41. 336 U.S. 220 (1949).

42. See Gerald Gunther, "Forward: In Search of Evolving Doctrine on a Changing Court: A Model for a Newer Equal Protection," *Harvard Law Review* 86 (1972): 1; Robert G. McCloskey, "Economic Due Process and the Supreme Court: An Exhumation and Reburial," *Supreme Court Review* (1962): 34. Cass Sunstein has argued that, in a clear case, the Court not only should but would overturn legislation that was purely for the private benefit of some narrow group. See Cass Sunstein, "Public Values, Private Interests, and the Equal Protection Clause," *Supreme Court Review* (1982): 127, 133–34. He reasons that the fact that the Court strains to find a *public* rationale or public value for legislation indicates that it would not sustain it where such a rationale or value could not be imagined. Perhaps. However, the key question is whether there are any cases where the Court's imagination is not up to the task of finding such a rationale or value.

43. See, e.g., Richard A. Posner, "Economics, Politics, and the Reading of Statutes and the Constitution," *University of Chicago Law Review* 49 (1982): 263.

44. Gunther, supra note 38.

45. See, e.g., Harold Bruff, "Legislative Formality, Administrative Rationality," *Texas Law Review* 63 (1984): 207, 226 (courts reviewing a particular statute cannot see the overall gains and losses to a given participant); Robert W. Bennett, "'Mere' Rationality in Constitutional Law: Judicial Review and Democratic Theory," *California Law Review* 67 (1979): 1049, 1067–69 (explaining but not endorsing this perspective as an obstacle to judicial review of legislative rationality).

46. 198 U.S. at 75–76 (1905).

47. M. D. Howe, ed., *Holmes-Laski Letters* (Cambridge, Mass.: Harvard University Press, 1953), 1:249.

48. For a sample of literature in this vein, see Jerry L. Mashaw, "Constitutional Deregulation: Notes Toward A Public, Public Law," *Tulane Law Review* 54 (1980): 849. Mashaw urges a criterion of "public regardingness" as a restraint on the use of public power to seek private ends. So, too, does Cass R. Sunstein, "Public Values," supra note 42; Sunstein, "Naked Preferences and the Constitution," *Columbia Law Review* 84 (1984): 1689. In the latter article, Sunstein appeals explicitly to the ideal of republicanism (civic virtue) and to the associated notion of deliberative politics as a

counter to interest-group pluralism. See also his later defense of republican ideals against liberal pluralism in "Interest Groups," supra note 18, and "Lochner's Legacy," *Columbia Law Review* 87 (1987): 873. A similar treatment of the conflict between interest-group pluralism and the republican ideal of civic virtue is Michelman, supra note 18. Richard Stewart argues for a "neutral" liberalism that bars the use of coercive state power to advance particular interests unless they are congruent with a general collective good. See Richard Stewart, "Regulation in a Liberal State: The Role of Non-Commodity Values," *Yale Law Review* 92 (1983): 1537.

49. On the higher law background generally, see Wood, supra note 18 at 273–305; Benjamin F. Wright, *American Interpretations of Natural Law* (Cambridge, Mass.: Harvard University Press, 1931), 1–148; Thomas C. Grey, "Origins of the Unwritten Constitution: Fundamental Law in American Revolutionary Thought," *Stanford Law Review* 30 (1978): 843; Edward S. Corwin, "The Higher Law Background of American Constitutional Law," *Harvard Law Review* 42 (1928): 149 and (1929): 265.

50. Calder v. Bull, 3 U.S. (3 Dall.) 386, 388 (1798). For similar judicial appeals to natural law in early cases, see Wright, supra note 49 at 293–99.

51. See Sunstein, "Lochner's Legacy," supra note 48, arguing that Lochnerian premises persist throughout constitutional law insofar as it is centered on the protection of certain "baseline" private rights that are fundamental and politically neutral (that is, anterior to positive law).

52. Griswold v. Connecticut, 381 U.S. 479 (1965).

53. Meyer v. Nebraska, 262 U.S. 390 (1923).

54. Ibid. at 399.

55. Pierce v. Society of Sisters, 268 U.S. 510 (1925).

56. It was abandoned insofar as the Court no longer treated the rational basis test as a meaningful limitation on legislative choices. See Williamson v. Lee Optical Co., 348 U.S. 483 (1955).

57. Griswold v. Connecticut, 381 U.S. 479 (1965). While Justice Douglas's opinion rests on "emanations" from the First, Third, Fourth, Fifth (self incrimination, not due process), and Ninth Amendments, Justice Goldberg, joined by the Chief Justice and Justice Brennan, accepted due process as the basis of the decision. So, too, Justices Harlan and White, in separate concurring opinions, acknowledged due process as the proper ground for the privacy right. Justices Black and Stewart, dissenting, both understood the case to be a revival of substantive due process à la *Lochner*.

58. Roe v. Wade, 410 U.S. 113 (1973). Justice Blackmun's opinion for the Court tracks Justice Douglas's opinion in *Griswold* in citing various provisions of the Bill of Rights as supporting a right of privacy, but it does recognize that the privacy right is textually grounded in the due process clause.

59. Moore v. East Cleveland, 431 U.S. 494 (1977). Justice Powell, writing for the Court, expressed the usual concern about reviving *Lochner* but emphasized that "appropriate limits on substantive due process come not from drawing arbitrary lines but rather from careful 'respect for the teachings of history [and] solid recognition of the basic values that underlie our society'" (ibid. at 503). Even Justice White, dissenting to the Court's decision, conceded that substantive due process had some role to play in constitutional review.

60. Bowers v. Hardwick, 478 U.S. 186 (1986). In *Bowers*, Justice White, for a majority of the Court, followed his opinion in *Moore* (supra note 59) about narrowly circumscribing substantive due process; the so-called privacy right was thus confined to matters of "family, marriages, or procreation," and did not embrace sexual activity. It is important to emphasize, however, that his opinion is addressed to the question of whether private sexual activity is a fundamental right that requires "strict scrutiny"; it was conceded that the law still required a "rational basis" (which the Court, following its usual pattern, found without difficulty).

61. See Webster v. Reproductive Health Services, 109 S.Ct. 3040 (1989). On the controversy over *Webster* see, e.g., Clare Collins, "Drawing up Sides in the Abortion Fight," *New York Times*, August 27, 1989, § 12CN at 1; "The Fearful Politics of Abortion," *Economist*, July 8, 1989: 21.

62. On this point, Ely's critique is powerful, even if his alternative conception of constitutionalism is unpersuasive. See Ely, supra note 1 at 43–72.

63. If one needed concrete evidence, the public controversy over the *Webster* case, supra note 61, supplies it.

64. Ely, supra note 1.

65. 304 U.S. 144, 152 n.4 (1938).

66. For a splendid analysis of the political background of the legislation, see Geoffrey P. Miller, "The True Story of Carolene Products," *Supreme Court Review* (1987): 397.

67. Ibid. at 399.

68. Judge Hans Linde has argued that legislatures are bound by some standards in Hans Linde, "Due Process of Lawmaking," *Nebraska Law Review* 55 (1976): 197, 222–51. However, apart from procedural requirements and standards for "legitimate lawmaking" (ibid. at 228–29), he is hard-pressed to identify any particular requirements other than the formal mechanics for enacting laws. The kinds of due process formalities required of courts and agencies are not binding on legislatures, as Linde concedes. See Ernest Gellhorn and Glen O. Robinson, "Rulemaking Due Process: An Inconclusive Dialogue," *University of Chicago Law Review* 48 (1981): 201, 222–26.

69. See McCloskey, supra note 42 at 50.

70. Bruce A. Ackerman, "Beyond *Carolene Products*," *Harvard Law Review* 98 (1985): 713, 719–31.

71. Ackerman, supra note 70 at 740–44, correctly notes that Justice Stone's emphasis on prejudice is precisely antithetical to process as pluralist bargaining in the manner endorsed by Ely. Ackerman points to Stone's acknowledgment of other "specific" prohibitions in the Constitution as a partial recognition of the role of substantive values in constitutional review.

72. Sunstein, "Lochner's Legacy," supra note 48.

73. Most of the bakers' unions already had comparable protection in their union contracts. The only bakers affected were the small, nonunionized bakeries, many of them employing immigrant bakers who, according to union rhetoric (much of it socialist), were "exploited." See Sidney G. Tarrow, "Lochner Versus New York: A Political Analysis," *Labor History* 5 (1964): 277, for a review of the political background of the New York bakery legislation.

74. See Mashaw, supra note 48 at 867.

75. See Bennett, supra note 45 at 1070.

76. Sunstein, "Naked Preferences,", supra note 48.

77. Epstein, supra note 33.

78. See Michelman, supra note 18.

79. For a philosophical perspective along these lines, see Richard Rorty, *Philosophy and the Mirror of Nature* (Princeton: Princeton University Press, 1979).

80. Grey, supra note 2.

81. Ibid. at 24.

82. Robert Browning, "Caliban Upon Setebos," *The Complete Poetical Works of Browning* (Cambridge, Mass.: Houghton Mifflin, 1897), 392.

83. The point is succinctly and ably argued by Richard A. Epstein, "Judicial Review: Reckoning on Two Kinds of Error," in *Economic Liberties and the Judiciary*, ed. James A. Dorn and Henry G. Manne (Fairfax, Va.: George Mason University Press, 1987), 39.

84. Schad v. Borough of Mount Ephraim, 452 U.S. 61 (1981) invalidated a local ordinance prohibiting commercial live entertainment, applied to coin-operated shows of live nude dancers behind a glass panel.

85. See McCloskey, supra note 42 at 53.

86. See Herbert Hovenkamp, "The Political Economy of Substantive Due Process," *Stanford Law Review* 40 (1988): 379.

87. Mancur Olson, *The Rise and Decline of Nations: Economic Growth, Stagflation, and Social Regulation* (New Haven: Yale University Press, 1982).

88. In budgetary terms, *entitlement programs* are not subject to annual appropriation. Politically, the term has a much wider compass, including all welfare programs. I use the term in the latter sense.

89. Theft, monopoly, and other rent-seeking behaviors all fall into this category of economic inefficiency insofar as they involve the wasteful consumption of resources to both effect the transfer and resist it. See, e.g., Richard P. Posner, "The Social Costs of Monopoly and Regulation," *Journal of Political Economy* 83 (1975): 807; Gordon Tullock, "The Welfare Costs of Monopolies and Thefts," *Western Economic Journal* 5 (1967): 224. No doubt theft stands apart from mere rent-seeking in the universality and the intensity with which we condemn it. But the moral distinction between simple theft and legislatively empowered wealth transfers depends critically, I think, on an assumption that the latter is legitimated by something beyond mere vote counts.

Chapter 3

1. Although the delegation doctrine issue has been associated with agency rule making as distinct from adjudication, there is no necessary connection to the form in which the agency chooses to exercise its delegated power. If a particular delegation of power to, say, the FTC were deemed to be so broad and unrestricted as to be unconstitutional (under Art. I, which vests legislative power in Congress), it would make no difference whether the FTC exercised that power by rule making or by adjudication. Agency adjudications might create a separate problem of delegation insofar as it gave judicial powers to a nonjudicial tribunal in supposed violation of Art. III, vesting the judicial power in the courts. However, the latter concern has been moribund since Crowell v. Benson, 285 U.S. 22 (1932) (adjudication of "public rights" involves no exclusively Art. III authority; for "private rights" Art. III requires only that the "essen-

tial attributes of the judicial power" be retained by courts). Despite a brief revival of pre-*Crowell* doctrine the Court has signaled that *Crowell*'s permissive, functional test remains intact. See Commodity Futures Trading Commission v. Schor, 478 U.S. 833 (1986). See generally, Richard H. Fallon, Jr., "Of Legislative Courts, Administrative Agencies, and Article III," *Harvard Law Review* 101 (1988): 916.

2. See Gordon S. Wood, *The Creation of the American Republic, 1776–1787* (New York: Norton, 1972), 388–89.

3. For Locke's formulation, see John Locke, *Two Treatises of Government*, ed. Peter Laslett, rev. ed. (Cambridge: Cambridge University Press, 1963), 408. For a brief discussion of the common law rule, see Louis L. Jaffe, *Judicial Control of Administrative Action*, abridged ed. (Boston: Little, Brown, 1965), 54.

4. After years of neglect, the delegation question has inspired a large modern literature. Pertinent legal doctrine and commentary is critically reviewed in Peter H. Aranson, Ernest Gellhorn, and Glen O. Robinson, "A Theory of Legislative Delegation," *Cornell Law Review* 68 (1982): 1. Half of a recent symposium, "The Uneasy Constitutional States of the Administrative Agencies," *American University Law Review* 36 (1987): 277, is devoted to exploring the pros and cons of restraints on the delegation of power.

5. J. W. Hampton, Jr. & Co. v. United States, 276 U.S. 394 (1928).

6. See New York Central Sec. Corp. v. United States, 287 U.S. 12 (1932) (ICC); Federal Radio Commission v. Nelson Bros. Co., 289 U.S. 266 (1933) (FRC, later the FCC); FTC v. R. F. Keppel & Bro., 291 U.S. 304 (1934) (FTC).

7. Panama Refining Co. v. Ryan, 293 U.S. 388 (1935).

8. A. L. A. Schechter Poultry Corp. v. United States, 295 U.S. 495 (1935).

9. Carter v. Carter Coal Co., 298 U.S. 238 (1936).

10. Ibid. at 311.

11. Yakus v. United States, 321 U.S. 414 (1944).

12. Ibid. at 424–26.

13. However, under state constitutions, state courts have sometimes employed the delegation principle to invalidate legislation. See, e.g., Chapel v. Commonwealth 197 Va. 406, 89 S.E. 2d 337 (1955); State Bd. of Dry Cleaners v. Thrift-D-Lux Cleaners, Inc., 40 Cal. 2d 436, 254 P. 2d 29 (1953).

14. Noteworthy examples of the occasional invocation of the delegation doctrine are the following: Industrial Union Dept. v. American Petroleum Inst., 448 U.S. 607 (1980) (opinion for the Court cites *Schechter* and *Panama* as reason for giving a narrow interpretation of broad agency power technique in order to avoid possibility of a delegation problem); American Textile Mfrs. Inst. v. Donovan, 452 U.S. 490, 547–48 (1981) (dissent by Justice Rehnquist arguing for invalidation of Occupational Safety and Health Act on delegation grounds because of absence of clear, limiting guidelines to OSHA); Arizona v. California, 373 U.S. 546, 603 (1963) (dissent by Justice Harlan, joined by Justices Douglas and Stewart, arguing for invalidation of law giving to the Secretary of the Interior sweeping power to allocate Colorado River water rights).

15. See, e.g., Industrial Union Dep't. v. American Petroleum Inst., 448 U.S. 607 (1980).

16. See, e.g., Arizona v. California, 373 U.S. 546 (1963); United States v.

Southwestern Cable Co., 392 U.S. 157 (1968). See generally Kenneth C. Davis, "A New Approach to Delegation," *University of Chicago Law Review* 36 (1969): 713.

17. INS v. Chadha, 462 U.S. 919 (1983).

18. Particularly useful critiques of *Chadha* include E. Donald Elliott, "INS v. Chadha: The Administrative Constitution, the Constitution, and the Legislative Veto," *Supreme Court Review* (1983): 125; Harold H. Bruff, "Legislative Formality, Administrative Rationality," *Texas Law Review* 63 (1984): 207; Peter L. Strauss, "Was There a Baby in the Bathwater? A Comment on the Supreme Court's Legislative Veto Decision," *Duke Law Journal*, 1983, 789.

19. 462 U.S. 919, 953 n.16.

20. Elliott, supra note 18 at 146, comments on the Lewis Carroll–like quality of the Court's treatment of lawmaking versus rule making.

21. In favor of some revival of constitutional restraint on broad delegations, see, e.g., Theodore J. Lowi, *The End of Liberalism: The Second Republic of the United States*, 2d ed. (New York: Norton, 1979), 300; Aranson, Gellhorn, and Robinson, supra note 4; J. Skelly Wright, "Beyond Discretionary Justice," *Yale Law Review* 81 (1972): 575; David Schoenbrod, "The Delegation Doctrine: Could the Court Give It Substance?" *Michigan Law Review* 83 (1985): 1223. See also the dissenting and concurring opinions referenced in note 14 supra. Against constitutional restraint on delegation, see, e.g., Jerry L. Mashaw, "Prodelegation: Why Administrators Should Make Political Decisions," *Journal of Law, Economics, and Organization* 5 (1985): 81; Richard B. Stewart, "Beyond Delegation Doctrine," *American University Law Review* 36 (1987): 323; Richard J. Pierce, Jr., "Political Accountability and Delegated Power: A Response to Professor Lowi," *American University Law Review* 36 (1987): 391.

22. Lowi, supra note 21 at 300.

23. Davis, supra note 16 at 713–29.

24. Woodrow Wilson, "The Study of Administration," *Political Science Quarterly* 2 (1887): 197, 214.

25. A contemporary argument in this vein is that of Bruce A. Ackerman and William T. Hassler, *Clean Coal/Dirty Air* (New Haven: Yale University Press, 1981), 4–12, 122–23.

26. On the role of casework see, e.g, David R. Mayhew, *Congress: The Electoral Connection* (New Haven: Yale University Press, 1974), 54–59; Morris P. Fiorina, *Congress: Keystone of the Washington Establishment* (New Haven: Yale University Press, 1977), 41–49.

27. On the strategy of ambiguity, see Morris P. Fiorina, "Legislative Choice of Regulatory Forms: Legal Process or Administrative Process?" *Public Choice* 39 (1982): 33.

28. See Fiorina, supra note 26; Morris P. Fiorina and Roger G. Noll, "Voters, Bureaucrats, and Legislators: A Rational Choice Perspective on the Growth of Bureaucracy," *Journal of Public Economics* 9 (1978): 239.

29. This is the central theme of the argument in Aranson, Gellhorn, and Robinson, supra note 4. A similar theme is implicit, in a more general fashion, in Lowi's critique inasmuch as he regards delegation to agencies as the central mechanism of "interest-group-liberalism." See Lowi, supra note 21 at 92–126.

30. On the basic episode of cable regulation, see Stanley M. Besen and Robert W. Crandall, "The Deregulation of Cable Television," *Law and Contemporary Problems* 44 (1981): 77.

31. For a critique of OSHA's performance, particularly its refusal to consider cost effectiveness in promulgating safety standards, see Albert Nichols and Richard Zeckhauser, "OSHA after a Decade: A Time for Reason," in *Case Studies in Regulation: Revolution and Reform*, ed. Leonard W. Weiss and Michael W. Klass (Boston: Little, Brown, 1981), 202.

32. On standards of identity generally, see the excellent critique in Richard A. Merrill and Earl M. Collier, Jr., "'Like Mother Used to Make': An Analysis of FDA Food Standards of Identity," *Columbia Law Review* 74 (1974): 561. Merrill and Collier are fairly charitable toward food standardization in that they give primary attention to their effects and inefficiency, inter alia their suppression of competitive innovation; they only incidentally notice that suppression of competition is a major objective of food standards sought by dominant or established firms as a curb on new product competition.

33. See Mashaw, supra note 21.

34. See, e.g., Motor Vehicle Mfrs. Ass'n. v. State Farm Mutual Automobile Ins. Co., 463 U.S. 29 (1983). Ordinary judicial review is examined in chapter 5.

35. In addition to *Chadha*, supra note 17, see Bowsher v. Synar, 478 U.S. 919 (1986) (exercise of executive functions by Comptroller General, an officer of Congress, unconstitutional); Northern Pipeline Constr. Co. v. Marathon Pipe Line Co., 458 U.S. 50 (1982) (adjudication of "private rights" by non-Art. III tribunal unconstitutional). This is not to suggest that the Court has been single-minded about separation of powers. Compare, e.g., *Bowsher* with Morrison v. Olson, 108 S. Ct. 2597 (1988) (exercise of investigative and prosecutorial powers by independent counsel constitutional). See generally Harold J. Krent, "Separating the Strands in Separation of Powers Controversies," *Virginia Law Review* 74 (1988): 1253.

36. Quoted in E. Pendleton Herring, *Public Administration and the Public Interest* (New York: McGraw-Hill, 1936), 12.

37. See Max Weber, "Bureaucracy," in *From Max Weber: Essays on Sociology*, ed. H. H. Gerth and C. Wright Mills (New York: Oxford University Press, 1958), 196–244; Herbert A. Simon, *Administrative Behavior*, 3d ed. (New York: Free Press, 1976).

38. See Anthony Downs, *Inside Bureaucracy* (Boston: Little, Brown, 1967).

39. See Simon, supra note 37 at xxxi. The word denotes a deliberate strategy of choosing suboptimal, but acceptable, objectives in contrast to the economist's model of maximization.

40. Downs, supra note 38 at 24–25.

41. See generally "Developments in the Law—Public Employment," *Harvard Law Review* 97 (1984): 1611, 1619–76; Hugh Heclo, *A Government of Strangers: Executive Politics in Washington* (Washington: Brookings, 1977).

42. Woodrow Wilson's own statement is an example. Responding to the possible objection that a professional civil service might become an "offensive official class," Wilson wrote:

The ideal for us is a civil service cultural and self-sufficient enough to act with sense and vigor, and yet so intimately connected with the popular thought, by means of elections and constant public counsel, as to find arbitrariness or class spirit quite out of the question. (supra note 24 at 217)

43. See Ludwig von Mises, *Bureaucracy* (New Haven: Yale University Press, 1944), 48–49.

44. On the principal-agent problem in private firms, see, e.g., Michael C. Jensen and William H. Meckling, "Theory of the Firm: Managerial Behavior, Agency Costs, and Ownership Structure," *Journal of Financial Economics* 3 (1976): 305; Eugene F. Fama, "Agency Problems and the Theory of the Firm," *Journal of Political Economy* 88 (1980): 288. In the public sector, the problem is typically discussed in the context of congressional control of agencies, which I will discuss subsequently. It is essentially an extension of the more general political problem that Buchanan and Tullock label "external costs" in their famous treatment of the costs of political action. See James Buchanan and Gordon Tullock, *The Calculus of Consent* (Ann Arbor: University of Michigan Press, 1962), chap. 6.

45. For a typical critique of the rational choice model in political science, see Robert T. Golembiewski, "A Critique of 'Democratic Administration' and Its Supporting Ideation," *American Political Science Review* 71 (1977): 1488. Criticism of rational choice models is not confined to its use in political science. Its use in mainstream economic theory (where it is virtually an article of faith) has also been criticized for its excessive stylization in dealing with complex economic behavior. See, e.g., Mark Blaug, *The Methodology of Economics* (Cambridge: Cambridge University Press, 1980), passim, especially 240–49 (critique of Gary Becker's application of economic models to nonmarket choices).

46. William A. Niskanen, *Bureaucracy and Representative Government* (Chicago: Aldine-Atherton, 1971), 38–39.

47. See William J. Baumol, "On the Theory of the Expansion of the Firm," *American Economic Review* 52 (1962): 1078.

48. Downs, for example, presents a rather elaborate typology of bureaucratic preferences and motives (Downs, supra note 38 at 88–111). On a less theoretical level, bureaucratic behavior is catalogued in Hugh Heclo, *A Government of Strangers* (Washington, D.C.: Brookings, 1977). See also James Q. Wilson, *Bureaucracy* (New York: Basic Books, 1989), chap. 4 (ideological beliefs, experience, and professional norms).

49. See Joseph P. Kalt and Mark A. Zupan, "Capture and Ideology in the Economic Theory of Politics," *American Economic Review* 74 (1984): 279, discussing such altruistic interests among legislators.

50. The precise meaning of *independent* has never been clearly defined. The Supreme Court has told us only that independent agency members, unlike other presidentially appointed officers of the United States, do not sit at the pleasure of the president and thus may not be removed without cause (Humphrey's Executor v. United States, 295 U.S. 602 [1935]). Whether this implies that the independent agency is beyond presidential control of policy choices is debated. See Geoffrey P. Miller, "Independent Agencies," *Supreme Court Review* (1986): 41, 94. Probably not much turns on the formal legal power, however, for there are other ways of indirect influence, through the power of appointment, budgets, and simply informal persuasion.

See Glen O. Robinson, "On Reorganizing the Independent Regulatory Agencies," *Virginia Law Review* 57 (1971): 917, 950–52; Harold W. Bruff, "Presidential Power and Administrative Rulemaking," *Yale Law Journal* 88 (1979): 451. While these means are not always used effectively by presidents to influence independent agency policy, that much is true of executive agencies as well. As a practical matter, both the character and the degree of control is the same for independent and executive agencies. See Glen O. Robinson, "Independent Agencies: Form and Substance in Executive Prerogative," *Duke Law Journal* (1988): 101.

51. Quoted in Richard Harris, *The Real Voice* (New York: Macmillan, 1964), i.

52. Pendleton Herring put it less delicately: "The 'voice of the people' sometimes suggests the squeal of pigs at the trough." Herring, supra note 36 at 3.

53. David B. Truman, *The Governmental Process*, 2d ed. (New York: Alfred A. Knopf, 1971), 65.

54. The tendency of commentators to associate "capture" with regulatory agencies may reflect the fact that these agencies have received more critical attention than other agencies, and also the fact that finding a capture relationship has more critical punch in a context in which agency and client are supposed, by the classical theory of regulation, to have an adversarial relationship. Be that as it may, the phenomenon of agency-industry alliance is scarcely unique to regulation or regulatory agencies, as any examination of the departments of Agriculture, Commerce, and Labor, and their nonregulatory (as well as regulatory) programs reveals.

55. Marver Bernstein, *Regulating Business by Independent Commission* (Princeton: Princeton University Press, 1955), 74–102.

56. See Glen O. Robinson, "The Federal Communications Commission: An Essay on Regulatory Watchdogs," *Virginia Law Review* (1978): 169, 189–93.

57. For Stigler's theory, see George Stigler, "The Theory of Economic Regulation," *Bell Journal of Economics and Management Science* 2 (1971): 3. Truman's classic work is cited supra note 53; Latham's key work is Earl Latham, *The Group Basis of Politics* (Ithaca: Cornell University Press, 1952).

58. An excellent history and critique of cable regulation is Stanley M. Besen and Robert W. Crandall, "The Deregulation of Cable Television," *Law and Contemporary Problems* 44 (1981): 77.

59. See Inquiry into the Economic Relationship between Television Broadcasting and Cable Television, 71 F.C.C. 2d 632 (1979), *affirmed sub. nom.*; Malrite T.V. of New York v. FCC, 652 F. 2d 1140 (2d. Cir. 1981), *cert. denied*, 454 U.S. 1143 (1982). The commission recently reneged on part of its 1979 opinion dealing with the carriage of syndicated programs. Essentially what it did was to provide a form of regulatory enforcement for copyright exclusivity provisions between program producers and local broadcast stations. See Program Exclusivity in the Cable and Broadcast Industries, 3 F.C.C. Rcd 5229 (1988), *on reconsid.*, 4 F.C.C. Rcd 2711 (1989), *affirmed sub. nom.*, United Video, Inc. v. FCC, 890 F.2d 1173 (D.C. Cir. 1989).

60. The FCC has recurrently expressed concern about network "dominance" of television programming, and promulgated various regulations ostensibly designed to enhance the role of non-network program supply. See generally Stanley M. Besen, Thomas G. Krattenmaker, A. Richard Metzger, Jr., and John R. Woodberry, *Mis-*

regulating Television: Network Dominance and the FCC (Chicago: University of Chicago Press, 1984).

61. Niskanen treats influence as a function of budget. This is too often incorrect to be a valid rule. In any case, it is clearly possible to increase influence very substantially without a major budget increase. One way of doing so is to do what the FCC did with cable: enact a regulatory program of fearsome complexity that requires constant referral to the agency for interpretation. Whether or not increasing the bureaucrat's control over rule interpretation expands the agency's budget according to Niskanen's law, it plainly does increase its effective sphere of influence—an end to which budget expansion is a mere means. For a highly technical "proof" of the bureaucratic tendency to promote rule complexity, see Richard E. Quandt, "Complexity in Regulation," *Journal of Public Economics* 22 (1983): 199. Quandt's argument proceeds simply from the divergence of bureaucratic and private preferences in regard to rule simplicity; it does not hypothesize any bureaucratic power function, as I have suggested.

62. See Martha Derthick and Paul J. Quirk, *The Politics of Deregulation* (Washington, D.C.: Brookings, 1985); Michael Levine, "Revisionism Revised? Airline Deregulation and the Public Interest," *Law and Contemporary Problems* 44 (1981): 179.

63. Derthick and Quirk, supra note 62, offer a detailed account of deregulation in the airline, trucking, and telecommunications fields in an attempt to explain how deregulation occurred in cases where accepted political theory (and common nontheoretical observation) indicated it could not. In each field, deregulation succeeded despite the fact that it enjoyed no well-organized political constituency, and was strongly opposed by industry (in the case of the airlines, some airlines did ultimately switch from their initial opposition to support, by which time it probably was not needed). Too, in defiance of conventional "laws" of bureaucratic behavior, in at least two instances—airlines and telecommunications—deregulation was instigated by the agencies. In the airlines case, the agency's initiatives were reinforced by presidential and congressional support, and were finally ratified by legislation. In the case of telecommunications, however, presidential encouragement was negligible and congressional support was uneven (the FCC did have substantial support from its oversight subcommittee in the House, but there was active opposition in other quarters); the deregulation measures have never been ratified by legislation. Derthick and Quirk's explanation of these deregulatory episodes is essentially an accurate account of what happened. It is not, I think, useful in understanding the puzzle of deregulation in theoretical terms. Their account relies heavily on personal narratives by involved parties, which tend to be anecdotal and somewhat simplistic, or at least incomplete, as explanations for the phenomena under study.

64. On the rules regulating transmission of syndicated programs see note 59 supra. On recent congressional efforts to lift restrictions on local regulation see "Last Rites for a Cable Bill," *Broadcasting*, October 22, 1990, 33–34.

65. The deregulation movement in telecommunications is reviewed in Glen O. Robinson, "The Titanic Remembered: AT&T and the Changing World of Telecommunications," *Yale Journal on Regulation* 5 (1988): 517.

66. 424 U.S. 1 (1976).

67. 478 U.S. 714 (1986).

68. 462 U.S. 919 (1983).

69. See Kendall v. United States, 37 U.S. (12 Pet.) 529 (1837). The president's own constitutional prerogatives in regard to law enforcement may constrain Congress's power to specify the ways and means of presidential enforcement, but that constraint has yet to be defined. For all practical purposes, Congress's power to control policy discretion is subject only to the president's power to veto the legislation that establishes such control. For instance, if Congress, by statute, directs the Department of Transportation to promulgate rules requiring the installation of airbags in automobiles, the president has no prerogative to direct the department to do otherwise. Even where there is a large area of administrative discretion, presidential prerogative is constrained by the outer limits of administrative discretion embedded in the statutory standards. See Motor Vehicle Mfr. Ass'n. v. State Farm Mutual Auto. Ins. Co., 463 U.S. 29 (1983).

70. For excellent, detailed analyses of these prerogatives, see Harold H. Bruff, supra note 50; Peter L. Strauss, "The Place of Agencies in Government: Separation of Powers and the Fourth Branch," *Columbia Law Review* 84 (1984): 573.

71. Niskanen, supra note 46.

72. For a highly theoretical model more or less along these lines, see John Ferejohn and Charles Shipan, "Veto and Congressional Influence on Bureaucracy," *Journal of Law, Economics, and Organization*, 6(1990): 1.

73. Matthew D. McCubbins, Roger G. Noll, and Barry R. Weingast, "Structure and Process, Politics and Policy: Administrative Arrangements and the Political Control of Agencies," *Virginia Law Review* 75 (1989): 431.

74. I give a more detailed critique of the McCubbins, Noll, and Weingast argument in Glen O. Robinson, "Commentary," *Virginia Law Review* 75 (1989): 483.

75. Barry Weingast and Mark Moran, "Bureaucratic Discretion or Congressional Control: Regulatory Policymaking by the Federal Trade Commission," *Journal of Political Economy* 91 (1983): 765. The Weingast and Moran study is criticized by Wilson, supra note 48 at 254–56.

76. See, e.g., Erwin G. Krasnow, Lawrence D. Longley, and Herbert A. Terry, *The Politics of Broadcast Regulation*, 3d ed. (New York: St. Martin's Press, 1982), 88.

77. For a good discussion of the FCC-Congress confrontation on the fairness doctrine and on several other major policy issues, see Paul Starobin, "FCC and Congress Clash Over Proper Roles," *Congressional Quarterly* 46 (1988): 479.

78. Congressional unhappiness with the FTC unfairness program, particularly the FTC's implementation of it through general rule making, led to the enactment of the Federal Trade Commission Improvement Act, 94 Stat. 374, 378 (1980) (codified at 15 U.S.C. § 57(a)(1)). Among other things, the act declared a moratorium on rule making proceedings involving the application of the unfairness doctrine to commercial advertising. It also subjected all agency rules to a legislative veto. The FTC continued to show some resistance to congressional committee preferences on the matter of the unfairness doctrine, as is illustrated by the fact that it forced Congress to exercise its newly enacted veto power to prevent implementation of the agency's politically unpopular used-car trade regulation rules. (The veto was invalidated just after the *Chadha* case. See Consumers Union of U.S., Inc. v. FTC, 691 F. 2d 575 [D.C. Cir. 1982], *aff'd*, 463 U.S. 1216 [1983]).

79. Morris P. Fiorina and Roger G. Noll, "Voters, Legislators, and Bureaucracy: Institutional Design in the Public Sector," *American Economic Review, Papers and Proceedings* 68 (1978): 256. For a more general treatment of congressional-bureaucratic interaction to distribute economic rents, see R. Douglas Arnold, *Congress and the Bureaucracy: A Theory of Influence* (New Haven: Yale University Press, 1979).

80. See Mayhew, supra note 26 at 52–54.

81. See Arnold, supra note 79, which focuses on distributed benefits such as military installations, water, sewer grants, and model cities grants. The bargain model is not necessarily confined to specific distributed benefits; it can be applied to the full gamut of policy or program choices over which agencies and Congress interact.

82. For a general, theoretical discussion of the bargain model and a critique of the Niskanen model, see Cheryl L. Eavey and Gary J. Miller, "Bureaucratic Agency Control: Imposition or Bargaining," *American Political Science Review* 78 (1984): 719.

83. Reagan's "hands-off" style of leadership has been the subject of endless journalistic as well as scholarly commentary, both admiring and critical. See, e.g., Donald T. Regan, *For the Record: From Wall Street to Washington* (New York: Harcourt Brace Jovanovich, 1988); David A. Stockman, *The Triumph of Politics: How the Reagan Revolution Failed* (New York: Harper and Row, 1986). On the contrasting Reagan and Carter styles of management see Stephen Hess, *Organizing the Presidency* (Washington: Brookings, 1988), 140–68; James G. Benze, Jr., *Presidential Power and Management Techniques: The Carter and Reagan Administrations in Historical Perspective* (New York: Greenwood Press, 1987), 55–95.

84. Bradley H. Patterson, *The Ring of Power* (New York: Basic Books, 1988), 60–61.

85. Two interesting cases in point are reported by Patterson, supra note 84 at 138–39. One case involved Solicitor General Irwin Griswold's resistance to White House review of a brief to the Supreme Court in a leading school desegregation case; the other case involved Attorney General Griffin Bell's similar resistance to White House review of Supreme Court briefs. In both instances White House review took place, which leads Patterson to imply that such White House monitoring is successful. In fact, however, the political sensitivity of active White House intervention in pending legal cases usually entails a hands-off attitude whenever there is reason to think that resistance by the officials directly involved would make the intervention public news. This sensitivity is why the White House never directed the Antitrust Division to drop its massive antitrust suit against AT&T in the late 1970s despite the strong opposition to the prosecution by, inter alia, the Defense Department, the Commerce Department, and the president's counsel. They were all acutely aware of the earlier scandal when the White House engineered a settlement of the antitrust case against ITT in return for campaign contributions. See Peter Temin, *The Fall of the Bell System* (Cambridge: Cambridge University Press, 1987), 223–28. The attorney general had recused himself from the case, and the president was obviously unwilling to take the politically delicate responsibility of directing the case to be dropped or settled on "easy" terms. The AT&T case was settled like the earlier ITT case, but this time it was on terms dictated by the head of the Antitrust Division, William Baxter.

86. Patterson, supra note 84 at 339, gives a figure of 568 (as of Fall, 1987) for the White House Office, which provides direct support of the president. A much smaller figure is reported in the official budget, 323 permanent positions in 1988. See Office of Management and Budget, *Budget of the United States Government, Fiscal Year 1990, Appendix* (Washington, D.C.: GPO, 1989), I-C1. The different figures presumably reflect the fact that many of the personnel working in the White House are budgeted outside the White House Office but are detailed to work there (Patterson, supra note 84 at 340). On the problem of White House size and bureaucratization generally, see Hess, supra note 83 at 171–91.

87. On the variation in presidential management styles and organization, see Hess, supra note 83.

88. Weber, supra note 37 at 233.

89. See Heclo, supra note 48 at 143.

90. On presidential influence of independent versus nonindependent agencies see note 50 supra.

91. See Steven Kelman, *Regulating America, Regulating Sweden: A Comparative Study of Occupational Safety and Health* (Cambridge, Mass.: MIT Press, 1981), 94–103.

92. In theory even the threat of presidential intervention, by exercising the veto, should be a constraint on interest groups by raising the costs of effective political coalition. See Harold H. Bruff, supra note 18 at 220. Of course, that threat must be credible, which means the veto must be exercised with some degree of regularity (which, as I will suggest, is precisely the problem).

93. See Bruff, supra note 18 at 233. See also Aranson, Gellhorn, and Robinson, supra note 4 at 41–42, pointing out the similarity between presidential and congressional political incentives in this respect.

94. See Richard P. Nathan, *The Plot That Failed: Nixon and the Administrative Presidency* (New York: Wiley, 1975). Incidentally, the title of Nathan's book is arresting. Characterizing the effort to gain political control over the bureaucracy as a plot suggests a politically nefarious purpose, a characterization hard to reconcile with the fact that the plot followed a landslide electoral victory in 1972.

95. A comprehensive departmental reorganization plan to consolidate domestic programs in four broad areas (in the fashion of Nixon's ill-fated consolidation plan) was vigorously opposed by those cabinet officers who stood to lose programs, as well as by congressional committees who stood to lose oversight responsibility and interest groups who feared loss of political clout. In the face of such opposition, the reorganization plan was dropped. See Benze, supra note 83 at 68–69.

96. In the Nixon administration, a "quality-of-life" review program required agencies to provide OMB with information concerning purposes, costs, and alternatives to regulations pertaining to environmental quality, consumer protection, occupational and public health, and safety. The Ford administration extended this review program to all major agency rules and formalized the review into a cost-benefit analysis (under the rubric of "inflation impact statements"). This review was continued with some changes by the Carter and Reagan administrations and is still in effect in the Bush administration. The program came under heavy congressional attack because of the increased level of OMB scrutiny initiated by the Reagan administration. For a review

of the background and current controversy over the regulatory reviews program, see Richard A. Harris and Sidney M. Milkis, *The Politics of Regulatory Change: A Tale of Two Agencies* (New York: Oxford University Press, 1989), 100–113; Marshall Goodman and Margaret Wrightson, *Managing Regulatory Reform: The Reagan Strategy and Its Impact* (New York: Praeger, 1987), 40–55.

97. See Richard E. Neustadt, *Presidential Power* (New York: Wiley, 1960).

98. For a general discussion of Reagan administration "management," see Benze, supra note 83 at 77–95.

99. For a good general summary see Carol F. Steinback, "Programmed for Plunder," *National Journal* (September 16, 1989): 2259.

100. Former FPC Chairman Lee White explained the process as follows:

A successful lawyer in Keokuk is appointed by the President to serve on an independent regulatory agency or as an assistant secretary of an executive department that exercises regulatory functions. A round of parties and neighborly acclaim surround the new appointee's departure from Keokuk. After the goodbyes, he arrives in Washington and assumes his role as a regulator, believing that he is really a pretty important guy. After all, he almost got elected to Congress from Iowa. But after a few weeks in Washington, he realizes that nobody has ever heard of him or cares much what he does—except one group of very personable, reasonable, knowledgeable, delightful human beings who recognize his true worth. These friendly fellows—all lawyers and officials of the special interest that the agency deals with—provide him with information, views, and most important, love and affection. Except they bite hard when our regulator doesn't follow the light of their wisdom. The cumulative effect is to turn his head a bit.

Quoted in Roger Cramton, "The Why, Where and How of Broadened Public Participation in the Administrative Process," *Georgetown Law Journal* 60 (1972): 525, 530 n. 14. White's engaging account misses one important point: bureaucrats do gravitate toward special interest groups, but they often also withdraw into a shell of bureaucratic insularity that is not necessarily dominated by special interests but may be quite as detrimental to wise public policy.

101. Henry A. Kissinger, *White House Years* (Boston: Little, Brown, 1979), 154. Patterson, supra note 84 at 61–62, cites this incident and others to draw the inference that White House monitoring is effective. I draw a different lesson: it is effective only when extraordinary effort and cost are expended, which almost guarantees that direct monitoring of operational echelons by the president or his immediate staff will be uneven.

102. The number cited here does not include judgeships or part-time members of boards and commissions. See Patterson, supra note 84 at 239–59, for a general breakdown and discussion of the process of finding and filling the positions.

103. In many cases even the patronage value is not obvious. Many of the appointments seem to be decided at a level in the Executive Office that obscures the rationale of the appointment. In any case, it is readily observed that appointments do not reflect any systematic search for persons with the "right stuff." See, e.g., Senate Committee on Commerce, 94th Cong., 2d sess., *Appointments to the Regulatory Agencies* (Washington, D.C.: GPO, 1976), 376.

104. The best survey of affirmance and reversal rates is contained in a recent study by Peter H. Schuck and E. Donald Elliott, "To the Chevron Station: An Empirical Study of Federal Administrative Law," *Duke Law Journal*, forthcoming. The Schuck and Elliott study is sophisticated and useful. However, because of the level of aggregation, the data do not give us a very sharp picture of the relationship between courts and agencies and the ways that they influence each other.

105. See, e.g., R. Shep Melnick, *Regulation and the Courts: The Case of the Clean Air Act* (Washington, D.C.: Brookings, 1983).

106. Interestingly, Schuck and Elliott, supra note 104, found some 40 percent of the judicial remands to agencies in the time period of their study did not result in further agency proceedings; either the agency abandoned the questioned course of action or settled with the complaining parties. To those like myself who believe in the general efficacy of judicial review this is gratifying. Of course, the point concerning evasive or strategic agency actions is not inconsistent with this finding. Indeed, it is corroborated by the fact that, in 60 percent of the cases, there was presumably some further proceeding or decision by the agency.

107. Compare the advice proffered to private parties seeking to influence agency decisions by James DeLong, "How to Convince an Agency," *Regulation* 6 (September-October, 1982): 27.

Chapter 4

1. The literature on procedural due process is immense. Two recent treatments provide excellent coverage and acute analysis of both theory and case law. See Jerry L. Mashaw, *Due Process in the Administrative State* (New Haven: Yale University Press, 1985); Edward L. Rubin, "Due Process and the Administrative State," *California Law Review* 72 (1984): 1044.

2. The legislative-adjudicative model is ably explored in Ronald A. Cass, "Models of Administrative Action," *Virginia Law Review* 72 (1986): 363.

3. See generally Hans Linde, "Due Process of Lawmaking," *Nebraska Law Review* 55 (1976): 197, 222–51. While Linde argues that there are some procedural requirements and standards for "legitimate lawmaking" (228–29), he is hard-pressed to identify any particular requirements other than the formal mechanics for enacting laws (e.g., majority rule, quorum requirements) that would seem to me to be "due process" requirements only in a very special sense. Certainly the kinds of due process elements associated with courts and agencies are not binding, as Linde concedes. See Fletcher v. Peck, 10 U.S. (6 Cranch) 87, 129–31 (1810) (expressing doubt as to whether a law can be invalidated merely because its passage was influenced by bribe).

4. Londoner v. Denver, 210 U.S. 373 (1908).

5. BiMetallic Invest. Co. v. State Bd. of Equalization, 239 U.S. 441 (1915).

6. Ibid. at 445.

7. See, e.g., United States v. Storer Broadcasting, 351 U.S. 192 (1956). See generally Glen O. Robinson, "The Making of Administrative Policy: Another Look at Rulemaking and Adjudication and Administrative Procedure Reform," *University of Pennsylvania Law Review* 118 (1970): 485, 496–506.

8. See, e.g., Heckler v. Campbell, 461 U.S. 458 (1983), where the Court sus-

tained HHS regulations setting medical-vocational guidelines to determine eligibility for disability benefits, but appears to have regarded it as critical that the rules did allow claimants to introduce evidence that the rule did not fit their particular situation.

9. In United States v. Florida East Coast Ry. Co., 410 U.S. 224 (1973), the Court in dictum said that, in general rule making, due process did not require an oral hearing as distinct from informal rule-making processes, but it did not address the question of whether due process required *at least* the informal notice and participation provided by the rule-making process.

10. See, e.g., Yakus v. United States, 321 U.S. 414 (1944); Amalgamated Meat Cutters v. Connally, 337 F. Supp. 737 (D.D.C. 1971).

11. Indeed, in Arizona v. California, 373 U.S. 546 (1963), the Court approved an extraordinarily broad delegation of power to apportion water rights where it appears there were no process constraints. Donald A. Dripps, "Delegation and Due Process," *Duke Law Journal* (1988): 657, proposes a kind of merger of delegation and due process, though it appears he is more interested in due process issues than in delegation concerns.

12. See William W. Van Alstyne, "The Demise of the Right-Privilege Distinction in Constitutional Law," *Harvard Law Review* 81 (1968): 1439.

13. See Richard A. Epstein, "The Supreme Court 1987 Term, Forward: Unconstitutional Conditions, State Power, and the Limits of Consent," *Harvard Law Review* 102 (1988): 4; Seth F. Kreimer, "Allocational Sanctions: The Problem of Negative Rights in a Positive State," *University of Pennsylvania Law Review* 132 (1984): 1293. There are two distinct, though related, ideas here. One is that the state's affirmative power as employer or "welfare agent" is almost wholly discretionary; individual beneficiaries do not have enforceable rights to the benefits conferred, or have only such rights as the government itself concedes in creating the employment or benefit programs. A second notion is that the government may impose, as a condition of granting such benefits, restraints on the exercise of other rights the individual may possess.

14. See Epstein, supra note 13, and Kreimer, supra note 13.

15. The early cases on property and liberty are reviewed in Glen O. Robinson, "Evolving Conceptions of 'Property' and 'Liberty' in Due Process Jurisprudence," in *Liberty, Property, and Government: Constitutional Interpretation Before the New Deal*, ed. Ellen Frankel Paul and Howard Dickman (New York: SUNY Press, 1989), 63.

16. See, e.g., Ex parte Robinson, 86 U.S. (19 Wall.) 505 (1873), holding that an attorney's "right to practice his profession" was protected by (procedural) due process.

17. See Stephen F. Williams, "Liberty and Property: The Problem of Government Benefits," *Journal of Legal Studies* 12 (1983): 3; Frank Easterbrook, "Substance and Due Process," *Supreme Court Review* (1982): 85.

18. I develop this further in "Evolving Conceptions," supra note 15. As a specific piece of historical evidence, it is now commonplace to cite Madison's rhetorical definition of property, which is sufficiently capacious to handle almost any type of interest that is likely to be a services candidate for protection (and some that are not). See James Madison, "Property," in *The Writings of James Madison*, ed. G. Hunt (New York: Putnam, 1906), 6: 101–03.

19. Goldberg v. Kelly, 397 U.S. 254 (1970).

20. Ibid. at 268 n. 8, quoting from Charles A. Reich, "Individual Rights and Social Welfare: The Emerging Legal Issues," *Yale Law Journal* 74 (1965): 1245, 1255.

21. Board of Regents v. Roth, 408 U.S. 564 (1972).

22. In a companion to *Roth*, Perry v. Sindermann, 408 U.S. 593 (1972), the Court reached a different result in the case of another university teacher who had been employed for four successive one-year terms and had been let go at the end of the last. In *Sindermann*, the university had no formal tenure system, but its guidelines, on which Sindermann claimed reliance, had promised permanent tenure to teachers so long as their service was satisfactory. The Court held this promise might be sufficient to create a "legitimate expectation of entitlement to continued employment," and, hence, a property right protected by due process. (Whether it did, in fact, create such an expectation was a question to be determined by the trial court.)

23. Most commentators have criticized *Roth* and its general premise that due process should turn on "rights," at least rights defined independent of the context in which the process questions are raised. While the precise arguments differ in detail, they essentially concur that the text of the due process clause should not be understood literally, but should be interpreted broadly to protect important interests (including dignitary interests in fair processes). See, e.g., Mashaw, supra note 1, and Rubin, supra note 1; Henry P. Monaghan, "Of 'Liberty' and 'Property'," *Cornell Law Review* 62 (1977): 405; William W. Van Alstyne, "Cracks in the 'New Property': Adjudicative Due Process in the Administrative State," *Cornell Law Review* 62 (1977): 445; Frank Michelman, "Formal and Associational Aims in Procedural Due Process," *Nomos 17: Due Process* (1977): 126; Robert Rabin, "Job Security and Due Process: Monitoring Administrative Discretion through a Reasons Requirement," *Chicago Law Review* 44 (1976): 60. Some commentators, however, insist on a stricter adherence to the rights language of the text. See Williams, supra note 17, and Easterbrook, supra note 17.

24. Perry v. Sindermann, 408 U.S. 593, 601 (1972).

25. See Jeremy Bentham, *Theory of Legislation*, trans. R. Hildreth, 6th ed. (London: Trubner, 1890), 112–13.

26. Williams, supra note 17 at 7.

27. Thomas C. Grey, "The Disintegration of Property," *Nomos 22: Property* (1980): 69, 81, 85, attributes the development of the bundle-of-rights concept to the legal realists who sought thereby to undermine the traditional sanctity of property. In this respect, the evolution of the property concept mirrors the general transformation of American legal thought away from natural law and toward a utilitarian, positivist perspective. See also Rubin, supra note 1 at 1086.

28. The judicial dispute can be traced through the following sequence of cases: Arnett v. Kennedy, 416 U.S. 134 (1974); Bishop v. Wood, 426 U.S. 341 (1976); Vitek v. Jones, 445 U.S. 480, 490–91 (1980); Logan v. Zimmerman Brush Co., 455 U.S. 422 (1982); Cleveland Bd. of Educ. v. Loudermill, 470 U.S. 532 (1985). Since *Loudermill*, the dispute has turned to questions of applying the "principles." See, e.g., Board of Pardons v. Allen, 482 U.S. 369 (1987); Kentucky Department of Corrections v. Thompson, 109 S. Ct. 1904 (1989) (the first involving parole rights [a liberty interest]; the second, prisoner visitation rights [not a liberty interest]). For a sample of the academic discussion on this issue see sources cited in note 23 supra.

29. The distinction is noted in *Roth* and in virtually all of the post-*Roth* cases, cited in note 23 supra.

30. In Bishop v. Wood, 426 U.S. 341, 349–50 n. 14 (1976), Justice Stevens, for the Court's majority, sarcastically rejected "Mr. Justice Brennan's remarkably innovative suggestion that we develop a federal common law of property rights." Stevens does not explain why a federal common law of property would be any more remarkable than a federal common law of liberty, which the Court has aggressively fashioned since *Allgeyer*. Indeed, as noted earlier, the Court has been traditionally indifferent to the distinction between property and liberty, particularly in procedural due process cases. This indifference must rest on an assumption that both terms have common foundations.

31. 470 U.S. 532 (1985).

32. Ibid. at 541.

33. Mathews v. Eldridge, 424 U.S. 319 (1976).

34. Ibid. at 335.

35. Goss v. Lopez, 419 U.S. 565, 579–82 (1975).

36. Ingraham v. Wright, 430 U.S. 651 (1977).

37. Mashaw, supra note 1 at 153.

38. Ibid.

39. Mashaw explores, supra note 1 at 172–82, several core values that a dignitary approach should serve, notably: equality of treatment, predictability, transparency, rationality, participation, and privacy. These values do not point unequivocally to any single set of procedures, as Mashaw recognizes. Moreover, he recognizes that they do point to a quite modest set of constitutionally required procedures, in many instances little more than a neutrally applied set of criteria and a requirement for reasons.

40. Mashaw, supra note 1 at 163–64.

41. Monaghan, supra note 23; Rubin, supra note 1; and Van Alstyne, supra note 23; and John Hart Ely, *Democracy and Distrust* (Cambridge, Mass.: Harvard University Press, 1980), 18–19, all argue to this effect.

42. Thomas C. Grey, "The Constitution as Scripture," *Stanford Law Review* 37 (1984): 1, 23, expresses a similar sentiment in admonishing us to think of federal judges—including Supreme Court justices—not "as priests, but as officials given more job security than other civil servants so that they can decide disputes fairly, taking account of a mass of institutionalized rules and precedents."

43. See, e.g., Griswold v. Connecticut, 381 U.S. 479 (1965); Roe v. Wade, 410 U.S. 113 (1973). I do not mean to suggest the Court's privacy jurisprudence is unproblematical; I do think it is fairly representative of the creativity that has characterized constitutional jurisprudence since virtually the beginning of judicial review. That same spirit of creativity has animated constitutional law scholarship even more.

44. Van Alstyne, supra note 23 at 487, proposes just such an interpretation.

45. On the English concept of natural justice, see, e.g., J. Beatson and M. H. Mathews, *Administrative Law: Cases and Materials* (Oxford: Oxford University Press, 1983), 191–286.

46. See, e.g., Connick v. Myers, 461 U.S. 138 (1983) (rejecting first amendment challenge to public employee dismissal because of employee's "private" dispute with supervisor; "private speech" insufficient basis for judicial intervention); Regents of the

University of Michigan v. Ewing, 474 U.S. 214 (1985) (rejecting substantive due process challenge to state university's refusal to permit student from retaking an examination required for graduation.)

47. Mashaw, supra note 1 at 50–51, uses the phrase in a somewhat different sense to denote the customary processes within a particular institutional setting that, being long conventionally accepted, are prima facie "due" in a constitutional sense. I use the word ordinary here to distinguish it from constitutionally mandated processes. While there may be an overlap between constitutional due process and ordinary process that is deemed to be appropriate as a matter of public policy, I do not want to get entangled in the debate about what norms are so fundamental as to be constitutional commands.

48. Office of Communication of the United Church of Christ v. FCC, 359 F. 2d 994 (D.C. Cir. 1966).

49. FCC v. Sanders Bros. Radio Station, 309 U.S. 470 (1940).

50. Actually this rationale was only suggested in *Sanders Bros.*, but two years later the Court explicitly put this gloss on it in Scripps-Howard Radio, Inc. v. FCC, 316 U.S. 4, 14–15 (1942).

51. In *Church of Christ*, the court assumed the criteria for standing in judicial and administrative forums as the same without examining the differences, both legal and practical, between access to the courts and access to agencies. On standing and participation in administrative proceedings generally, see, e.g., Ernest Gellhorn, "Public Participation in Administrative Proceedings," *Yale Law Journal* 81 (1972): 359; Richard B. Stewart, "The Reformation of American Administrative Law," *Harvard Law Review* 88 (1975): 1667.

52. The separation-of-powers concern in federal law is constitutionally crystallized in the requirement of Art. III limiting the judicial power of the United States to "cases or controversies." Administrative agencies are not constituted, as Art. III tribunals and agency adjudication is not regarded as an exercise of Art. III power. See Commodity Futures Trading Comm'n v. Schor, 478 U.S. 833 (1986). See generally Richard H. Fallon, Jr., "Of Legislative Courts, Administrative Agencies, and Article III," *Harvard Law Review* 101 (1988): 916. The case or controversy requirement thus has no application to agency proceedings.

53. The mere recognition of a person as having standing does not of itself entail a hearing; the hearing requirement turns on whether the person seeking standing or other party has raised sufficient grounds to warrant a hearing. See Stone v. FCC, 466 F. 2d 316 (D.C. Cir. 1972). Quite commonly, however, the standing issue is raised in a context like *Church of Christ*, where a hearing has been instituted and the question is whether a particular individual or group is entitled to participate in it.

54. Mill embraced both the individual liberal perspective, which sees participation as a means of protecting individual interests, and the view that participation (in the wider sense of political activity generally, not simply voting) promoted public-regarding attitudes and responsible citizenship. See Dennis F. Thompson, *John Stuart Mill and Representative Government* (Princeton: Princeton University Press, 1976), 13–53. Donald W. Keim, "Participation in Contemporary Democratic Theories," *Nomos 16: Participation in Politics* (1975): 1, develops these twin themes of preference voting and citizenship education, though he distinguishes three functions: "self-protection, self-rule, and self-realization." It is not clear to me whether there is any

operational difference between the first two. For an excellent discussion of these themes in a different political context, that of local plebiscite voting, see Clayton P. Gillette, "Plebiscites, Participation, and Collective Action in Local Government Law," *Michigan Law Review* 86 (1988): 930.

55. The distinction here is roughly Hanna Pitkin's distinction between *acting* for another and *standing* for another; see Hanna Pitkin, *The Concept of Representation* (Berkeley: University of California Press, 1967): 59.

56. See Stewart, supra note 51 at 1759–60, rationalizing public participation along these lines.

57. Mashaw, supra note 1, is a leading proponent of this view.

58. Albert O. Hirschman, *Exit, Voice, and Loyalty* (Cambridge, Mass.: Harvard University Press, 1970).

59. Charles M. Tiebout, "A Pure Theory of Local Expenditures," *Journal of Political Economy* 64 (1956): 416.

60. These and other conditions are explored in Tiebout's seminal paper, supra note 59 at 419–23. See also James M. Buchanan and Charles J. Goetz, "Efficiency Limits of Fiscal Mobility: An Assessment of the Tiebout Model," *Journal of Public Economics* 1 (1972): 25.

61. I have in mind something in the spirit of Rawls's use of contract theory. See John Rawls, *A Theory of Justice* (Cambridge, Mass.: Harvard University Press, 1971).

62. See David Hume, "Of the Original Contract," in *Essays: Moral, Political, and Literary*, rev. ed. (Indianapolis: Liberty Classics, 1984).

63. The seminal work here is that of Anthony Downs, *An Economic Theory of Democracy* (New York: Harper and Row, 1957).

64. The extraordinarily low, and declining, level of electoral voting in the United States has been the subject of extensive empirical investigation into the social and political conditions and attitudes underlying voting behavior. For a recent empirical analysis, see, e.g., G. Bingham Powell, Jr., "American Voter Turnout in Comparative Perspective," *American Political Science Review* 80 (1986): 17.

65. See, e.g., William H. Riker and Peter C. Ordeshook, "A Theory of the Calculus of Voting," *American Political Science Review* 62 (1968): 25.

66. Illustrative is Mancur Olson's influential model of group activity, *The Logic of Collective Action* (Cambridge, Mass.: Harvard University Press, 1965). Applying the logic of public goods theory, Olson argues that broadly organized political and social groups are not sustainable on the basis of their general objectives unless they also provide other specific, divisible benefits to their members. The general benefits secured by the group are, by their nature, "public goods" that the affected individuals can enjoy without being contributing members, that is, they can "free ride" on the contributions of others. Despite the logical force of Olson's model, it requires more than a little massaging of the data to make it fit observed reality. While we do not see Earth Day celebrations, civil rights marches, or mass demonstrations by farmers every day, we see such activity often enough to send us searching for a richer model of collective activity. Albert Hirschman has ironically remarked that, just as Olson's book appeared, "the Western world was about to be all but engulfed by an unprecedented wave of public movements, marches, protests, strikes, and ideologies" (*Shifting Involvements: Private Interest and Public Action* [Princeton: Princeton University Press, 1982], 78).

67. I take this to be the sense behind the argument that the net social value of each individual vote, no matter how small its marginal contribution, must be considered positive. See Derek Parfit, *Reasons and Persons* (Cambridge: Cambridge University Press, 1985), 73–75.

68. Again, I have in mind Pitkin's distinction between acting for and standing for. The latter envisions the representative as a mere surrogate of the represented, essentially a pure process theory of democratic governance. The former envisions a more substantive conception of governance in which representatives are judged by their actions on behalf of the public welfare, not simply by how well they mirror the characteristics of their constituencies. See Pitkin, supra note 53 at 60–91, 112–43.

69. For instance, a state statute limiting the right to vote in school district elections to owners of taxable property in the district or parents of children who went to school in the district was held unconstitutional in Kramer v. Union Free School Dist. No. 15, 395 U.S. 621 (1969). On the other hand, the Court has upheld similar interest limitations in water district elections. See Ball v. James, 451 U.S. 355 (1981). Whether the Court has appropriately drawn the right line in these cases is controversial. See Laurence H. Tribe, *American Constitutional Law*, 2d ed. (Mineola, New York: Foundation Press, 1988), 1086–88. However, this is irrelevant for present purposes; the basic point remains that interest limitations on the franchise are disfavored.

70. For a helpful survey of some of the practical aspects of designing participation, see Gellhorn, supra note 51.

71. Office of Communication of the United Church of Christ v. FCC, 425 F. 2d 5431 (D.C. Cir. 1969).

72. See, e.g., Ohio Bell Tel. Co. v. Public Utilities Comm'n of Ohio, 301 U.S. 292 (1937) (evidence not divulged to parties); Gibson v. Berryhill, 411 U.S. 564 (1973) (conflict of interest).

73. For a general view of the problem, see Ernest Gellhorn and Glen O. Robinson, "Rulemaking 'Due Process': An Inconclusive Dialogue," *University of Chicago Law Review* 48 (1981): 201.

74. See Dr. Bonham's Case, 8 Co. Rep. 113b, 118a, 77 Eng. Rep. 646, 652 (C.P. 1610).

75. See, e.g., Berger v. United States, 255 U.S. 22 (1921) (bias); Gibson v. Berryhill, 411 U.S. 564 (1973). On the evolution from conflict of interest to a more general bias standard, see Gellhorn and Robinson, supra note 73 at 215. General acceptance of the bias principle does not imply frequent application; at least in the case of federal judges and administrators, disqualification for bias or interest is quite exceptional. See Gellhorn and Robinson at 219 n. 79. Whether or not this suggests a lack of occasion for disqualification, it does reflect a generally high standard of proof for obtaining it, even in adjudicatory cases. See, e.g., United States v. Grinnell Corp., 384 U.S. 563 (1966).

76. Association of National Advertisers, Inc. v. FTC, 627 F. 2d 1151 (D.C. Cir. 1979), *cert. denied*, 447 U.S. 921 (1980). For a thoughtful analysis of this case and major adjudicatory bias cases preceding it, see Peter L. Strauss, "Disqualification of Decisional Officials in Rulemaking," *Columbia Law Review* 80 (1980): 990. See also Gellhorn and Robinson, supra note 73 at 206–10, 215–37.

77. The use of an adjudicatory standard was deemed especially appropriate here

because the statute specified a hybrid type of rule making in which there were some elements of adjudicatory formalities.

78. 627 F. 2d 1151 at 1170.

79. See Morgan v. United States, 313 U.S. 409 (1941). See also National Nutritional Foods Ass'n v. FDA, 491 F. 2d 1141 (2d Cir. 1974).

80. See *Morgan v. United States*, supra note 79.

81. See, e.g., Cinderella Career & Finishing Schools, Inc. v. FTC, 425 F. 2d 583 (D.C. Cir. 1970); Texaco Inc. v. FTC, 336 F. 2d 754 (D.C. Cir. 1964), *vacated on other grounds*, 381 U.S. 739 (1965). Both of these decisions involved public speeches by the agency chairman (the same one) that showed prejudgment of a pending case.

82. See, e.g., *Cinderella*, 425 F. 2d at 591.

83. On ex parte communications generally, see Gellhorn and Robinson, supra note 73 at 210–15, 237–58. As in the case of bias, the occasions for invoking restrictions on ex parte communications in adjudicatory cases where they have long been outlawed have been few; in the federal arena it became a noteworthy problem only in the late 1950s with a series of episodes (ibid. at 210). For a discussion of those early cases and their immediate fallout, see Cornelius J. Peck, "Regulation and Control of Ex Parte Communications with Federal Agencies," *Harvard Law Review* 76 (1962): 233.

84. Sangamon Valley Television Corp. v. FCC, 269 F. 2d 221, 224 (D.C. Cir. 1959).

85. Home Box Office v. FCC, 567 F. 2d 9 (D.C.Cir.), *cert. denied*, 434 U.S. 829 (1977).

86. See Action for Children's Television v. FCC, 564 F. 2d 458 (D.C. Cir. 1977). The court avoided an open conflict by holding simply that the rule would not, in any event, be applied retroactively, hence not to the case before it.

87. See Sierra Club v. Costle, 657 F. 2d 298, 387–410 (D.C. Cir., 1981). See also United Steelworkers of America v. Marshall, 647 F. 2d 1189 (D.C. Cir. 1980), *cert. denied*, 453 U.S. 913 (1981), where the court refused to disapprove ex parte communications between internal staff "advocates" and decision makers and also between outside consultants and decision makers.

88. I opposed most of the pay television rules on the merits. See Subscription TV Rules, 52 F.C.C. 2d 1, 72 (1974). So, to my great satisfaction, did the court of appeals.

89. For a discussion of the inherent tendency toward distortion of information as it passes through successive layers of bureaucratic staff, see Gordon Tullock, *The Politics of Bureaucracy* (Washington, D.C.: Public Affairs Press, 1965), 137–41; Anthony Downs, *Inside Bureaucracy* (Boston: Little, Brown, 1966), 112–31. Downs comments on the importance of outside information sources as a means of reducing this distortion (119).

Chapter 5

1. Ernst Freund, *Cases on Administrative Law*, 2d ed. (Chicago: University of Chicago Press, 1928), v.

2. Some idea of this centrality is suggested by a standard text on administrative law in which over half of its content falls under various judicial review headings. See

Richard J. Pierce, Jr., Sidney A. Shapiro, and Paul R. Verkuil, *Administrative Law and Process* (Mineola, N.Y.: Foundation Press, 1985).

3. Oliver W. Holmes, "The Path of the Law," *Harvard Law Review* 10 (1897): 457, 461.

4. For an account of the legislation (the Walter-Logan Act) and its background, see Paul R. Verkuil, "The Emerging Concept of Administrative Procedure," *Columbia Law Review* 78 (1978): 258.

5. The generic standard for review of all agency action is the arbitrary-capricious test, which translates into a requirement that the agency's action have a "reasonable" basis—that there be "a rational connection between the facts found and the choice made." See, e.g., Motor Vehicle Mfrs. Ass'n v. State Farm Mutual Automobile Ins. Co., 463 U.S. 29, 43 n. 9 (1983).

6. See Bowen v. American Hospital Ass'n, 476 U.S. 610 (1986), specifically distinguishing the rational basis test in administrative law from the constitutional standard of minimal rationality under Williamson v. Lee Optical, 348 U.S. 483 (1955). The more rigorous standard for review of agency rule making is a product of positive law—specifically the Administrative Procedure Act and common law embellishments thereon—not constitutional law. In fact, a half-century ago, the Court specifically held the *constitutional* standard (under substantive due process) to be the same, in Pacific States Box & Basket Co. v. White, 296 U.S. 176 (1935). *Pacific States Box* notwithstanding, it has been recently argued that the more rigorous standard for agency rule making is constitutionally necessary inasmuch as agencies, unlike Congress, are not politically responsible. See Sidney A. Shapiro and Richard E. Levy, "Heightened Scrutiny of the Fourth Branch: Separation of Powers and the Requirement of Adequate Reasons for Agency Decisions," *Duke Law Journal* (1987): 387, 425–28. However, we have little reason to constitutionalize standards for review of agency action; as a general proposition, the nonconstitutional sources of review are quite adequate authorization for a vigorous review of agency action.

7. Cass Sunstein argues to the contrary: the Court will, in an appropriate case, strike down a purely private-regarding statute that makes no appeal to public value. See Sunstein, "Public Values, Private Interests, and the Equal Protection Clause," *Supreme Court Review* (1982): 127, 132–38. The possibility of that occurring must be discounted by the fact that the Court has shown itself to be remarkably adept at finding (imagining) public values sufficient to sustain legislation.

8. See, e.g., Jonathan R. Macey, "Promoting Public-Regarding Legislation through Statutory Interpretation," *Columbia Law Review* 86 (1986): 223; Cass R. Sunstein, "Interest Groups in American Public Law," *Stanford Law Review* 38 (1985): 29, 59–68; Richard B. Stewart, "Regulation in a Liberal State: The Role of Non-Commodity Values," *Yale Law Journal* 92 (1983): 1537; William N. Eskridge, Jr., "Dynamic Statutory Interpretation," *University of Pennsylvania Law Review* 135 (1987): 1479.

9. See Richard A. Posner, "Economics, Politics, and the Reading of Statutes and the Constitution," *University of Chicago Law Review* 49 (1982): 263, 285–86.

10. See, e.g., Kent v. Dulles, 357 U.S. 116 (1958), a standard authority for this unremarkable principle. See also National Cable Television Ass'n v. United States, 415 U.S. 336 (1974).

11. Ronald Dworkin, *Law's Empire* (Cambridge, Mass.: Harvard University Press, 1986), 52–53.

12. Modern conservatives are not wholly of one mind on the question of judicial restraint. Conservatives of the libertarian persuasion defend judicial interventionism as a means of curbing government initiatives that interfere with individual rights and liberties (which are broadly defined). The contrast between the two strands of conservatism on the question of the judicial role is illuminated by a debate between Richard Epstein and Justice Antonin Scalia (the latter representing the more conventional conservative view that decries the illegitimacy of activist review). See Antonin Scalia, "Economic Affairs as Human Affairs," *Cato Journal* 4 (1985): 703; Richard A. Epstein, "Judicial Review: Reckoning on Two Kinds of Error," *Cato Journal* 4 (1985): 711. For another example of "conventional" conservatism, see, e.g., Frank H. Easterbrook, "Statutes' Domain," *University of Chicago Law Review* 50 (1983): 533.

13. For some recent commentary on statutory interpretation generally, see, e.g., Eskridge, supra note 8; Richard A. Posner, "Statutory Interpretation in the Classroom and in the Courtroom," *University of Chicago Law Review* 50 (1983): 800. On statutory interpretation in the context of administrative programs—which is basically part of the scope of review of agency decisions (which are themselves interpretations of statutes)—see, e.g., Colin S. Diver, "Statutory Interpretation in the Administrative State," *University of Pennsylvania Law Review* 133 (1985): 549; Cynthia R. Farina, "Statutory Interpretation and the Balance of Power in the Administrative State," *Columbia Law Review* 89 (1989): 452; Cass R. Sunstein, "Interpreting Statutes in the Regulatory State," *Harvard Law Review* 103 (1989): 405. I will return to questions of statutory interpretation in discussing the scope of review issue.

14. See, e.g., William M. Landes and Richard A. Posner, "The Independent Judiciary in an Interest Group Perspective," *Journal of Law and Economics* 18 (1975): 875. This view of the courts is not unique to public choice theory. Earlier interest-group theory similarly saw the courts as agents of the legislative process and judicial review as an extension, more or less, of the political process. See, e.g., Earl Latham, *The Group Basis of Politics* (Ithaca: Cornell University Press, 1952). Ironically, in view of its fundamental antagonism to liberal interest-group political theory, classic pre-American republican theory also viewed the courts as agents of the legislature. Thus, in James Harrington's republican utopia, judges are regarded as mere assistants to the legislature. See "The Commonwealth of Oceana," in *The Political Works of James Harrington*, ed. J. G. A. Pocock (Cambridge: Cambridge University Press, 1977), 309.

15. Greater Boston Television Corp. v. FCC, 444 F. 2d 841, 851 (D.C. Cir. 1970), *cert. denied*, 403 U.S. 923 (1971).

16. See Abbott Laboratories v. Gardner, 387 U.S. 136 (1967), embracing a broad presumption of review except where there is "clear and convincing evidence" of congressional intent to preclude review or the action is "committed to agency discretion." Although "clear and convincing evidence" of intent to exclude has not been confined to explicit statutory language, courts have been loathe to find such evidence outside explicit statutory terms; indeed, they have sometimes gone to extraordinary lengths to interpret explicit statutory limits on review so as not to preclude the particular action in question. See, e.g., Johnson v. Robison, 415 U.S. 361 (1974). As always

there are deviations from the norm. For example, in Block v. Community Nutrition Institute, 467 U.S. 340 (1984), the Court found an implied preclusion of review by particular parties based on evidence that could be honestly described as clear and convincing only if the presumption of reviewability were reversed. However, inasmuch as the case involved not generic review but preclusion of review by certain parties, the case may best be treated as a standing case. Apart from the unusual case where Congress attempts specifically to preclude all judicial review, review may be foreclosed on any issue that is "committed to agency discretion." Again, however, the Supreme Court has given this a narrow interpretation. Review is foreclosed only where an agency has been given such broad discretion that there is "no law to apply" to its choice of action. Citizens to Preserve Overton Park Inc. v. Volpe, 401 U.S. 402 (1971), finding law to apply, is the authoritative reference. Webster v. Doe, 108 S. Ct. 2047 (1988), not finding such law, is the exception.

17. More detail can be found in the sources cited in note 1 supra. See also Joseph Vining, *Legal Identity* (New Haven: Yale University Press, 1978); Lee A. Albert, "Standing to Challenge Administrative Action: An Inadequate Surrogate for Claims for Relief," *Yale Law Journal* 83 (1974): 425; Mark V. Tushnet, "The Law of Standing: A Plea for Abandonment," *Cornell Law Review* 62 (1977): 663; Richard B. Stewart, "The Reformation of American Administrative Law," *Harvard Law Review* 88 (1975): 1669, 1723–46; William A. Fletcher, "The Structure of Standing," *Yale Law Journal* 98 (1988): 221; Cass R. Sunstein, "Standing and the Privatization of Public Law," *Columbia Law Review* 88 (1988): 1432.

18. For more elaboration of these purposes, see Fletcher and Sunstein, supra note 17.

19. See, e.g., Allen v. Wright, 468 U.S. 737 (1984).

20. The evolution of standing is detailed (albeit with some interpretations that are debatable) in Sunstein, supra note 17; leading precedents are extensively examined by him and by Fletcher, supra note 17. Most of the major points touched on here can be found elaborated at length in these two excellent critiques.

21. FCC v. Sanders Bros. Radio Station, 309 U.S. 470 (1970). See also Scripps-Howard Radio, Inc. v. FCC, 316 U.S. 4 (1942).

22. The "private attorney general" label was added by Judge Frank in Associated Indus. of New York, Inc. v. Ickes, 134 F. 2d 694 (2d Cir. 1943), *vacated as moot*, 320 U.S. 707 (1943), and later approved by the Supreme Court in Association of Data Processing Services Org. v. Camp, 397 U.S. 150, 154 (1970).

23. At this point, it is important, if elementary, to distinguish private standing to seek review of agency action from the creation of a private right of action to enforce the statute that the agency is charged with enforcing. The former permits individuals to seek judicial intervention to control the agency's policies and enforcement choices. The latter permits a separate system of private enforcement in addition to administrative enforcement. See generally Richard B. Stewart and Cass R. Sunstein, "Public Programs and Private Rights," *Harvard Law Review* 95 (1982): 1193.

24. See Association of Data Processing Services Organization, Inc. v. Camp, 397 U.S. 150 (1970).

25. Clarke v. Securities Industries Ass'n, 479 U.S. 388 (1987). The Court granted standing despite the absence of any particular congressional intent to protect

plaintiff's interest. The Court said the test was not meant to be "especially demanding"; review is denied only to plaintiffs whose interests are "so marginally related to or inconsistent with" the purposes of the statute that it cannot be assumed Congress intended to permit the action.

26. 405 U.S. 727 (1972).

27. Mark V. Tushnet, "The Sociology of Article III: A Response to Professor Brilmayer," *Harvard Law Review* 93 (1980): 1698, 1708–21, makes these arguments with great skill, and with supporting examples, in criticizing the position that standing should be limited to individual litigants representing their own rights or interests.

28. For an example of the Court's equating of nondistinct injury with abstractness of issues, see Allen v. Wright, 468 U.S. 737 (1984), where the Court contrasts "distinct and palpable" injury with "abstract, conjectural or hypothetical" claims.

29. See ibid. at 1709–13.

30. See United States v. Students Challenging Regulatory Agency Procedures (SCRAP), 412 U.S. 669 (1973).

31. See Duke Power Co. v. Carolina Environmental Study Group, Inc., 438 U.S. 59 (1978).

32. See Simon v. Eastern Ky. Welfare Rights Org., 426 U.S. 26 (1976).

33. See Allen v. Wright, 468 U.S. 737 (1984).

34. Compare, e.g., Linda R. S. v. Richard D., 410 U.S. 614 (1973) (mother denied standing to demand prosecution of father of child for nonsupport), with Planned Parenthood of Central Missouri v. Danforth, 428 U.S. 52 (1976) (physicians granted standing to challenge statute requiring parental and spousal consent to abortions); and Arlington Heights v. Metro Housing Develop., 429 U.S. 252 (1977) (individual given standing to challenge restrictive zoning based on alleged interest in moving into houses that could not be built because of zoning), with Allen v. Wright, 468 U.S. 737 (1984) (individual denied standing to challenge tax benefits for segregated schools).

35. 467 U.S. 340 (1984).

36. 479 U.S. 388 (1987).

37. Ibid. at 757.

38. Frank H. Easterbrook, "Forward: The Court and the Economic System," *Harvard Law Review* 98 (1984): 4, 51–54. See also Easterbrook, supra note 12.

39. The indeterminacy of the bargain model is pointed out by Richard B. Stewart, "Regulation in a Liberal State: The Role of Non-Commodity Values," *Yale Law Journal* 92 (1983): 1537, 1551–53. Even employing a bargain model, Easterbrook's characterization of it is somewhat misleading insofar as it implies that the deal in question is essentially a matter of identifying winners and losers. It is the essence of private bargaining that the parties see it as a positive-sum, not zero-sum game. From this perspective one would logically ask not who lost, but how the parties sought to maximize their interests by joint commitment. This perspective about the particulars of the "deal" in question gives us a quite different interpretative framework than Easterbrook's. See Eskridge, supra note 8. As Eskridge shows, even accepting the private bargain model as a description of legislation, it would not follow that there is no room for creative (in Eskridge's phrase, "dynamic") interpretation, just as there is in ordinary contract interpretation and reinforcement.

40. See, e.g., the Albert, Fletcher, and Sunstein articles cited in note 17 supra.

41. See Kenneth E. Scott, "Standing in the Supreme Court—A Functional Analysis," *Harvard Law Review* 86 (1973): 645.

42. I do not argue that this public resource is, or should be, wholly subsidized, but merely that rationing it by manipulation of standing is inappropriate unless it is done within the context of a fuller evaluation of how the judicial resource is allocated—the degree to which it is (or should be) supported by litigants or public taxpayers respectively. On the economics of the judicial system and legal rules, see generally, Richard A Posner, *Economic Analysis of Law*, 3d ed. (Boston: Little, Brown, 1986), chaps. 19, 20.

43. Justice Scalia is a noteworthy and ardent supporter of this view. See Antonin Scalia, "The Doctrine of Standing as an Essential Element of the Separation of Powers," *Suffolk University Law Review* 17 (1983): 881. For a good critique of the argument, see Sunstein, supra note 17 at 1469–74.

44. See Sunstein, supra note 17 at 1471.

45. 108 S.Ct. 2597 (1988).

46. See, e.g., Easterbrook, supra note 12, who makes this point as an argument for narrowly construing statutes that are alleged to create private rights of action for public offenses.

47. As it happens, Congress specifically provided that compliance with NHTSA's standards does not immunize the manufacturer from tort liability, so there is no general preemption of common law standards. However, that still leaves open an argument for preemption where tort liability is sought to be grounded on some design feature specifically approved by the agency. See, e.g., Wood v. General Motors Corp., 673 F.Supp. 1108 (D. Mass. 1987).

48. The history of *qui tam* suits is analyzed in Harold J. Krent, "Executive Control Over Criminal Law Enforcement: Some Lessons from History," *American University Law Review* 38 (1989): 275.

49. Sunstein, supra note 17 at 1471.

50. See, e.g., Sunstein, supra note 17 at 1461–75.

51. See Tushnet, supra note 17, proposing to eliminate standing restrictions generally.

52. On nonacquiescence generally, see Samuel Estreicher and Richard L. Revesz, "Nonacquiescence by Federal Administrative Agencies," *Yale Law Journal* 98 (1989): 679.

53. This is precisely what the FCC did in a prolonged "dialogue" with the Court of Appeals for the District of Columbia in a series of discussions involving agency policy regarding changes in "unique" radio program-formats. The agency finally succeeded in having its position sustained by the Supreme Court, ending the dialogue. See FCC v. WNCN Listeners Guild, 450 U.S. 582 (1981). A similar, but briefer episode, occurred in respect to the renewal of licenses in comparative hearing cases. See Central Florida Enterprises, Inc. v. FCC, 598 F. 2d 37 (D.C. Cir. 1978), *cert. dism'd*, 441 U.S. 957 (1979); Central Florida Enterprises, Inc. v. FCC, 683 F. 2d 503 (D.C. Cir. 1982).

54. The phrase originated with Judge Harold Leventhal in Greater Boston Television Corp. v. FCC, 444 F. 2d 841, 850 (D.C. Cir. 1970), *cert. denied*, 403 U.S. 923 (1971), in the context of review of agency adjudication. See generally Cass R. Sunstein, "Deregulation and the Hard-Look Doctrine," *Supreme Court Review* (1983):

177; Harold H. Bruff, "Legislative Formality, Administrative Rationality," *Texas Law Review* 63 (1984): 207, 238–40.

55. Illustrative of this rather formalistic version of judicial review is Bernard Schwartz, *Administrative Law*, 2d ed. (Boston: Little, Brown 1984), 592–603, 650–68.

56. A classic discussion of this ambiguity, expressed in the traditional dichotomy of "findings of fact" versus "conclusions of law," is Jaffe, supra note 2 at chap. 14.

57. The obligatory citation here is Hans-Georg Gadamer, *Truth and Method* (New York: Seabury Press, 1975).

58. 467 U.S. 837 (1984).

59. See, e.g., Kenneth Starr, "Judicial Review in the Post-*Chevron* Era," *Yale Journal on Regulation* 3 (1986): 283. The effect of *Chevron* on lower court affirmance/reversal rates in agency review cases is examined by Peter H. Schuck and E. Donald Elliott, "To the Chevron Station: An Empirical Study of Federal Administrative Law," *Duke Law Journal*, forthcoming.

60. See, e.g., Farina, supra note 13 at 467–76, who criticizes *Chevron* for its broad statement about deference to agency interpretation in the case of statutory ambiguity. She notes that such deference does not follow as a matter of legislative intent: the absence of legislative specification does not necessarily signify an intent to leave resolution of the issue to the discretion of the agency; it could equally mean that Congress did not see the issue, or that Congress decided to leave the gap filling to itself, or even to the courts. This is correct as far as it goes, but it misses the central point that this "interpretation" is necessarily a joint task. The court cannot initiate a decision; it can only review one that has been made (affirmatively or negatively) by the agency. Given the absence of any statutory specification, the responsibility of review is to determine if the agency's substantive policy choice is "rational," in the sense of conforming to the best sense it can make of the statutory scheme. What else can a reviewing court do? Essentially the same comments apply to Sunstein's criticism that *Chevron* is inconsistent with separation of powers. See Sunstein, "Interpreting Statutes," supra note 13.

61. See, e.g., Immigration and Naturalization Service v. Cardoza-Fonseca, 480 U.S. 421 (1987), where the Court, per Justice Stevens (author of the *Chevron* majority opinion), held that a "pure question of statutory construction" was for the courts to decide without deference to the agency. Deference to the agency only arises where the court has determined that there is no clear statutory meaning applying "traditional" tools of statutory construction. The definition of "clear meaning" is thus as important as the definition of deference—whether the agency interpretation is based on a "permissible construction" of the statute. See Antonin Scalia, "Judicial Deference to Administrative Law," *Duke Law Journal* (1989): 511, 521.

62. 463 U.S. 29 (1983).

63. See Stephen G. Breyer, "Judicial Review of Questions of Law and Policy," *Administrative Law Review* 38 (1986): 363.

64. See 463 U.S. at 43 n. 9 (rejecting NHTSA's argument) and note 6 supra.

65. Schuck and Elliott, supra note 59.

66. See Diver, supra note 13 at 562–64. See also the comprehensive survey of interpretive principles (not uniquely in the context of reviewing agency decisions) in Sunstein, supra note 13.

67. Diver's argument here draws on the positivist analysis of Landes and Posner, supra note 14.

68. Diver, supra note 13 at 583–92.

69. See Dworkin, supra note 11.

70. Diver supra note 13 at 589.

71. This is based on measures of affirmance/reversal rates before and after the *Chevron* case, the assumption being that the case materially changed the deference standard. See Schuck and Elliott, supra note 59.

72. Particularly noteworthy on this score is the study by Jerry Mashaw and David Harfst showing how the highly restrictive review of NHTSA safety rules resulted in an agency shift to automobile recalls as a regulatory strategy. See Jerry L. Mashaw and David Harfst, *The Struggle for Auto Safety* (Cambridge, Mass.: Harvard University Press, 1990). See also R. Shep Melnick, *Regulation and the Courts: The Case of the Clean Air Act* (Washington: Brookings, 1983), critically reviewing judicial review of EPA clean air decisions.

Conclusion

1. James Landis, *The Administrative Process* (New Haven: Yale University Press, 1938), 24.

2. Robert G. McCloskey, "Economic Due Process and the Supreme Court: An Exhumation and Reburial," *Supreme Court Review* (1962): 34, 46.

3. In United States v. Eichman, 110 S. Ct. 2404 (1990), the Supreme Court held that Congress could not constitutionally criminalize flag burning (or other forms of knowing mutilation). Congress's attempt to protect the flag as a special national symbol was found to be squarely in conflict with the First Amendment's protection of free speech, extended to expressive conduct, such as flag burning as a protest of domestic and foreign policy.

4. It is pertinent to note that the statute struck down in *Eichman*, supra note 3, was a congressional response to the Court's earlier invalidation of a state flag burning law. Congress self-consciously addressed the constitutional issue, at the same time trying to avoid the constitutional problem of narrowing the scope of the statute.

5. James Harrington, "The Commonwealth of Oceana," in *The Political Works of James Harrington*, ed. J. G. A. Pocock (Cambridge: Cambridge University Press, 1977), 257–58.

Index of Cases

General Index

Ackerman, Bruce, 15, 60, 208n, 211n
Adair, Douglas, 201n
Adams, Samuel, 44
Adjudication. *See* Due process
Administrative agencies. *See* Bureaucracy; Bureaucrats *and names of individual agencies*
Administrative due process. *See* Due process
Administrative law, 3, 5, 110, 185
Administrative Procedure Act (APA), 1, 6, 113, 126, 143, 151, 171–72, 175, 177
Administrative state, 1
Agriculture, Department of, 13–14
Albert, Lee, 230n
Appleby, Joyce, 200n
Appointments, to agencies, 107, 219n
Aranson, 195n, 210n, 218n
Arnold, Douglas, 217n
Arrow, Kenneth, 2, 20, 34, 52, 90, 200n

Bailyn, Bernard, 35, 201n, 203n
Banning, Lance, 203n
Bargains, interpretation of statutes as, 163–64, 182–83, 231n
Baumol, William, 85, 199n
Baxter, William, 217n
Beatson, J., 223n
Bell, Griffin, 217n
Bennett, Robert, 206n
Bentham, Jeremy, 26, 118
Benze, James, 217n
Berger, Raoul, 202n
Berlin, Isaiah, 198n

Bernstein, Marver, 89
Besen, Stanley, 197n, 214n
Bias. *See* Due process, bias of decision maker
Bickel, Alexander, 47, 188, 205n
Black, Duncan, 200n
Borah, William, 81
Bork, Robert, 202n
Braeutigam, Ronald, 197n
Brams, Steven, 22
Breit, William, 199n
Brennan, William, 116–18
Brest, Paul, 202n
Breyer, Stephen, 233n
Bruff, Harold, 104, 211n, 218n
Buchanan, James, 2, 196n, 199n
Buck, Solon, 192n
Bureaucracy, 1, 2, 5, 18; courts and, 108–10; delegation of powers to, 69–80; growth of, 9–17; political control of, by Congress and president, 95–108; rule of law and, 151–57. *See also* Bureaucrats; Due process; Judicial review
Bureaucrats, 80–87; autonomy of, 82–83; clientele of, 87–95; preferences of, 84–86, 213n
Bush, George, 15, 106

Carroll, Lewis, 34
Carter, Jimmy, 16, 18, 105
Cass, Ronald, 220n
Cavell, Stanley, 45
Chase, Samuel, 54
Civic republicanism, 4, 34–38, 44, 60–61, 203–4n

239